Smile
Daddy-
I am Dying

BY

ROBIN HOOD

Grosvenor House
Publishing Limited

This book is published by
Grosvenor House Publishing Ltd
28-30 High Street, Guildford, Surrey, GU1 3EL.
www.grosvenorhousepublishing.co.uk

A CIP record for this book
is available from the British Library

ISBN 978-1-78148-357-2

Notes: Some sources including some scientists and researchers describe EB as a 'disease'; Wikipedia similarly uses 'disease' in relation to EB. At other times in this story the word 'condition' is used. Robyn Perham insists that EB is a 'condition'. Rather than cause offence or argument I have therefore used both terms.

CHAPTER ONE

Like his namesake of centuries earlier Robin Hood had sacrificed all for love. The outlaw of folklore, driven by injustice, was said to have gathered a fortune to buy the freedom of his sovereign. And the modern day man, for whom that name had once been a millstone, had raised a king's ransom to save his own child. But while legend recorded that the first had succeeded, the second failed.

His daughter Alexandra had died after battling an illness so cruel that the Devil himself might have devised it. Apart from sleep or unconsciousness there was not a minute during the 7104 days, the 170,496 hours of her existence when she was free from agony. Not a moment when pain was all the future held. The appalling condition left its little victims with skin as tender to the touch as that of a butterfly. But now that death had given relief from her nightmare, her father could at least hug what he held of his Butterfly Child, even if that was in a little grey urn.

Until the moment when life left her, not once had he dared cuddle his daughter in the nineteen years of her agonising life in the way a father would. Even now, that simple act of holding his child was his only consolation.

Because in trying to save not just her, but all the other afflicted children, he had lost his family, his home, his savings, and his livelihood. No wonder friends constantly asked whether the cost to him and those closest to him was all worth it.

And then what of the hope he had forever dangled before his child? Until his own dying day he would carry the memory of knowing that barely a week had passed when he had not told his little girl that her misery would end, not in death but with the discovery of a cure. But she had died with that promise unfulfilled, his freedom to cry being the cost of her passing. Yet he found even that simple act of grieving difficult, maybe because for most of her life he had been too busy with the business of trying to save her to find time for emotion. Now, his face was damp, but that was from raindrops which seemed to want to wash away his own pain.

Memories that yearned for tears streamed through his thoughts. Even when she was newly born he had known this day might come; had carried the terrible inevitability that her mother Virginia and he would outlive their daughter. Wasn't the worst fear of any parent that of having to be present at the funeral of their child? He had given his all to try to save her and had lost the fight. Now it was time to let his lovely Alex go for ever.

He had brought her ashes to the beautiful home that he and Virginia had hoped would be an idyllic spot in which to mature. Their house nestled on a loch. Fish swam. Deer played. Birds sang. Gentle waves lapped just a few feet from their door. But always present too was the suffering of their girl. True there had been golden days when her childhood laughter had rung out. But they were a rarity and then even their home life had turned

2

into a nightmare until he had been abandoned to solitude, loneliness and desolation.

As she had grown, his desire to rid her of pain had changed from that of the innocence of the caring helper into a raging obsession that had driven away all he loved. His motivation to fund the finding of a cure had been the determination to avoid the very act that he now prepared to perform. Well, now at least Alex was back. This time to stay.

Through the wind and rain and under a grey sky with clouds shrouding distant hills rang out the sound of a solitary piper playing a lament. Slowly and with great care he trickled the ashes of his child on to the lake allowing it to envelop her for a first and final time. It was a very personal act but he would use even that to further his craving for the publicity that fed his dream of a cure. And so just a few yards off, discreetly recording his every move, was a film cameraman.

Robin had become a specialist in manipulating the Media, using news of the suffering of others to further his quest for a solution to the misery that afflicted every Butterfly Child the world over. Just as the Lincoln Green outlaw had once traded their hunger as his weapon to win the populace to his cause, ruthlessly he sought to use the pain of children to save others yet unborn from the same tragedy. Alex might be gone, but she was still the banner behind which he campaigned.

In just minutes the last trace of her disappeared beneath the lapping waters.

"Goodbye Alex, I love you" was his final parting and now, it was only as he rose to leave her that the first tears appeared. I was privileged to be there that day and as he walked the few yards to his home Robin stopped and briefly hugged me before moving on. It would have been natural to ask what the future held for him, natural but pointless. I already knew the answer. His addiction to funding an antidote to the illness that decimated his daughter had destroyed his own family. But like a junkie hurtling headlong into oblivion on heroin or crack cocaine, Robin Hood had long ago pressed his own self destruct button. Even in her last agonies his dying daughter recognised that inevitability. In an hour, as the last traces of her remains still drifted, he would be back on the fundraising trail.

CHAPTER TWO

In February 1989 Robin Hood drove a heavily pregnant Virginia twenty miles east from their loch side home to the little town of Dumfries in the south west of Scotland. He pulled to a stop outside the highly regarded Cresswell Maternity Hospital and helped his wife inside where she would give birth to their second child, a sibling for their hale and happy son also named Robin.

It was a time of great joy for the couple and one especially precious to Virginia who, as her fortieth year approached, was convinced her conceptive clock was ticking ever faster towards the point where she would no longer bear children and this chance to complete her family might well be the last.

Just a few weeks earlier the town had found itself desperately plunged into the centre of world focus. On December 21 1988 the Pan Am airliner, Clipper Maid of the Seas, packed with 259 passengers and crew, their thoughts filled with the impending thrills of spending Christmas at home with loved ones, had blown up as she flew over Dumfries. The remains of the giant jet and all those on board rained down on the nearby town of Lockerbie, the exploding impact of the fuel filled fuselage obliterating homes and human beings on the ground where another eleven souls perished.

Those bodies that could be retrieved from fields, gardens, farms, the local golf course and even rooftops were taken to a makeshift mortuary at Dumfries to await identification. It was still hard to keep that terrible disaster out of even casual conversations among hospital staff, many of whom had been involved in caring for and counselling the injured and bereaved. The terrorist outrage had condemned thousands of friends, family members and loved ones to lifetimes of grief and hurt. Yet on a personal level the Hoods were about to undergo an equally devastating experience. And that too would emerge from the anticipation of great happiness.

As she lay in the delivery room trying to relax, her husband by her side, Virginia had no reason to doubt that other than the normal birth of a normal baby awaited. Tests had indicated she was carrying a healthy female foetus, that there was nothing to give concern. Indeed so confident were the parents of an uncomplicated arrival that they had already chosen a name for the new addition to their family, Alexandra. Virginia laboured for seven hours at the end of which the birth went smoothly and into the world appeared a beautiful child weighing seven pounds and two ounces. Before the baby was taken away to be cleaned and then given to her overjoyed mother, her father briefly held her, his face glowing with pride and happiness. Now his world was complete. He had a successful business, a stunning home, a wife he desired and admired and two loving children, a boy and a girl. He drove home bursting with emotion and almost as he arrived the telephone was ringing. It was to be the worst call he had ever taken; in a tick of time his world fell from the pinnacle of ecstasy into a chasm of fear.

The message from hospital staff was simple. Something was wrong, seriously wrong, with Alexandra. Robin raced back to his wife to discover his child in intensive care. Skin had peeled from a foot and the infant's skin was red and blistered. Worse still, nobody knew what was wrong. It would be almost five weeks before the cause of the horror would be confirmed. Five weeks of blackness and despair not just for mother and father but for hospital staff who never ceased to be excited by every birth. The baby's parents felt as though they were in a condemned cell awaiting the axe to fall on the life of their little girl.

When the waiting ended, the diagnosis was as grim as it was possible to be.

Alex was the victim of the most lethal form of Epidermolysis Bullosa, commonly known as EB. One in every 50,000 babies was affected. There was no cure and she would be dead within six months. Her life, however long or short, would be one of unremitting pain. Her skin would fall off; ingesting food would be likened to digesting thorns, getting rid of her bodily waste a miserable agony. Never again would either parent be able to cuddle their infant daughter because the merest touch on her butterfly skin would cause it to violently redden and blister. Every blister would have to be pricked with a needle and burst. Her tiny body would need to be swathed in bandages.

For Virginia and Robin, caring for their baby would need not merely a patience and tenderness far beyond that of any average parent, but an ability to immediately adapt to coping with seeing their infant in eternal suffering. Not only would they need to handle their daughter's misery, but stow away their own distress. There was no hope. The only prognosis was one of excruciating pain and ultimate death. On the horizon six depressing months devoid of hope with, at the end, the certainty of a little coffin. What was this evil that threatened to blight their lives? And why them?

CHAPTER THREE

No sane person feels anything other than distress over the suffering of a child. We may categorise the various degrees of pain from slight to unbearable, but to a parent the cry of an infant is still hurtful regardless of the cause.

Most bouts of childhood torment last only a few minutes. For victims of Epidermolysis Bullosa, EB, though there is no relief from unrelenting agony. No hope of ever having freedom from pain other than death. Discovering that a new born baby has the disease is the worst conceivable nightmare of any parent. The only consolation for those with the most severe form of the condition is that they die early. EB has been around for as long as the human race has existed. We know now why children are born with it, but for centuries what caused it, what could be done to treat and even prevent it remained steeped in mystery.

Doubtless in the middle ages the standard treatment would have been to bleed the patient and in doing do actually worsen the effects. But it was not until late in the nineteenth century that doctors and scientists began investigating, studying and understanding the causes. The French skin specialist, Francois Henri Hallopeau was one of the pioneers of conduct studies into EB from the early 1870s until his death in 1919. Since then experts worldwide have devoted increasing resources to researching the problem. In the United Kingdom, one of the leaders in this field is John McGrath, Professor of Molecular Dermatology at King's College Hospital in London. Another is Irwin McLean, Professor of Human Genetics and head of the Division of Molecular medicine at the University of Dundee. There are many others as equally eminent, skilled and dedicated. Despite their brilliance, the fact is that although we now know what triggers EB, there is still no cure.

While this story will deliberately not delve deeply into the complexities of the disease, it is necessary to give a fairly basic understanding of this terrible condition.

The skin is made up of three layers. The outside is known as the epidermis. Beneath it is the dermis and below that the hypodermis also known as the subcutaneous. Normally tiny anchors known as the basement membrane and made of a naturally occurring protein called Collagen VII, hold on to these layers, preventing them from moving independently. In other words all three should move together in the same direction at the same time. Without these anchors, the layers would chafe painfully against one another. Where there are no anchors decides the severity of the disease.

EB sufferers in general have no anchors in varying parts of their skin area and the result is that the slightest movement, even a touch, means the epidermis and hypodermis rub together and bring out dozens of agonising blisters and sores.

These blisters have to be burst within hours otherwise they swell and literally roll about worsening the gap between the two outer layers. Yet the very act of bursting creates more problems, because unlike that of healthy children, the skin of those with EB has problems healing and repairing itself. The result is increasing areas of the body where there is no skin that needs to be gently bandaged to fight the risk of infection. And bandaging alone, in particular the removal of bandages and dressings can be a nightmare ordeal. Many with EB liken their sores to third degree burns and yet they must be endured from birth until death.

Why do children fall to EB? It affects all racial and ethnic groups, males and females equally. Quite simply, it is passed from parents who carry a defective gene. Normally having this rogue gene would not create a problem. If a carrier and a non carrier meet, fall in love and have children there is no risk.

It is when two carriers produce a baby that the danger arises, although even then it does not necessarily mean the production of an EB child. Because there is just a one in four chance of their offspring being born with the condition. An affected couple might even have four healthy children.

Unless one or other parent is aware that he or she is a carrier of a defective gene then there can be no warning of the impending horror. The first indication they will normally have will come when they hold their child for the first time only to discover skin being ripped from limb or discover cruel vivid red marks on a baby's face where the skin has pulled away during the actual birth. The shock to any parent is awesome and from that first moment their lives will change dramatically because they will never know freedom from the suffering of their child.

Debra, the UK charity that helps victims and which plays a huge role in our story, has categorised the three main forms of the disease as EB simplex, junctional EB and dystrophic EB, although it points out that each main type can again be divided into several variations and currently, 27 clinical sub-types are known. Of an estimated 5000 EB victims in the United Kingdom, around 70 per cent suffer from the commonest and mildest type, simplex. In terms of relative severity it ranks as the least, although that is no comfort for those who have to live with it. Pain is pain.

Simplex is characterised by lack of adhesion of the skin right above the basement membrane. Most forms of simplex are inherited as dominant traits which is to say that the parents visibly have the condition. Because of this, the family history has already shown that there is a possibility of their having a child with EB simplex. However, sometimes a child is found to have the disorder for the first time in his or her family, a so-called new mutation. Generally EB simplex in its most prevalent form has blistering confined to the hands and feet. These patients usually do not seek medical assistance because the disorder is mild and because it is well known in the family due to the dominant inheritance.

In another sub strain of EB simplex, blistering can occur all over the body. It can appear during the neonatal period, those first days of a child's life, but may also reveal itself in later childhood (or even in adult life). Rubbing tends to be the main cause for blistering and especially rubbing of the feet by footwear. Rubbing is worse in warm weather.

About one quarter of EB sufferers have the dystrophic variety. One form of dystrophic EB, known as Recessive

Dystrophic Epidermolysis Bullosa or in short RDEB, can lead to major handicaps and a relatively short and painful life. However, there are many exceptions to this rule. Dystrophic EB gets its name from the tendency of the blisters to heal with scarring and the eventual nightmare of there simply being no skin left to scar or heal making the body vulnerable to cancerous tumours. There are other devilish consequences including contraction of the joints, fusing together of fingers and toes, contraction of the mouth membranes and narrowing of the oesophagus, the organ that delivers food and breath from the mouth to the stomach.

There is a wide variation in the severity of dystrophic EB. In general, it is not life-threatening in childhood and at its least severe the patient can lead an almost normal life. However, the severity of the disorder increases at a later age due to scarring, fusion of fingers and wastage of skin tissue resulting in such wear and tear on the body that the outlook is bleak. In the recessive type of dystrophic EB there is a high chance of developing Squamous Cell Carcinoma, SCC, – an aggressive skin cancer – before the age of 35. Eventually two fifths of those with this type of EB die from the effects of SCC.

Junctional EB is the worst of the worst and around one in twenty EB victims suffer from this dreadful form. Once again parents carry the defective gene unknowingly and show no physical signs of the condition. As a result the birth of a child with junctional EB is totally unexpected. Once the rogue genes meet, it becomes a lottery whether the result is a normal child, one affected by EB junctional or EB dystrophic.

According to Debra: "The outlook of junctional EB is usually rather bleak; half of the children die within the first two years as the result of malnutrition and anaemia which are caused by serious blistering in the pharynx and the oesophagus. Characteristic clinical features are damage to and marking of the skin tissue on the face. These defects only develop after a couple of months. There are only a few patients with this severe type that survive the second or third year of life."

There can be no worse ordeal for any parent than to watch and listen to the screams of a new born baby, its outer skin and internal organs ripping and blistering at even the most tender of touches as lips are torn off while the mother tries passing milk to her child knowing the infant she has nurtured for nine months will survive only days.

The fact is the prospect for anyone with EB is grim even though huge advances have been made in recent years in understanding the disease and both developing ways of alleviating the suffering of its victims and researching a cure. As far as many of those bearing the crosses of junctional and dystrophic EB are concerned, they fight not just the disease but time. Because if a cure is not discovered they will die, their prayers for even the chance to experience normality for a few hours unanswered.

CHAPTER FOUR

Like the vast majority of parents who discover their child has EB, there was nothing in the background of Robin or Virginia to suggest each was the carrier of a gene that would ultimately cause such devastation. The parents of his mother, Barbara, had pulled up their roots in south east Ireland and moved to the English Midlands in search of work and hope. The family head, her father John Joseph, was a devout Catholic who ruled over his wife and six children with a rod of iron serving as an Army reservist with the Coldstream Guards in the early 1920s.

With the outbreak of the Second World War in 1939, John Joseph was called into service with the ill-fated British Expeditionary Force and quickly found himself huddling on the beaches of Dunkirk, desperately trying to avoid the merciless and unceasing strafing, bombing and shelling from the encircling German forces. He was wounded and although he eventually made it back over the Channel, never recovered and died of his injuries in March 1941.

Six years later Barbara met 21-year-old insurance salesman Dennis John Hood. His family originated in the shipbuilding district of Govan on the banks of the

River Clyde. Friendship blossomed into love and they married in November 1949. The couple moved to Surrey after a family member offered Dennis work and seven years later on June 15 1956 Barbara gave birth to Robin John Gerard, his first forename being her choice despite the reservations of her husband. It is not unusual for parents to name their children after well known personalities from whatever walk of life, maybe in the hope they will follow in the same footsteps as their namesakes. There are, after all, countless Winston Churchills, Robert Bruces, David Livingstons. The Hoods simply followed the trend, but it was a decision that would later cause problems for their son. When Robin was two the family moved back to the Midlands, to Birmingham, eventually taking over a cafe, where customers would hold the youngster while Barbara cooked breakfasts. Two years later they became owners of a thriving fish and chip shop, making such a success that they were able to buy a second.

He loved his father but soon after starting primary school found himself with a stepfather, businessman Trevor Bufton, after his parents split up and then divorced. Bufton owned shops but Robin would come to hate him.

"My parents and I lived above one of the fish shops and they were doing really well. This was in a poor part of Birmingham in back to back houses with three families sharing an outside toilet.

My Mother wanted the best for me and was not satisfied with the local state school, so I was packed off to Chigwell House, a public school in the Edgbaston district. The fees were paid out of the profits from the chippies. I was given a bright purple uniform which

I used to hang up in the back of the fish and chip shop. School wasn't far away. I made some friends there but mostly their fathers were doctors, dentists, gynaecologists and barristers and when I met up with them they'd ask one another, 'Can you smell fish and chips?'

After school I had to run a gauntlet of stones thrown by the local gangs in the poorer part of the city, I was a prime target in my bright purple school uniform.

"At school I wasn't very bright, not doing well. My mother was determined I'd pass the Eleven Plus. She and my father had spent a lot of money on my education through public school fees and had even arranged to pay for extra tuition. Bufton wanted nothing to do with helping to bring me up, and so my mother decided something needed to be done. She said, 'Robin needs some fatherly advice so Dennis is going to come around and see him each evening'. Although they were no longer married, my parents still ran the two fish and chip shops so they saw each other all the time. So my father would come when he'd finished work and he and I would eat our dinner in the kitchen of my stepfather's mother's house while Bufton and my mother ate in the living room.

"What she didn't know was that one of the reasons why I did badly was that Bufton was never very nice to me; he would go out of his way to humiliate and embarrass me and did other things which should not have happened. "

The extra tuition helped him pass the Eleven Plus examination and he found himself at Kings Heath Boys Technical School "I had the most miserable time at school it was though I was the school punch bag. I did make one friend who I did not know then but would be a great person in the rest of my life." Graham Bird was the local greengrocer's son and we soon found we had a lot in common as we matured.

Dennis Hood gave up selling fish and chips and went into business as a timber merchant with his brother Geoffrey. Robin worked there on Saturdays, sweeping and doing odd jobs for pocket money. At school teachers constantly reminded him he was an academic failure, but, just as in adult life, when faced by a tough challenge he stepped up to the mark.

"One day during swimming lessons at the local pool, my cousin Simon who was in the class after mine got into difficulties. He was drowning and I dived in to rescue him. One of the mothers, who had been there and saw what had happened, told the school headmaster I'd saved Simon's life and the result was I was given a standing ovation at school, but that was one of the only good things I remember about schooldays."

Bufton's once thriving businesses went into decline, and the strain of keeping them afloat spread to his marriage. With the family home about to be repossessed by the bank he ran off and left Barbara at the mercy of his debtors. Dennis, who had never ceased to love her, came to the rescue, settling debts, moving in, giving Robin a full time job in the timber yard and re-marrying Barbara on December 28, 1974, much to the delight of the best man, 18-year-old Robin, and they remained happily together until Dennis died in 2005.

Barbara is still alive but has dementia.

CHAPTER FIVE

As a schoolboy he had been tagged a failure. Now, maturing into his late teens, Robin began showing signs of the stubbornness and determination to succeed that would have such dramatic consequences in later life. He started working full time at the timber yard run by his father and uncle, the classic case of the boss's son encouraged to start at the bottom and head upwards. "It wasn't glamorous, but what it did give me was a fantastic physique, I developed muscles on my muscles." His good looks and strength also attracted women. One in particular, was about to enter his life. But his account of his first meeting with Virginia in 1977 differs from that told by her. According to Robin, "What I found attractive in ladies was confidence and elegance and Virginia had both. One night I was in a club when I saw this girl who had stunning legs. We started chatting and at the end of the night I took her home and asked her out." But Virginia remembers the meeting as, "I was the last person he asked to dance with all evening. He didn't like dancing, He was a typical man. Once you've met them, and they've used the excuse of a dance to meet you, they never want to dance again."

The couple might only have danced once, but Robin was smitten. Virginia Murphy had waltzed her way into his heart. "Virginia was 24 and I was 21. She was a woman and I was still immature. Basically she was going to be another conquest for me."

As their courtship began and developed, he found it difficult to come to terms with the fact he was falling in love with her and became very jealous. And Virginia was quick to recognise it. "Frankly he was a pain in the arse a lot of the time, but I did love him." He asked her to marry him and she accepted. "What attracted me to Robin? He was very different. And he is very personable and when you meet him, if he decides he wants to, he can charm you to death. If he doesn't want to then he'll have nothing to do with you."

They set a date and bought their first house in Royal Leamington Spa. Renovating the property left little time for a social life, less still for watching television or reading newspapers. So it was little wonder that they failed to notice an item in 1978 that made a few paragraphs in a number of the broadsheets, but which would ultimately have worldwide implications and become the hub around which their own lives would revolve. In England, kindly Phyllis Hilton, daughter of a Bournemouth shopkeeper, had given birth to three children with her Spanish husband. When the couple divorced Phyllis re-married and in 1963 was shattered when, at the birth of her fourth child, a daughter she had decided to name Debra, the baby's skin peeled away and her body was covered in blistered and sores. Eventually EB was diagnosed.

Baffled and confused, not having encountered the condition previously, doctors advised her, 'Sorry, but there is nothing we can do. We'd advise you to take the child home and nurse her until she dies.' Such a grim prognosis may have left most mothers too distraught to do other than follow the advice. But Phyllis Hilton's love for her new-born child filled her heart with a wonderful desire for the baby to be given the chance of life. If miracles exist, Phyllis Hilton performed one by caring for her daughter with such devotion, using cotton bandages to gently cover her skin, that word gradually spread about her efforts to seemingly defy nature and keep her child alive.

One day another young mother of a newly born child found to be suffering from EB sought help from Phyllis having been also told there was no hope for her baby. Phyllis decided it was time to act. She wrote to newspapers and magazines pleading for the parents of other EB victims to get in touch and the result was a meeting in 1978 to which 98 people turned up. And so a charity was formed that would campaign for help for victims and seek to raise money to research a cure for the sickening disease. Coverage of the meeting was scant, but those newspapers that did report it said the new charity would be named after Phyllis's daughter, Debra.

While Phyllis and a handful of volunteer workers started raising money and awareness, Robin and Virginia were preparing for their big day. They were married on December 16, 1978 and went off to honeymoon on Mull, the Inner Hebridean island off the west coast of Scotland. There Robin went stalking and shot his first deer.

As the young couple settled down to married life, Robin threw himself into his work with gusto, but found it at first difficult and then impossible to conceal a driving ambition to climb the promotion ladder, to achieve his aim of leaping from the work floor to the boardroom. Throughout his life he would set a target and rush through a self-made tunnel to achieve it, along the way using any means and anyone to reach his destination. When he took a decision he threw himself into the task of completing it with total devotion, immune at times to the consequences.

His interest in stalking became a passion. Virginia, a nursery nurse and qualified swimming teacher, was working at a public school in the Midlands.

One of her colleagues was a member of a prestigious deer stalking club called the St Hubert Club.

One highlight of membership was attending a club dinner one evening and meeting a young man named Rory Morrison, a multiple sclerosis sufferer.

"He couldn't walk but had a lovely personality, a nice nature. I found myself sitting next to him and asked him if he wanted a beer. 'I can't have a beer,' he said. 'Because I can't walk and the toilets are downstairs. How am I going to get to the loo?' I told him, 'Do not worry about that, I'll carry you to the loo.' And that's just what I did." He and Rory became close friends. They would stalk together on a private estate in the Scottish Borders, Robin being allowed to indulge for free his love for the pastime in return for looking after his friend. "Rory used to get on a quad bike, cover it in camouflage netting, wait for the deer and when he'd shot one I'd drag it back. Then I'd cook his breakfast. I learned much from reflecting on Rory's attitude to adversity. It would come to help me so much in the future."

Robin began seeing more and more of Scotland and fell in love with the desolate hills and forests that teemed with wild life. Meanwhile at work he could not see eye to eye with his uncle and cousin Roger who were also part of the business, so he just left a well-paid job with a company car.

It was May 1980, and just a few weeks earlier Virginia had told him she was expecting their first child. Now the couple were facing the imminent addition to their family with no apparent income. Robin invested their savings in a haulage company but found keeping seven ancient lorries on the road a financial burden. There was a further complication. During one of his frequent stalking trips to Scotland, Robin had bought a tumbledown bungalow near Lochmaben, a market town four miles from Lockerbie, intending to rebuild it as a family holiday home. Now he began travelling regularly to Lochmaben and had started work on the near ruin with timber supplied free by his father. He had treated the news of his wife's pregnancy with some dismay. "Virginia felt she needed a baby because she said she was getting older. But I never wanted a child. I wasn't ready for a baby, I was too young for children. When Virginia had said, 'I want a baby' I told her, 'No we don't'. I was working all hours, trying to hold the haulage business together and every week-end driving up to Lochmaben to work on the bungalow. At the same time, Virginia was great. She handled the books for my business and put up with so much from me. A lot of wives would simply not have coped."

As the months of her pregnancy passed without complication and the Hoods awaited the new arrival into their midst, a hundred miles to the south Phyllis Hilton lost the daughter to whom she had given so much of her love and devotion with the death of Debra. The girl, whose life expectancy had been given as just days or weeks, had survived to the age of 18 but as was tragically so often the case, the drain on her body's resources of EB finally took its toll. At least Debra would never be forgotten. The setting up by her mum and other stricken parents of the charity bearing her name had been no short lived germ of enthusiasm. Debra was by now firmly established. It was small. But it had arrived and the strength of its supporters would ensure its growth and survival.

Epidermolysis Bullosa meant nothing to Virginia and Robin Hood. It was a term they had never encountered and had no reason to do so. And yet in the conception of the child Virginia now bore, the couple had come frighteningly close to tragedy. Unknown to them, each carried the defective gene that had the potential to create EB. There was a one in four chance of Virginia giving birth to an infected baby. As was the norm she had undergone regular checks during routine visits to her antenatal clinic. But none of these had been to discover whether the foetus was infected with EB. There had, after all, been no cause to do so.

As it transpired, luck was on the side of the couple and on October 24 1980 Virginia gave birth to a healthy son. It was her decision to name the boy Robin, simply because she liked that name. She was 27 and had felt the need to conceive because her biological time clock was ticking towards 30. There was, of course, time for her to mother again, but what would be the odds against a second baby being healthy and normal? She and Robin did not know it, but in gambling terms, they would be betting blind, risking their stake on a hand they had not seen.

CHAPTER SIX

Despite his passion for Virginia, his longing to be with her, Robin admits he had not been ready, mature enough, for marriage and still wanted to see his father who he admired, go to karate training and see Graham his friend. "I think I was a bit of a fool. I wasn't ready to settle down and could see all my friends of my age being still unmarried and being able to go off and do their own thing. "As far as business was concerned, I was on track to being a successful guy, but on that journey I think I lost my way a bit and maybe still wanted to be a free.

"Virginia deserves a medal for putting up with me. I was a total idiot and, arrogant. If she didn't cook the food the way I liked it cooked, I wouldn't eat it. I was just like a spoiled brat. The crazy thing was that when I'd say to Virginia, 'I want to go away for a week-end with the boys', she'd say, 'Great, do it.' She would never tell me, 'Oh you've got to do this, do that, and stay at home.' "So I could do as I wanted and as a result the first couple of years of our marriage had been the happiest of my life, a time I will always remember."

However the arrival of their child meant a traumatic change in the relationship. Up until then, Robin felt as though Virginia's world revolved around him and him alone. Now it was as though he had a rival for her affections. "I'd been having a good time, not fooling around with other women but going out, seeing my friends and spending three nights a week studying karate. I felt I earned my fun because I was working so hard at trying to build up the haulage business, but it was an uphill struggle. And then once Robin was born, Virginia began spending lots of time with her mother and I felt excluded. I don't think I had ever been her parents' favourite choice for their daughter."

In fairness to Robin, he tried to be the father his own dad had been to him. "I used to do fatherly things and I loved my son. When Robin junior was about 18 months old Virginia and I hired a camper van and travelled up to Glencoe. I strapped him on my back and we went climbing. It was such a fun time." But the fact was that gradually Robin and Virginia were spending less time together; she devoted to their son; he a workaholic running his own business, helping that of his father and trying to find time to visit Lochmaben and work on the renovation of the bungalow.

It was almost inevitable that the marriage broke up. Virginia remembers: "When my son was about two and a half, Robin decided he didn't want to be with us anymore and went to live with his mother and father. I have never been able to work out why. He said he didn't know what to do with his life. He wanted to do his own thing and so he went off. While we were living apart he told me he was planning to go on holiday to Majorca with his mother and I said to him, 'If, by the time you come back, you haven't made up your mind whether you want our marriage to continue, that will be it as far as I'm concerned. I'll get a divorce.' And I was serious."

Robin admits: "Virginia was a fantastic wife and mother. She looked after me physically and emotionally; she'd see to my food, my clothes, everything. She was so talented. She could make curtains, clothes and had even made her own wedding dress. But back in those days I was an arrogant fool. I was a great provider, but not a very nice man. Everything had to be my way or it didn't happen. I was very demanding. I was confident I was on my way to being successful, but maybe at the same time I wanted to be a free. Then when Robin was born I felt pushed out. She was going off to her mum's a lot and I'd come home exhausted after working away at the haulage business and she wouldn't be there.

"And so we drifted apart. I'd got myself in the mind-set where I thought that by getting married so young I'd missed out. The fact was I hadn't. I'd had plenty of girlfriends, there had been physical relationships and I'd sown plenty of wild oats. But I began convincing myself I didn't want to be a father with a mortgage to pay, that I simply wanted to get my businesses up and running, earn some money and do what I wanted when I wanted. The truth was Virginia let me do all those things anyway but I was not wise enough to see how lucky I was."

"My father, who was my best friend, said, 'If you don't get back with Virginia I'll never forgive you, I know he remembered the situation where I had seen my own parents break up after he and my mother split when Bufton came on the scene and he didn't want his grandson Robin to go through the same experience as I had. And so we got back together." He and Virginia bought a stunning 16th century thatched cottage in the beautiful nearby village of Radford Semele and moved once more.

Robin began breeding chocolate Labradors, a venture that would prove successful and significant later on. At one time he had eight Labradors. But before long Virginia realised cracks in their relationship were beginning to re-open. During weekdays her husband would rise early and go off to the business delivering goods on one of his lorries often visiting his parents after finishing work in the evenings and then spending time with his father in a local bar before coming home to his wife and son.

Robin often remembers when his mother was away at weekends with Bufton and his father would spend all weekend doing things with him horse riding swimming, looking for conkers. His haulage business was an increasing drain on his time and resources as lorries began breaking down ever more frequently while he himself was spending more and more week-ends in Scotland, sometimes with Rory Morrison, leaving the Midlands on a Friday evening, sleeping rough, stalking over the week-end and returning home late on a Sunday night. "Robin was never really very happy," says Virginia. "He never seemed a happy person."

By the time Robin junior reached school age, he was left alone with his mother every other week-end. "Robin said to me one day, 'I've been away 26 week-ends this year shooting in Scotland' and I knew I must have been a good wife to put up with that. So I said to him, 'Why don't we move to Scotland? If that's where you really want to be why don't we live there?' He said he'd think it over."

Robin told Virginia a move was out of the question because of the business tie up with his father. However a year later, in 1986, fate resolved the issue. As Dennis Hood neared his 60th birthday he decided it was time to relieve himself of the workload and go into semi-retirement at least. He offered his business to Robin but was taken aback when his son told him, 'If I take this on it will mean my spending even less time at home with Virginia and Robin. Sell it, I don't want it.'

The calls on his time had by this time been increased by his decision to fulfil a long held ambition to join the Territorial Army as an officer cadet, his fitness enabling him to easily pass an Assessment Course that younger men failed. Meanwhile the announcement by his father to opt out of business had encouraged an idea that had been growing within the mind of his son for some time, that of settling in Scotland. Virginia supported her husband in this dream and they went house hunting.

Driving along country lanes and side roads they came upon the beautiful Loch Ken, a thirteen miles long stretch of freshwater in Dumfries and Galloway and forty five miles from Lochmaben. Motoring around the loch, they passed a spot known as Mossdale. There, on the edge of the water, at the end of a short drive leading from the road, stood a solitary house, Lochside Cottage, and by it a 'For Sale' notice.

It was a sunny May day and they were immediately entranced by the remarkable view over the loch, but not impressed by the condition of the house. Robin remembers: "It was in tatters. There was no mains electricity, just a dilapidated and failing generator and only calor gas heating and as a result the house was very damp.

There was no kitchen, a very poor bathroom and it was little other than a two-bedroomed dump."

But with the house came a couple of potential gems. The property was built on just under two acres of land lying alongside the loch. On the other side of the road running past the property, were another five acres and, potentially more valuable still, was a kilometre of fishing rights to the well stocked water. An attempt by previous owners to develop the spot into a sailing centre had been rejected by local planning officials and so the property went on sale.

I said to Virginia, 'That is where we are going to live'. It was obvious the building would require lots of remedial work. The Hoods discovered the asking price was £90,000. They arranged a survey and valuation, which recommended a ceiling of £60,000, the figure they offered. They immediately placed their own home in Radford Semele on the market and quickly found a buyer. Now they needed a new home but their offer for Lochside Cottage was rejected. It meant more visits to Scotland and a seemingly endless trek around seeking 'For Sale' signs. They found nothing that pleased them so much as the property by the side of Loch Ken, but as the months dragged on gave up hope of buying it, refusing to increase their offer, arguing why pay more than the survey had suggested.

Then out of the blue in April the following year came a telephone call asking if their bid of £60,000 was still on the table. By now desperate to find a new home, the Hoods agreed, but another call some time later caused anger and dismay. "We were told that if we wanted Lochside Cotttage it could cost us another £5,000. So I said, 'Okay, we'll pay the £5,000 but just tell the people

SMILE DADDY – I'M DYING

responsible not to be there when I get in'." They moved to Scotland on November 6, 1987, eighteen months after first seeing the property.

Virginia and young Robin were the first to fully live there, because a new home was not the only change in the lives of the family. Robin had announced that like his father he too was selling up and for three months commuted between Scotland and the Midlands helping Dennis dismantle his company and arranging the sale of his own. The proceeds of his firm and money given to him by his father, together with the sale of the thatched cottage in Radford Semele, meant he was able to have the security of a reasonably sized bank balance. In addition, as a form of reserve, he still had the bungalow at Lochmaben in which he and Virginia had never lived.

The couple moved permanently to Scotland a few weeks before Christmas 1987 and set about bringing warmth and comfort to their new home. A central heating system was installed and a touch of paint here and there brought colour and a welcoming feel. "We had a great Christmas and Virginia and I fell back in love. I even have letters from her saying, 'Thank you for bringing me to such a beautiful place'. Money was not a problem. In addition to what he had in the bank, Robin was still earning a salary from his father's business while he continued to help with its dismantling and sale. But there lurked in the background the uncertainty of what he would do when his links with the Midlands business came to an end. "Virginia asked me, 'What are you going to do for a living?' and I had to tell her, 'Virginia, I haven't a clue.'

But as one door closed, another opened. One night while he and Virginia dined with friends, Robin was introduced to a local land agent who said he was looking after acreage near Mossdale. 'There's not much game on it and so the rent is low, it's £200 a year', he said. Curious, Robin went off to look it over. At first he saw only a few pheasants but, climbing higher he discovered a positive treasure trove. "At the top of this hill the grouse and black cock were everywhere. 'Got to have some of this,' I thought. I rang the agent and said, 'You're right, there's nothing there and you want £200? I'll have it on a six-year lease.'

"He asked, 'Why do you want it for six years?' I told him, 'Well, I'll put some birds down and it will take time for them to breed and for me to get a decent return on my outlay.' He said, 'Go on then' and I got it for six years at £100 a year. "I put an advert in Shooting Times. 'Grouse Shooting. £50 a gun per day.' The area was so big I used to take two parties a week up there. No more than four men. I was getting £400 a week. It suddenly took off."

He expanded the ever thriving business by renting more land with deer and organised stalking parties. A mobile home was bought and used as accommodation for the generously paying guests.

"I was doing okay, but it was a very demanding business. When you are feeding pheasants, when you release them you have to feed them twice a day. The result was I never saw much of my son." He was also seeing less and less of his wife who began feeling the pressure of looking after a home, a young demanding son, feeding and cleaning for constant parties of strangers and helping with the business paperwork. Almost as if to rub salt into the wound Robin was determined to continue his Territorial Army links. He loved soldiering and arranged to transfer his TA base from the English Midlands to Dumfries and was pleasantly surprised to be invited to join 1/52 Lowland Volunteers (TA) , an infantry battalion attached to the King's Own Scottish Borderers.

Virginia raised no objection but was once more wondering whether her future and that of their son lay with her husband. At times she saw no relief from her workload and then in the summer of 1988 discovered she was once more pregnant. None of the family had any inkling of the trauma that now lay before them.

CHAPTER SEVEN

As her pregnancy advanced, Virginia became increasingly disillusioned. It may have been that her natural concern over the forthcoming birth on top of the daily and wearing workload added up to uncertainty over whether to remain at Lochside Cottage. She had even taken a practical step towards quitting. "In the midst of everything I had gone to my doctor and asked for my notes because I was leaving. I don't think Robin understood what women go through at these times, that they have their moments. If a man cares then he will understand and I didn't feel that was the case. So I was going to go."

She decided to delay her decision until after the birth, an event to which she looked forward because once again the normal checks and tests had indicated no sign of any abnormality. She had been given a standard amniocentesis in which a hollow needle had been gentle probed into her womb to extract fluid. The test would show up any defects but the outcome had been that she was told all was fine and well.

"Ours was just a small, two-bedroomed cottage and the hospital staff asked whether we wanted to know what sex the baby would be," said Robin. "We told them, 'Yes' because we realised that if we had another boy then the two boys could share while if we had a girl then we had a problem and would, at some stage, need to create another bedroom. "The result came back and we were told it was to be a little girl. "We chose clothes and discussed a name for our baby. Virginia chose 'Alexandra' and I picked a middle name, 'Rebecca' and so we just waited for the arrival of Alexandra Rebecca Hood."

As far as Virginia and the doctors and midwives at hospital in Dumfries were concerned all would run smoothly; Gerard Majella, the patron saint of childbirth and expectant mothers had no cause to intercede. In reality in any case she had no time to worry about whether anything might go wrong. As well as caring for her husband's guests and the multitude of her other tasks, she was preparing for Christmas and even trying to find time to decorate Lochside Cottage. It would be the last normal Christmas for the Hood family, just as it would for thousands of other families throughout the world when a bomb exploded in the hold of Clipper Maid of the Seas as she cruised through the starlit sky nearly six miles above Lockerbie, leaving bodies to shower down over the town like snowflakes in a storm from Hell. A few miles off, going about the task of wrapping presents, Virginia Hood could not have known that a tiny, human unborn time bomb grew within her.

At the beginning of February 1989 Robin drove his wife to Cresswell Maternity Hospital and soon after received a telephone call advising him the birth was imminent. He had wanted to be present, as he had with the birth of Robin junior, and on Sunday the fifth,

Alexandra – she would come to known as Alex – was born.

"As soon as Alex came into the world, the midwife handed her to me and so I was the second person to hold her. She was beautiful. Everything was absolutely perfect. My parents had travelled from the Midlands to look after our son and help out while Virginia was in hospital and so I drove back out to Lochside Cottage to tell them they had a lovely grand-daughter. Then I rang up Virginia's mum and dad to give them the news."

Back in hospital nurses were quickly realising all was not well with the new baby. Immediately she had been taken from the delivery room, her tiny body had begun to show angry blisters and skin had ripped from a foot which had been held during delivery. Clearly something was seriously wrong, but nobody knew what.

"I hadn't been home very long when the telephone rang and the hospital staff said I needed to get back very quickly. All they could tell me was that Alex was unwell. It was a terrible drive back there; all sorts of things were racing through my mind. When I arrived I discovered Alex in an incubator in intensive care and Virginia, obviously in shock, wearing a mask and gown standing over her. I saw where the skin was missing from our baby's foot and the blistering. Even the maternity staff were treating this as though they had a leper on their hands, and I suppose you had to see it from their point of view. They could not possibly know that what Alex had been born with, was infectious.

"This was the beginning of very dark days and we had a really bad time, especially because nobody had a clue what was amiss, what was the cause of the blisters which just kept showing up on Alex's body. I remember coming in through the car park one evening to see Alex and Virginia when a guy came over and threatened me, He said, 'If my baby catches what your baby has got then you're a dead man.' Virginia had stayed on at the hospital where the staff were carrying out tests to see if they could diagnose the problem, but she was allowed home for her birthday on the 20th of the month. But even by then we did not know what was wrong with Alex.

"We had been living at Lochside Cottage just under 18 months and had made a good many friends, but did not realise just how good those friends were. "Everybody locally knew something was wrong. I just didn't know what to do for Virginia's birthday. I wanted to make it special because of what she was going through and as, at that stage, without knowing what illness Alex had, we thought our baby was going to die. A friend Leslie Wykes rang and said, 'Just come to the lochinvar in Lochinvar Hotel, we have a surprise for you'. Virginia and I went along and walked in to find all the locals had gathered to welcome us as if to say, 'Come on, we're thinking of you, don't worry'. It was the best thing that could have happened. We knew we had friends, but all of a sudden we had so many more new friends and it was great for Virginia. Both of us felt as if the entire community had stretched out its arms to hold us and say, 'We're with you in this'. It was such a warming feeling and especially great for Virginia, who could at last talk to some of the women she had come to know and tell them about Alex. This night gave us a massive fillip. We felt we weren't alone."

They still, though, remained on tenterhooks wondering just what was wrong with their baby. Finally a hospital dermatologist was able to tell the couple, 'Your child has a condition known as epidermolysis bullosa.' It was such a rare disease that little was known about it. In many cases, it was a lottery whether or not maternity hospital staff could even diagnose it. Those few hospitals where an EB baby had been born previously would be able to tell parents almost immediately what the problem was. But to the great majority EB was an unknown, and only diagnosed through a series of tests.

At Dumfries the full extent of the various types of EB was, logically perhaps, not fully understood which made the initial verdict desperately cruel. The Hoods were told Alex had been born with the worst form of EB, junctional.

"We were advised to prepare ourselves for the death of our daughter within six months," said Robin. "Virginia and I were devastated. The hospital was trying to be as helpful as it could, but was only able to tell us about the existence of a charity called Debra. Of what Debra was, who ran it, what it did or how it had come about, we knew absolutely nothing."

Robin was given a telephone number for Crowthorne, Berkshire, in the south of England for the charity and remembers his first conversation with an organisation that would come to dominate the lives of every member of his family. "I rang up and spoke to a man named John Dart. I found from that first chat that Debra was a small charity with a staff of four or five and an income of about £90,000 a year. "I said, 'Look, I don't know why I'm ringing you but my child has EB' and John said, 'We'll send a nurse up to see you. It doesn't necessarily mean your daughter might die quickly because there are several types of EB and we will have to wait for the results of a skin biopsy'.

"He was as good as his word. The nurse arrived, educated the maternity staff about the condition, how to care for and bandage Alex, and assured everybody EB was not contagious. That was a huge relief for everybody, not least ourselves, because now it meant we were effectively accepted back into society. It's not until you are treated as though you are a leper that you realise how dreadful an experience that can be. Even so, I was shell-shocked when the nurse explained the full implications of having a child with EB.

"She told us Alex did not have the chemical Collagen VII, that the reason she had born with the condition was because Virginia and I both carried a defective gene. When we asked why Robin had not been born with the disease she explained the odds of us having a child with the defect were one in four. In a sense, Robin had been one of the lucky three."

If it is possible for parents to be given good news under the circumstances of discovering their baby has EB, then the Hoods were the recipients of some relief when the results of the skin biopsy showed Alex did not have the worst, but the second most serious form of the condition. She was diagnosed as suffering from dystrophic EB. Confused, frightened and still struggling to come to terms with having had their lives turned upside down they asked, 'What will this mean?' and were told, 'Your daughter will live until adult mid-life'. 'How long will that be?' they wondered, but the answer was forgivably vague. There was no guarantee that she would survive beyond her late teens.

If the news was a nightmare for her parents, how much more would it be for the daughter for whom they had so longed once she grew up and understood what lay in store for her? Until that time her education would be painful, dire and without relief from torment.

Meanwhile every tick of time of her life would mean her needing to be wrapped in bandages; not a day would go by when she would not have to suffer the awful bursting of the blisters that swelled up at the slightest pressure on her skin. For every moment of her existence she would require to be protected against those joys given to every parent who watches a child grow and tumble and has the marvellous wonder of transforming cries to laughter. Because for an EB child, even the very act of wiping away a tear can bring untold pain and misery.

In the chaos of the mental pain that would never leave them, an eight-year-old voice, the owner curious as to the obvious sadness and fear of his parents, was heard. "One day, when I came home from seeing Virginia and Alex in hospital, my son could see I was upset and asked, 'Daddy, what's wrong?' I told him, 'Your sister's not very well' and all the times he had said to me, 'Daddy, will you come and play football?' or 'Daddy can we go out? flashed through my mind. I'd told him, 'Tomorrow', not fully aware of his needs but perhaps inwardly persuading myself I was too exhausted from building up the business to kick a ball around with Robin or take him out on the loch fishing.

"Now, all of a sudden, I realised nature had denied me something that I'd taken for granted, the freedom to play with my children, to laugh with them, run with them, pick them up when they fell and hug the tears away. 'I'll never be able to play football with Alex' I thought and now everything was coming home to me, all the missed opportunities with Robin. I should have done this and that with my son. And if by the arrival on the scene of my daughter I had any thoughts of sharing with her all those times I had missed with my son, then it was too late. It was all about regret; for the first time I was having regrets about not doing things with Robin that I should have done because I was too busy or just hadn't wanted to. Instead of spending time with him, I'd maybe wanted to do what I wanted ."

Once the initial shock of discovering the bleak future that awaited his daughter had passed, anger set in. "Am I religious person? Yes, I am even though I don't go to church other than to someone's christening, a funeral or a wedding. But I do believe that if God can do all he is said to have done by creating the world and everything in it in just six days, then you can talk to him, and my parents always brought me up to say my prayers every evening, and I did. But when Alex was born, I remember saying to my father, 'There's no such thing as God. The same God who can create the world in six days can do this to a new-born baby? It's all rubbish.' I was very resentful, very aggressive, 'Why has he done this to us? What have I done to deserve this?' I just couldn't see what the answer was." However in the years that followed, it was a question to which he himself believed he had found the solution.

For Virginia, pondering over the prospect of leaving her husband after the birth of their daughter, a new realisation now appeared before her. She would need the unstinting and generous help and support of her husband through the unremitting years of toil that lay ahead.

Her memories of those first days are fragmented. She recalls being in the lift taking her to her ward; then the birth; at some stage being told her daughter had an illness so serious she would die within a few months; and then the horror of facing the consequences of that illness alone. "I said to Robin, 'Please can we stay together because I can't cope with this on my own?' So we did end up staying together and tried to get on with living as normal a life as possible."

In those early days, Robin was convinced the prognosis of his daughter dying, at best having reached mid adult life, would change. He felt sure there must be an urgency about the need to find a cure for such a terrible condition that decimated and destroyed the lives of children. The fact was that apart from the efforts of Debra and the dedicated volunteers who worked to support the charity, there was little if any progress. Like so many of the most dreadful defects in the human body, their very rarity left them well down the list when it came to dishing out public money on research. There was care available, but the expensive business of allocating National Health Service funds for searching out a solution had to take a back seat while its very rarity meant investigating EB was not a viable or attractive commercial proposition to the giant companies who made their millions and billions offering cures or the alleviation from suffering. It was just not good business to spend a fortune and tie up valuable resources for many years developing a cure that ultimately only a relative few would have need to buy.

At this stage Robin saw Debra as a well-intentioned but very small operation doing its best to cope on extremely limited resources. He and Virginia were grateful for its existence, and for the help it offered, but it was as if they were students starting out on a new course, there was so much to learn and sadly much of their education would have to be at the expense of their infant daughter. If mistakes were to be made, then it would be Alex who suffered.

One requirement made clear to them at the very outset was that the baby would need a clean environment in which to have her bandages changed, a twice daily routine into which Virginia soon settled. Her daughter was aged six weeks when Virginia was allowed to bring Alex home, but it was clear the extra bedroom that she and Robin knew would be needed at some stage, was now an immediate essential. Their daughter had to have a room of her own and so her brother gave up his bedroom and shared that of his parents. He did so willingly, but over the years Robin junior made countless sacrifices for the love of his sister and he did so gladly and without complaint; indeed his devotion to Alex was plain to all to see. Brother and sister were close from the very beginning until her last breath.

The need to quickly build an extension to Lochside Cottage became crucial. Funding was never a problem; Robin simply sold the Lochmaben bungalow to his parents for £25,000. The family doctor wrote a letter to local planners confirming the couple urgently needed an extra room for their disabled child. "The planners were brilliant," said Robin. "We were given permission to go ahead almost immediately."

He shopped about the area for a builder, but in the end recruited a team from the Midlands who lived in the caravan that, during the shooting season, was used to accommodate stalking parties. At least they were a captive audience and with nothing else to do but build, set about completing the work in double quick time in order to return home. Robin and Virginia would move into the extension, Alex have their original bedroom and Robin return to his own room. But the arrival of the builders meant extra work for Virginia who discovered herself in her old routine of looking after her home, her family, helping with her husband's business and catering for guests. Only now she had the additional strain of acting as near full time nurse to her infant daughter. It was a burden that would soon tell as problems began to mount.

CHAPTER EIGHT

Along with the mental agonies they suffer day after day, the parents of children with disabilities face the fact that their marriages are in greater peril. Some statisticians estimate the divorce rate among couples with disabled offspring to be as depressingly high as 80 per cent. While others believe this to be a heavily inflated figure – some even suggest that the rate is lower than the average – the consensus is that these couples are more likely to divorce.

Marriage guidance specialists suggest that married couples finding themselves with a disabled child need to make a greater than normal effort to stay married; to give more time to the needs of one another and to understanding the feelings of the other party. This is all very well, but parents in these environments invariably need more time to devote to their children. Giving less time to their children will lead to arguments between parents and the need to put the needs of the children to one side while they resolve their own difficulties. It was the type of Catch-22 situation in which Virginia and Robin found themselves.

At least they would never go down the road, as do so many other parents, of wondering whether one or the other was the cause of their daughter's illness. "We'd never have blamed each other in any case, but when it was explained that we both carried the defective gene we knew it was one of those situations where neither of us could have done anything. It wasn't as though we'd done anything wrong purposely. All we wanted was to get on with dealing with what now confronted us," said Robin.

As the weeks and months passed, they found just how demanding was the task of caring for little Alex. Their home was not connected to the mains electricity supply. Power came from an ancient diesel powered generator. If it needed to be cranked and Robin wasn't at home, Virginia struggled to turn the stiff handle. Until the birth of Alex they had been able to cope adequately but now the need for a reliable supply of power became increasingly evident.

"The generator we had bought with the house was long past its sell-by date," said Robin. "Virginia's father paid £8,000 for a new model and we just got on with it. I was still running my shooting and stalking business. Virginia was doing the bandaging of Alex. In hindsight, where we went wrong was that we did not bring our son Robin into things. I used to say to him, 'Get away from your sister, don't go near your sister, don't do this, don't do that.' Virginia had little time to give to him because she seemed to be constantly doing Alex's dressings. Alex was starting to grow and became aware, could understand at an early age, what she could and could not do.

"Any parent remembers the first time their child begins to crawl. But when Alex first began, she was taking the skin off her knees and hands. Taking parties deer stalking meant getting up at two in the morning. We'd start stalking at three o'clock and carry on until seven or eight in the morning. Then I'd drop them off for their breakfast and go and do other things, administration or feeding pheasants then at seven in the evening take them out once more before I got to bed. Three hours later, I was getting up and doing it all again. This was my routine week in, week out, but it was really good money, a grand a week and letting Virginia get on with things at home.

"I could see Alex was struggling, but didn't really think anything about it. I thought, 'If that's what she's got then we'll somehow cope.' But I began taking more notice of other children. What used to irritate me was being out and about, say, in the supermarket and seeing somebody with a healthy child and, as children do, the child would maybe pick up a bag of sweets when the parents didn't want it to. The child would be reprimanded and maybe given a smack and then I'd think to myself, 'You don't know how lucky you are to have a healthy child to hit. But why hit a child over a bag of sweets?' There were many times when I just had to bite my tongue and look the other way."

For Virginia, there was no time to introduce herself gradually to the daily task of tending to her daughter. The vivid blisters, the vivid red bare flesh where the skin had rubbed off were there every morning and evening. There was no escaping from the nightmare, the squeals of pain each time she pricked a blister with the specially sterilised needles issued by the hospital. She learned to become immune and practical, realising it was a task that had to be done and the sooner it was over the better for her daughter and for her.

47

ROBIN HOOD

Every night she would be woken up by the cries of her baby as Alex turned over in her cot, each movement causing friction, agony and another blister.

Virginia has always played down the role she took in the care of her daughter, adopting the attitude of however distressing the situation in which she found herself, there was no escape, so why not simply face up to the problem and do whatever needed to be done. For example the simple act of her child sleeping brought no relief. "During the first three years Alex would wake about sixteen times during the night. It meant I wasn't getting much sleep and made things very difficult."

And as spring turned to summer and the weather warmed, that difficulty became all the greater. Swathed in her bandages the baby would sweat, the wrappings becoming wet and liable to create even greater friction. It was a concern that, as Alex grew older, the Hoods would need to meet face on. Then came another hurdle. Once Alex reached the age where she could begin taking solid foods, her parents discovered a new and awful difficulty as Virginia found. "She couldn't swallow. It took her simply ages to feed because she was blistering in her mouth and throat. Her oesophagus had narrowed and shortened and because she had lots of medication to take, she would sometimes bring everything back up and it would block the throat. All of this combined to mean she just wasn't putting on weight.

"She had splints on her hands to protect the skin and these would have to be removed and then replaced. The toilet could take a long time because she would blister her back passage and used to get very constipated and would be in floods of tears because she couldn't go. I don't even know that she was constipated. Maybe she

48

just didn't want to do the toilet because it hurt so much, but using the toilet generally took about 45 minutes. The dressings took about an hour and a half in the mornings. Throughout the day she was taking medication and then in the evenings we would need about three and a half hours to place her in the bath so the dressings could be soaked off, then the blisters needed to be burst and her new bandages put in place. It sounds very quick when you simply say it like that."

That she coped was remarkable because, as the stalking business flourished, Virginia also had the task of catering for parties accommodated in the caravan outside their home on top of the normal chores of any mother. Robin cooked breakfast for his customers, but the greater chore of providing evening meals was still left to his wife. Added to those was her extraordinary care of Alex. She had begged her husband to stay with her, and he had never considered any other course. But she needed a husband to be there for her physically, a shoulder on which to lean in the few moments when she had time to feel dispirited.

However his business that had begun on a small scale had grown at an astonishing rate until it became a monster eating up his time and munching into the needs of his family. If Virginia rightly had cause to feel tired, so did her husband and sometimes when weariness led to frustration he took his irritation out on his daughter. "When breakfast time came after Alex had come off the bottle, we'd give her half a Weetabix and it would take her up to an hour to eat it. It was frustrating. Lots of other children play with their food and their parents become annoyed. But Alex wasn't playing and I'd bang the table and shout at her."

In a sense the situation might be interpreted as a husband and wife going their separate ways, each pursuing their individual tasks; she of home maker and child carer, he of breadwinner; then occasionally meeting. Their days seemed to be comprised of work and worry with no solution or end in sight. "I was getting on with the business, trying to make ends meet but the amount of land I was renting, and some of the rents I was paying, sometimes £10,000 and £15,000 a year, meant I needed the £1,000 a week I was getting. By now I was renting about 90,000 acres around Scotland. I had land at Torridon, Perth, at Lochmaben and 17,000 acres at Gatehouse of Fleet, with some other smaller holdings. The business had really taken off and the only day I didn't go shooting was a Sunday.

"I just let Virginia get on with it. I was doing what I was doing and she was looking after the kids and I was bringing in money. We were dedicated to our respective jobs. I expected her to get on with it. The way I saw it, I was doing my bit. I was bringing the money in and without the money we were going to go under. "I can see it now; looking back I must have been so inconsiderate to her. I must have appeared to be so selfish. Did I feel guilty? Could I have done more to support her? Could I have been there for her more? The way it seemed to me then, I couldn't do anything about it. I had to make the business work otherwise we would have been in trouble. Both sets of our respective parents used to come to Lochside Cottage to help out. And Virginia had friends who did whatever they could. But there always seemed to be something else to do."

And along with everything else, there was his prized membership of the Territorial Army, a sideline in which he had long wanted to participate. But was it right or fair to continue with a duty that demanded so many precious days and nights? Before their birth of their daughter, Robin had begun a rigorous training programme with the ultimate goal of being commissioned as an officer cadet. In September 1988 he was one of 180 hopefuls who began the programme stretching over a series of week-ends and a strenuous two-week long course designed to test the fitness of those taking part. As the programme progressed, more and more men were told they did not meet the strict criteria and expectations needed. The numbers were whittled down but Robin retained his place.

However the birth of Alex and subsequent discovery she was a victim of EB caused him to wonder whether he could justify continuing. His age alone would have given him the ideal excuse to call it a day. At the very outset, a Colonel in the training centre at Edinburgh had poured doubt on his ability and value. "I was now touching 33. But I was very fit. I was taking people deer stalking and was a black belt in karate, I was as fit as a butcher's dog. The officer suggested, 'I don't think Her Majesty's Government is going to get its money's worth out of you, Hood. You'll be too old to do anything by the time you get commissioned.' The regular staff there, who were watching me train, had noticed I was a very fit guy who fitted in with the rest of the group and urged him to let me go on and he agreed.

"Then Alex was born and I said to Virginia, 'I'll give all this up, messing about with the TA. Our daughter has this illness.' At that time we thought Alex was going to die. Virginia was a very, very wise woman and asked, 'If you give this up, will it stop Alex dying?' And I said,

'No, of course it won't.' And she said, 'Well don't give it up. It's something you've always wanted to do, carry on with it.' So I did. All the training staff knew about Alex and her illness and thought she was going to die. They were convinced I'd bottle the course and throw in the towel."

They reckoned without his determination and ingenuity, facets many, many more would come to recognise in Robin in later years. He was not a man who gave up, even when the odds cried out against him. An example of his cunning came when course entrants went in batches for a two week long series of exercises at the Royal Military Academy at Sandhurst in Surrey. "I asked some of my pals, who had already completed this part of the course, what had happened. They told me, 'You are all given your own room and during your first week they run you ragged. They get you up at six o'clock in the morning with a room inspection, get six or seven changes of kit daily, have lectures and are made to crawl around the Barossa training area. There are 80 guys and just four washing machines so people are fighting each other to get their gear washed because every morning you face a kit inspection. Then your room is checked every day and there's only one vacuum.' My answer to this was to beg, borrow and steal seven sets of kit so every day I didn't have to do any washing. I just threw the dirty kit in a bin liner and stuck it in the back of my car. And I took with me a hand held vacuum. So I was going to bed at ten or eleven o'clock every night, while at three or four in the morning the other poor bastards were still ironing their clothes then sleeping on the floor because they didn't want to mess their beds up.

"This information gave me the insight enabling me to prepare and get a good result and the best thing for me was to make my father so proud to come to Sandhurst and watch the parade.

Five months after Alex was born Robin, having received the blessing of his wife to continue in the Territorials, was commissioned at Sandhurst, one of just 17 who had survived the course from the initial 180. He walked the same corridors and performed in the same the same ceremonies as illustrious predecessors who included actor David Niven, 007 creator Ian Fleming and Winston Churchill. Among the proud families watching the Passing Out parade was Second World War veteran Dennis Hood. Robin will remain on the Army reserve list until the age of 60.

Meanwhile Virginia and Robin had continued their contact with Debra and, impressed by the help the charity had given them soon after Alex was born, decided they owed it to give what backing they could. "We did a little bit of fundraising, when I had enough time. Virginia and I held a dinner and raised money and I sent them £1,000. But we just got on with looking after Alex and keeping the business that supported us going. "Then we began attending Debra meetings, including their annual conference. There wasn't a Debra in Scotland; in fact as far as Debra was concerned, what was happening took place in England. Any money generated in Scotland was sent to England and yet there were EB victims in Scotland.

"Obviously most of the people at these gatherings were the parents of EB children or members of their families. They were really nice, genuine people sincerely concerned with trying to help, but for me they just didn't have enough drive. On our way home from one meeting, I said to Virginia, 'They need to get their act together if they are going to raise the money to find a cure. They are lovely people, really good people, genuine, dedicated and caring, but they just don't have enough oomph.' Something needs to happen." Robin Hood would change all that. But the cost would be heart-breaking.

CHAPTER NINE

As if the suffering of the Hoods over Alex had not taken them to their allotted quota of ill luck, there was more to come. Virginia hoped for another baby. She was 38 years old and her daughter just over two when she found she was pregnant again. An outsider might have reasoned that she was entitled to expect a healthy baby, the one-in-four odds now being in her favour. But life was about to deal another terrible card.

"We had been told we were going to lose Alex quite early to EB. We didn't tell anyone Virginia was pregnant, because we lived in a small community and didn't want everyone knowing, particularly in case something happened to go wrong again. Even Virginia's parents and my parents didn't know she was pregnant. She was encouraged by her doctors and by Debra to undergo a skin biopsy, a test that would show whether the baby she was carrying had EB, or if there were any other problems expected. So when Virginia was 19 weeks pregnant, we went to an eminent specialist, Professor Robin Eady in London – he's now Emeritus Professor of Experimental Dermatopathology at King's College London – who inserted a needle into her womb and took a tiny amount of fluid containing foetal tissue. The fragment of tissue was so small, you couldn't see it with the naked eye. I only knew it had been taken because I watched a tiny reaction from the embryo. I was with Virginia and we watched on a little screen as he performed this very delicate operation."

Terrified of a repeat of the ordeal they had gone through after Alex's birth, the couple continued to keep the pregnancy and amniocentesis test strictly under wraps. But the whole saga would have a very unpleasant backlash.

The amniocentesis test had been scheduled to be carried out during the second week of a Territorial Army camp at which Robin was required to be present. But both he and Virginia wanted him present during the hospital procedure and this would necessitate his being given special permission to be briefly absent. To avoid embarrassment we are not identifying the officer concerned, instead we will only refer to him as ' Major A'.

"What happened would have a knock on effect on my Army career. 'A' was an absolute clown. I told him, 'I need a day off for personal reasons'. He wanted to know, 'What personal reasons?' and I said, 'No, I'm not telling you.' He said, 'Look, it's like talking to your doctor, you can tell me.' So I told him in absolute confidence. So, while I'm away and we are awaiting the results of the test, a friend visits Virginia and tells her, 'Oh by the way, I hear you are having a baby.' It was obvious that 'A' had been blabbing. He knew people who were our friends.

"When I telephoned her she demanded to know, 'What the hell are you doing. I thought we had agreed that nobody was to know.' So when I came back from camp Virginia, who had come to collect me, was not happy with me.' I wasn't happy with 'A' either. He was there too and I told him, 'You bastard, why did you have to tell people."

A week later the Hoods were elated to be told the baby, another little girl, was clear of EB. At least they felt able to tell family and friends about their wonderful news. Days later came a bombshell. Further tests on the fluid taken from the embryo and the amniotic fluid revealed the baby would have been deaf, dumb, blind and deformed and had a condition known as Trisomy 13, a chromosome disorder. "It was simply bad luck, nothing to do with EB. We listened to medical advice and the baby was aborted. That was the end of the pregnancy and the end of the babies for Virginia and me. How did we feel? I think it was a bigger blow to Virginia than it was to me. At least we still had Alex and Robin. "I'd felt euphoric when we were told we were going to have a healthy baby. But I'm a great believer, and Alex was the same, that if something is wrong, get off your backside and change it. Don't sit there crying."

Virginia loved her daughter. Twice each day as she removed Alex's bandages, helplessly watching strips of skin tear away from the tiny body and then gently re-bandaged the raw flesh, a remarkable bond grew between them. It was a closeness that went beyond the normal relationship between a mother and daughter, as if the umbilical cord that had passed life from one to the other was still in place. She and Robin had listened intently to every scrap of advice given by the knowledge-able and helpful nurse who had travelled from Debra headquarters to see them and pass on her expertise and listen to their fears. They took in the words of hospital specialists, but at the end of the day had to learn for themselves from experience, very often at the expense of their baby's agony.

A major worry was that Alex was not gaining weight. She could not tell them just how much it hurt to swallow, to have morsels of even the softest food rip her throat. But her cries, when she tried to swallow, told them more than a thousand words. Their baby was in terrible pain. The solution was to create a means of feeding that would bypass her oesophagus and that required an operation at the world renowned Great Ormond Street Hospital. The hospital, in Bloomsbury, central London, is acknowledged as the finest centre in Europe for research into and treatment of child ailments. Much of the work is funded by donations and in 1929 J.M.Barrie gave Great Ormond Street the rights to the wonderful children's fantasy Peter Pan, or The Boy Who Wouldn't Grow Up, a gesture which has brought significant and much needed income over the years.

Surgeons talked to the Hoods and described how they would perform a gastrostomy, effectively creating a hole in Alex's midriff, close to her tummy button, through which specially blended mixtures of liquid food and medication could be delivered. It was an operation they had carried out frequently and they spent time calming the fears of Virginia and Robin over how their baby, aged just two, might react. The well-tried procedure involved passing a thin tube with a microscopic camera at the end known as a gastroscope down her throat and into Alex's tiny stomach, which was then enlarged by having air gently pumped into it. A hole was made in the wall of her abdomen and the gastrostomy tube threaded down her throat and out through this same hole. A connector was fitted through which food and other needed solutions could be passed from the outside into her stomach.

In practical terms it was as if Alex now had a tiny petrol cap just above her navel. When the cap was opened, inside was a tube slightly bigger than the diameter of a ball point pen.

Once carried out, the gastrostomy was simple to operate, merely requiring a tube from the food container to be linked into the connector. Then a brown concoction, disgusting in appearance but packed with goodness, was pumped inside her. It meant Alex could begin putting on much needed body weight. But with it came problem. Normally food entering the stomach via the throat passes through a ring of muscle at the stomach entrance. This opens to allow food in and then closes. When the muscle is not fully developed some food can return through the food pipe into the throat and even mouth. It is a problem common in babies and is known as acid reflux. Adults often experience this as a form of heartburn. Because Alex was receiving some of her food directly into her stomach, the muscle frequently would not recognise the need to close and as a consequence she regularly suffered from acid reflux leaving her with a burning sensation, feeling uncomfortable and sickly.

Meanwhile the introduction of the gastrostomy meant she needed extra antibiotics to counter any risk of infection. And it had another side effect. "The gastrostomy was fitted so she could develop the correct weight for her height and for a girl of her age. But because her use of her oesophagus had diminished, the back of her throat used to shrink until she couldn't even swallow her own spit. That would then entail Alex being treated at Great Ormond Street or St Thomas' Hospital in London to have her throat stretched so she could swallow her own saliva," said Robin.

As Alex grew out of infancy, Virginia became aware of new problems for which she had not been prepared. She would tell her husband, "There are so many things that we do which we take for granted but mean misery for Alex." Alex's hands would be a problem for her throughout her life and again Virginia would come to be aware of a problem for which she had not been prepared. She had known it as hamstring finger through a former work colleague who suffered from the problem. To others it is trigger finger. It is otherwise recorded as Dupuytren's disease or, more technically, palmar fibromatosis, and is usually caused by the tissue just under the skin of the palm becoming thickener and pulling the fingers towards the palm.

"Actually when Alex was small I saw she had a finger which bent over a little bit," said Virginia. "Although I had tried reading up as much as I could about EB, maybe I didn't read enough. Nobody had ever said this might happen and when I had visited a consultant dermatologist in Edinburgh he had not mentioned it. But one day he sent me a newspaper cutting showing a hand with splints on it after an operation to correct the problem. Evidently for anyone with EB, hamstring finger was a possibility yet I had never been warned it was going to happen. That was a real shock. But then if we'd known about it before and about all the other side effects, we wouldn't have been able to cope. Because the list of problems just went on and on. More and more of them. It was just one thing after another. You'd find something wrong, get it sorted and then there would be something new that needed to be taken care of."

SMILE DADDY – I'M DYING

One day, while accompanying her mother on a shopping expedition, Alex slipped. Instinctively Virginia grabbed her daughter by the hand and was horrified to realise she was holding not flesh and blood and her child but simply a glove of skin. In place of Alex's tiny hand was a red mass of flesh which took around three months to heal.

The incidence of heartbreak mounted. Those of us fortunate enough not to be EB victims will think nothing of rubbing our eyes, perhaps one of the first acts of the day. That simple movement, Virginia found, could cause acute distress to her daughter because the skin around her eyes would blister and peel away. If the youngster even blinked too hard, blisters would develop on her eyeballs. "If she did that, she wouldn't be able to open her eyes for five or six days and she would be in agony. And as she got older it meant she wouldn't be able to go to school because she couldn't see to read or go to the bathroom, in fact she couldn't see to do anything." Alex was prescribed special medication that she needed to gently caress into her eyes each night. But on occasions the only relief was for her to sit in a darkened room for days on end. Even the very basic womanly act of having her hair cut had to be carried out with great delicacy while making sure contact with her scalp was avoided. Fortunately a close friend of Virginia carried out the task with gentleness and understanding.

Did Virginia develop immunity to emotion at seeing her daughter's suffering? Did she become upset? "Yes, but in order to deal with situations like that it's no good being in floods of tears, you've got to get on with it. You know I'm in front of a daughter that has got a condition. I don't want to upset her." She hid that upset until Alex's bedroom door had closed and she could grieve in private.

At least the Hoods, intelligent and practical, were able to accept that there was always someone worse off, an acknowledgement that seems to come more readily to the parents of children with disabilities. "We felt sorry for ourselves. But one day Virginia and I had taken Alex to Great Ormond Street for a hand operation. We were second on the waiting list and I can never forget the look on the faces of the couple whose appointment was immediately before ours. They had Siamese twins, joined at the shoulder, about 18 months or two years old. One baby was as bright as a button taking note of everything in the room, the other quiet and unresponsive. We later found out the parents were there to have the children separated because time was pressing, and knew only one could survive. Maybe the choice as to which one should live and which die sounds easy. Easy, that is, to anybody not affected. But what must that choice have caused those loving parents? I never learned the outcome. But that was a situation worse than the one in which Virginia, Alex and I found ourselves. For me personally, it was a huge learning curve."

Just how well they had taken heed of the lesson that no matter how black they seemed, things could always be worse, was about to be put to the test.

CHAPTER TEN

During the off season when, due mainly to adverse weather conditions, paying parties were few and stalking and shooting pulling in little income, Robin was able to supplement the family finances with attachments to regular Army units. As such he was entitled to Second Lieutenant's pay, equivalent to £30 or £40 a day with the opportunity for this to increase. It was highly useful money and work which Robin enjoyed.

On the evening of Tuesday, January 16 1992, while on his way to his local TA centre and driving south of the village of Dalmellington, near an notorious accident black spot perhaps appropriately named Black Rock, he was involved in a head on collision with an articulated lorry carrying tons of newly forested timber. The impact was horrendous. For years afterwards Robin was convinced he was immediately knocked unconscious and had woken up in Glasgow's Southern General Hospital. But four years ago he met up with a nurse who had been following him and arrived on a scene of utter carnage almost certainly in time to save his life. It was immediately clear to her he had suffered horrific injuries to his head and right leg and as she began administering emergency first aid until the arrival of paramedics and an ambulance, she began talking to the desperately ill man who had been dragged from the mangled wreckage of his motor.

"She had asked me my name and when I told her 'Robin Hood' she thought I was delirious. She continued talking to me and I was evidently conscious for about 15 minutes. Because I believed I had been unconscious from the start and not able to remember what had happened, I had been unable to argue against the account of the lorry driver as to what took place. He said the accident was my fault. Had I been aware that I had been conscious I would have been able to dispute his version and say the blame lay with him. But as it was through stating I had been unconscious there was nothing I could do and I was informed I would be unable to claim compensation." That outcome would add to the devastating effect on the Hood family of the accident.

An ambulance took Robin to hospital in Ayr and, once doctors were satisfied his condition had been stabilised, he was transferred to the Southern General Hospital in Glasgow. X-Rays showed worrying symptoms. The front of his skull had been smashed and so great was the pressure on his brain that it was beginning to swell alarmingly causing dangerous clotting. He was given the Last Rites. At around midnight, when his condition had begun to deteriorate seriously, surgeons performed an emergency procedure to remove a blood clot from his brain.

At home in Lochside Cottage, Virginia had been with Alex, then two but only a few weeks from her third birthday while Robin junior, then eleven, was at school. She was contacted by police who informed her that her husband had been seriously hurt in a road accident and was in hospital. "I have a disabled daughter and can't go to hospital now," she was forced to reply. Robin was unconscious for several days and probably only survived because walking the hills and woods with his parties of deer stalkers had made him extremely fit, even for a man of 35 and in his prime.

Unable to rouse him from his coma, the doctors suggested to Virginia that hearing the voices of his children might stimulate their father's brain and encourage him back to consciousness. And so in the cottage, the children sang the 1930s favourite, 'You Are My Sunshine', desperately trying to hide their fears by emphasising 'You Make Me Happy When Skies Are Grey' and recorded it on to a cassette which was then played to the unconscious Robin at his bedside. Did that loving gesture from his son and daughter bring him back to life? No one can ever know, but soon after hearing it Robin came round.

"I woke up in the Southern General, not remembering a thing about the accident, but bursting for a pee. I spotted a toilet and went in, so desperate that there wasn't even time to switch on the light. But then I looked into a mirror and in the light shining from my bedroom saw myself. My face was minced, and covered in scars. So was my head. My nose was smashed." He did not know it, but beneath the bandages wrapped around his head, lay a deep indentation where surgeons had performed the emergency operation to remove the life threatening blood clot. Nor did he or his family know just how devastating would be the effects his injuries would have on their lives.

"I was in hospital for a couple of weeks recovering from a fractured skull, blood clotting and severe knee damage. My right knee was swollen up like a football and I was unable to bend the knee. At first I could not walk and had to be pushed around in a wheelchair. I had been warned that one of the side effects from serious head injuries could be severe depression and when eventually I was allowed to go home I became severely depressed. I was absolutely vile to all of them my son, daughter and my wife Virginia.

"I became convinced Virginia was having an affair with a local man. She wasn't of course. She'd always worn nice underwear and now I would demand to know, 'Why are you putting that on? Who are you seeing?' The law insists that if a driver has suffered a serious head injury then he or she must inform the Driving and Vehicle Licensing Agency, the DVLA, and when I explained the severity of my condition my licence was suspended for a year until I was able to provide medical evidence that I would not be prone to black outs.

"Loch Ken was virtually in the middle of nowhere and one day, after she had driven off, I got my bicycle out because I was going to follow her, sure I knew that I would find the car outside the business of the man I had told myself she must be seeing. "Because my right leg was so swollen, I could only pedal with one leg. I was effectively a cripple trying to cycle. I started pedalling along the road in pursuit of Virginia when suddenly my life seemed to change. I thought, 'You fool. What are you doing? If there is something happening, by the time you get there it will be all over.' So I just turned around and went back.

"Things were difficult at home, especially as I was there all day not working and with all the land I was renting still to support. A really good friend, Albert

Winn, who lived in Lincolnshire, was driving up to Scotland every week-end to feed the pheasants and take parties out stalking. Albert was brilliant, a wonderful guy and friend. He also gave Virginia moral support while I moped around, feeling sorry for myself, and not giving a toss. I made regular visits to hospital to have checks done on how my injuries were healing, but the fact was that specialists had told me I was going to be a cripple, that the damage to my leg would get progressively worse so that by the time I was 40 I'd be confined to a wheelchair. It wasn't the sort of news I wanted to hear because the success or otherwise of my business depended on my ability to walk over often difficult terrain with stalking and shooting parties and it would be unfair to expect Albert to continue indefinitely.

"Money became a problem. Once all the rent and bills were paid there was nothing left over and our savings began to suffer. We needed an income but came up against a double edged sword involving an insurance company and the Ministry of Defence. I had an insurance policy which covered me for any accident whether on a bus, train, boat, any form of travel. It stipulated I would be entitled to receive £100 for every day I was in hospital and then £100 a week after that for a period of up to two years. I had to show I was on duty and, in addition, the Ministry insisted that if I was in any way to blame for the accident then they wouldn't pay me.

"Nobody was prosecuted over the crash but I was in an impossible situation. I explained my predicament to a friend who was a regular soldier and an officer. He asked if I could prove the accident wasn't my fault but I had to admit I could remember nothing. This man was a gem, a brilliant guy. He contacted the lorry driver and explained he was carrying out an investigation into the incident on behalf of one of his officers. He told the man, 'I've been to the scene and measured both the width of the road at the point where the collision occurred and the width of your vehicle. If you were entirely on your correct side of the road there should have been signs of your tyre impressions on the grass verge. Can you explain why there weren't?' "The driver told him, 'Maybe I was over on his side of the road a little bit'. The guy had the decency to be honest and that was all we needed to show I had not been at fault. As a result I was awarded a lieutenant's pay for six months.

"I was still determined to fight the insurance company. I'd paid into the policy for years but when it came to making a claim they just didn't want to pay up. By now I estimated they owed me £2000 but hadn't paid a penny. They kept telling me to fill out forms and said they needed the results of a blood test and so we arranged for that to be sent. Each time I rang them to find out what was happening, I seemed to speak to somebody different, someone higher up the chain. It was frustrating and eventually I spoke to somebody who asked, 'We've seen your blood test, which shows you hadn't been drinking, but you weren't breathalysed. We need a form showing why not.' I said, 'Because I was unconscious'.

"I was trying to make him understand that lying unconscious and covered in blood in the road made it improbable I'd be giving a breath sample, but it seemed to make no impression on him. 'Yes, but you could have had a drink,' he said and I told him, 'A blood test showed I was clear of alcohol.' 'Ah, yes, the blood may be clear but you could have just had a drink and it hadn't had time to get into your blood stream,' he said. 'Why weren't you given a breath test?' 'Because I was unconscious,' I told him again. By now, I'd had enough. I said, 'I'll tell you what, forget it. Don't worry. Your head office is in the south of England but I'll come down tomorrow morning. I have a disabled daughter who is dying and a son at school. I haven't worked for three months. We are destitute. I have been paying premiums for fifteen years and the moment you have to pay out, you do everything possible to avoid it. You want us to pay in but you won't pay out. I'll be in front of your building tomorrow showing my smashed up face, holding my daughter in my arms and telling everybody you are refusing to pay up.' I hung up, and half an hour later the telephone rang and a voice said, 'Mr Hood, there's a cheque in the post'.

"I must have been so difficult to live with. In the early days after leaving hospital I was very conscious of being in a wheelchair and certain passers-by were staring at my face or the dent in my head because it was so disfigured. If I caught someone peering I'd shout, 'What are you looking at?' When I was unable to walk, I'd feel so sorry for myself that I'd look at Alex and think, 'Oh, you've just got that skin thing, look at me, I'm the one who's going to be a cripple for the rest of his life.'

"Virginia was doing literally everything and eventually, one day told me she was going to leave. It came as a terrible shock. 'I can't tolerate you anymore,' she said. 'We're off, I can't cope. We're going. You're such a miserable bastard'. The truth was that if she had gone there was nothing I could do and I couldn't argue against her leaving. I was at home all day, not working and had all the land I was renting to support. But when she said that, I changed. The shock of thinking I was going to lose her made me change overnight."

For Virginia, holding the family together in the face of her husband's tirades was a nightmare. She had faced so much but if there was any consolation in the loss of her baby, she saw it now. "I actually think it was fate because I would never have coped with the baby, Alex, Robin after his accident and everything else that was going on around us. What happened after the crash was very intense and Robin's mother always said the accident changed him. Well, I think he was like that anyway and the accident just accentuated the way he felt about things. But when he first had it he was a nightmare. He was right to try getting back into the normal way of things as soon as possible, but he used to pick on the children dreadfully, really, really badly and Alex all the time. He just kept going on and on at them and it was really hard because I was trying to deal with him when he wasn't well, with Alex and with our son."

CHAPTER ELEVEN

Being at home, for much of the time at the beginning unable to move about with any degree of freedom, meant Robin became much more aware of the effects of his daughter's condition. Virginia had been told Alex would certainly develop osteoporosis, if it had not already infiltrated her bone structure. Osteoporosis is mainly thought of as a disease affecting the elderly, in particular women, who begin to suffer as the body slowly begins to run down and wear out. Lower than necessary levels of proteins leaves the bones brittle and prone to fracturing.

In the case of Alex, and EB victims generally, the open sores resulting from skin being peeled or torn away results in vital nutrients escaping or being used up to fight to repair this damage. The proteins her body needed to continue to function effectively were being replaced and fed into her through the gastrostomy tube.

Most of her food was pumped in through the same tube, but Virginia found her daughter was able to cope with eating and swallowing a very limited selection of edibles. The problem was not so much with chewing, she could perform this task which healthy children take for granted slowly and with some difficulty, but the problem then came with digesting her food. This caused severe pain as it brushed against the sides of her oesophagus. She was able to swallow mashed potatoes and gently drink soup, but these were fed to her more for social reasons. For example, if the family went out or invited Alex's friends to her home for a party or celebration, then being able to join others in eating gave her a feeling of some semblance of normality.

The installation of the gastrostomy tube did much to cheer the Hoods. Not long after Virginia began using it her daughter perked up, flourished even. "She developed a lovely complexion," said Robin. "She looked great, really, really great."

It was not all plain sailing though. "The down side of her gaining weight was that as she did, her skin could not support the extra weight and as a result she had no skin on either cheek of her buttocks, so in order to get by had to have a pad on each cheek."

A close friend who visited Robin one day watched in near horror as Virginia peeled back some of the bandaging on her daughter. "The man was fairly religious and he said to me, 'God is constantly fighting evil, he needs people to help him in that fight. I believe you are one his helpers. This is an evil, help him fight it.'

"I said nothing but then began wondering if it was purely bad luck that had left Alex as she was. Was it a sort of random luck of the draw or had we been chosen to be parents to a child who needed very special care? Was this a test for us? I felt if I went around claiming to be some sort of chosen one people would think I was barking mad. But maybe this was a test to see how we'd react."

SMILE DADDY — I'M DYING

It was a year and well into 1993 before Robin was fit enough to actively resume running his business. By then, thanks to injections of Army pay and insurance policy compensation, the family finances which had been draining fast, looked considerably healthier. They could now at least pay their bills. The threat by his wife to leave had shocked him and he knew he needed to get out from under her feet at home. The loss of his driving licence for a year had been a bitter blow because he had always enjoyed the freedom owning a car gave and in any case knew that until the suspension was lifted it would be impossible for return to supervising stalking and shooting parties.

"My leg was giving me a lot of trouble and Virginia introduced me to a local lady, an aromatherapist, who began treating me by rubbing oils into my knee, back and back of my neck. She was highly skilled and capable and performed wonders. At hospital I had been told to prepare for being a cripple, but within weeks of starting her treatment I was fully riding my bicycle, not struggling to pedal as on the day I'd intended following Virginia. During the regular checks at the Southern General, I underwent a series of tests wearing what looked like a spaceman's helmet. The purpose was to examine my reactions, to see if I could identify lights and respond to them. It was all intended to see just how well my brain was working. The results were so good that I was able to successfully apply for the return of my driving licence after six months instead of having to wait a year.

"Now I felt I was playing with a full deck of cards and started back with the business. But at first it was difficult, my strength and level of fitness had dropped through so much inactivity while I was recuperating. One of the conditions attached by my insurers to my taking out parties was that I had to be with them, so with groups of stalkers I'd take them to the moor, point them in the right direction and tell them, 'There you go.' So they'd disappear while I sat in the car and fell asleep because I was absolutely shattered. I had not realised just how much the accident had taken out of me."

Determined to get back to his former level of income he found himself working ceaselessly. "I was working literally every day. For more than thirteen weeks I did not have a day off because my backside was up against the wall financially." Of course Virginia worked every day of every month of every year. His resumption of the business had a knock on effect for her. Once groups of clients began returning to Lochside it meant her already gruelling workload increased once more.

"I'd get really, really exhausted. Once again when Robin had shooting or stalking guests in the caravan, I'd be expected to feed them. I'm a very capable person, which was just as well. I'd do things like laying slate tiles for the kitchen floor; I always seemed to be decorating. These were things I had to do because it was obvious nobody else was going to do the work and while Robin wasn't working we couldn't afford to bring people in. The people who stayed in the mobile home needed to be fed. It had to be cleaned. Robin had to be taken to school and brought home. In addition to everything else I was so much involved with looking after Alex. There was always something new to be learned about how to look after her. My life seemed to be taken over by everything, I'd be on the go until 11.30 at night when I'd go to bed, but even then Alex's cries in the night would keep me awake.

"Robin would go off with the shooting and stalking parties, come back home, sit down and think that he had done his bit for the day. That used to get to me. But I still put up with it, still carried on. I don't see where it's written that the woman has to do everything. Why was it that other fathers of EB children got so involved? Sometimes Robin would have friends in the Army to dinner and I'd go all out to make it a really special evening. This was on top of all the other jobs I had. Robin would do the drinks and when they'd gone, he'd go off to bed saying he needed to be up in the middle of the night for his shooting parties, so I had all the washing up to do. But if I had people round he wouldn't even get the drinks. He'd expect me to interact with his guests but he wouldn't want friends of mine to visit, even though the only reason I'd come to know them was through him."

It was a fatiguing roundabout from which there seemed to be no relief, and she took a short break by visiting her parents with the children. "When I returned to Scotland I said to Robin, 'I nearly didn't come back because I don't need this, it's not on'. He seemed to pull himself together a little, which helped."

Elsewhere, another family was about to begin the same hurtful journey along which the Hoods and countless other parents of EB children were travelling. At Ninewells Hospital at Dundee in the north east of Scotland, one of the largest and respected teaching hospitals in Europe, staff were shocked by the appearance of a newly born baby whose face and body was coated in blisters and during birth skin had peeled away. The condition was eventually diagnosed as EB and the baby's mother began the routine of bandaging, dressing and listening to the cries of her infant.

Dianne Forsyth meanwhile, knew Dundee well. Happily married, she and her husband Peter often visited the city to shop. While the parents of the EB child had cause for deep concern, no such worries clouded the lives of Dianne and Peter. She had given birth to their first child, a bubbly baby girl they named Tanis having fallen in love with the name, that of the ancient city on the Nile Delta in Egypt and well known to cinemagoers as the site of the Ark of the Covenant in the movie, Raiders of the Lost Ark. The couple were thrilled and looked forward to watching their daughter grow into a happy and healthy young woman. Their lives, that of the EB mother and the Hoods would become intertwined.

Robin, doing his best to resume a normal life, had been shocked to learn of the terrible death of his old friend Rory Morrison. The pair had shared a love of the outdoors and had a common passion for stalking the wildlife that abounded in the acres Robin leased. Rory had faced his physical difficulties with courage and dignity. But when he was unable to resolve other affairs, he one day took his own life, much to the sorrow of those who knew him.

Robin too had his concerns. As his strength recovered he found himself increasingly capable of building up the business to the level of success it had achieved before his accident; but with success came problems. The busier it became for him, the heavier the workload for his wife. On top of her many other tasks, as 1993 neared a close, she found herself preparing for Christmas. Alex, by now approaching the age of five, was becoming ever more aware of her condition, hardly surprising considering that there was never a moment of relief from pain.

Nights could be particularly awkward. It was winter and Lochside Cottage could be cold. While her brother could wrap his blankets around him and snuggle into warmth, not so Alex. Already cocooned in bandages, the bedding made her sweat. The answer was of course the installation of air conditioning, but without mains electricity that was a dream too far. As a consequence she was uncomfortable and hot and as she thrashed around in her bed seeking relief the skin ripped and tore. Often she could wake up in the morning with her nose and cheeks devoid of skin.

When their father asked young Robin and Alex to write down what they wanted for Christmas, his son handed him a list containing the sort of games he would have expected from any adolescent boy just entering his teens. Alex, despite her bandaged and deformed hands, had made a huge effort and gave her dad a letter. The fact she had tried so hard to be normal and interact with us made me want to change things for her.

The letter had a stunning effect on her father. He had always been aware of how desperate was the plight not just of Alex but of any child with EB. Now it was as if her piteous plea reached a part of him that had lain dormant. He had watched his wife bandage their daughter and had occasionally assisted with, but never performed the task himself. Doing it required being oblivious to the youngster's shrieks and cries. "I realised I had been selfish and reluctant in another way, by never doing the bandages. Virginia had always done this, I never took my turn. I'd walk in to the room where she was working with Alex, have a little look and then walk out.

"I considered this to be Virginia's job. I didn't see myself as running away from it because Virginia always did it, and she did a very good job. Now I realised that unless something was done she would go on bandaging Alex for ever, that Alex would never be free from pain and our daughter would die. We had continued going along to meetings of Debra. They were fine people but it just wasn't going along in the way that I wanted. Giving advice to parents who found themselves with an EB child was fine, but I wanted Debra to be doing much more than that. Giving treatment and advice was fine, but why not do something to make sure no child had to live with EB? At meetings I'd think, 'Why don't they do this? Why not try that? Why not do it this way, or that way?' I'd come away feeling frustrated because Debra just didn't have the funds to pay for researching a cure. How much that would take I did not know. But I did know something needed to be done.

"I left one Debra meeting feeling, for some reason, especially unimpressed and as we drove home said to Virginia, 'Are these people going to raise the money to find a cure for our daughter?' I was always a great 'Get in there and get on with it' person. Lots of people, asked a question to which they don't know the answer, are too frightened or even ashamed to admit, 'I don't know.' If I don't know something or I don't know how to do something then rather than tell a white lie I'll say, 'I don't know'. But too often people I'd be speaking to at meetings when asked what they would be doing to find a cure for EB would be answering, 'Well, we're going to do this' or 'We're going to do that' and it just didn't ring true.

"What I had learned about EB, what I had seen of how it affected Alex and then my being so thankful at surviving the car accident convinced me I had to do something to help. It was a very defining moment in my life. I could see Alex deteriorating, saw other children who were victims or heard about them from their parents. I knew there were other kids worse off than Alex and the newsletters Debra regularly sent us always seemed to be carrying a obituary column saying some youngster or other had died aged twelve or thirteen and I'd think of Alex and ask myself, 'She'll be five in just a few days from now. Is that all she has to look forward to?'

"My car accident had taught me much about priorities. Now, looking at Alex every day and seeing what Virginia was having to do brought home just how important your health was. I'd always been fit and healthy, I'd taken my good health for granted, as most of us do but now I realised that without good health you had nothing."

By February 1994 and the fifth birthday of his daughter, Robin had made a life changing decision. "I said to Virginia, 'I want to wind up the shooting business and start doing some work for Debra.' She said, 'Ok. Your choice.' We talked about it and she went along with what I was proposing, but she didn't realise, indeed neither of us did, just what would be involved."

What Robin was proposing was to offer his services to the charity for free. To work for nothing, take no salary. As far as he and his family were concerned, instead of having around £50,000 a year coming into their coffers, they would have nothing. It would mean living off savings that had dwindled since his accident.

From the very outset of their married life, Virginia had left financial matters with her husband. He had always provided. Now he was telling her he would no longer be an earner. "We were not in a good financial state anyway and now he was announcing he would work for Debra without a salary. I didn't know how he thought we were going to survive but then Robin was always something of a wheeler and dealer."

Robin never doubted his ability to be a successful fundraiser. And he was confident in his ability to speak in public, a crucial asset if he were to address meetings and plead for money. That had not always been the case. He recalled his schooldays and how he would feign illness whenever he was chosen to address his fellow pupils. Now of course he had the greatest of incentives, a mission to save Alex's life and end her suffering. He and Virginia had already held a couple of successful fundraising functions on behalf of Debra. He had spoken movingly about his daughter, although most of the audience comprised friends. But he spoke from the heart. He had first hand knowledge of what EB meant. He had watched Alex from the moment she was born, seen her condition fluctuate, her tiny beautiful face contort in pain day after day. It would have been easy and understandable for him to have wallowed in pity, for Alex, Virginia, Robin and himself. But what was wanted was for the pity of others to be translated into hard cash. He needed to be a super salesman, persuading strangers to hand over money for a cause of which most had never heard.

"I remembered the conversation with my religious friend about taking up the struggle to defeat evil. Maybe some people will probably think I'm bonkers, and if they want to believe that then it's up to them. But the truth was that by now I had become convinced I was given the job of helping to raise the money to find a cure, and as time went by I became wholly certain I would get Alex cured. I was about to set out on a mission that could not fail." But had he considered the price his family would pay?

CHAPTER TWELVE

Each day, as he looked at his daughter and saw her beautiful innocent face contorted in pain Robin Hood became more certain that he had made the right decision. Her hands had caused problems from the day she was born. In addition to the inherited trigger finger deformity, the skin between her fingers had fused together until they had the appearance of belonging to a duck with webbed feet. In trying to explain their appearance to strangers Robin would liken them to a pair of drumsticks at the end of her arms and even suggest his listeners try spending a day with their hands wrapped in mittens.

"She had no skin on her feet and all her toes were fused together too. You couldn't identify her toes, simply see the bones underneath the coating of what skin there was. She had no toenails or fingernails. Her digits wriggled around underneath but as her fingers became clenched due to Stenosing tenosynovitis we found we were taking her to Great Ormond Street when she was a child and then St Thomas's in London once she reached adulthood, where the surgeons would separate the skin between her fingers to try to get back the use of her digits.

"In hindsight I believe this may have contributed to the decline in her health once she reached her teens. My opinion is that when they separated the fingers, the doctors needed to get skin from somewhere on her body to use in skin grafts. They used to take skin from her leg and when they took that skin then the area from which it had been removed never healed. When you have open wounds for more than ten years then you have a more than even chance of developing skin cancer. So if we hadn't taken her to hospital for these operations and the skin had not been removed from her leg, would the story of her life have had a different ending? It's all ifs and buts, and the only certainty is that we'll never know the answer."

If Virginia had objections to her husband's decision to drain the family of their savings by working for Debra for free, it seems most likely that she did not initially voice them for the simple reason that she had too many other tasks to occupy her to add that of provoking and indulging in a lengthy argument. As far as she was concerned, there was nothing heroic in the way in which she took care of her daughter. Alex was ill, she needed help and Virginia simply went ahead and did whatever was needed. Robin admired his wife as he watched her carefully tend to Alex. The youngster needed to be bathed each day in special fluids formulated to try to remove any traces of infection from the wounds and open sores that covered her body. Over some wounds she tenderly soothed Aloe Vera, the cream extracted from the plant of that name and sometimes used in the production of cosmetics. Some scientists doubt its effectiveness; others argue it has healing and soothing properties and can even rejuvenate. Regardless of the various arguments, Virginia and Robin believed it helped their daughter and that was what mattered.

Once Virginia had drained the blisters of fluid, which was then mopped up with cotton buds, these areas and those areas bare of skin needed to be covered with specially prepared bandages, sometimes four layers of them before the final wrapping, a K Bandage. Talented though she was, it was a routine for which Virginia's background had not prepared her. Before her marriage her good looks and smart appearance had gained the attractive French speaker occasional work as a hostess at the annual British International Motor Show at Birmingham's National Exhibition Centre and then there were assignments at major London venues. After she and Robin tied the knot, Virginia had worked as a swimming instructress and in Scotland had taught line dancing. Those early days of wedded bliss had seen them jet off in search of the sun to exotic locations such as Lanzarote and Corfu. They lived and loved well, worked hard and played hard.

Now there seemed no task to which she could not turn her hand successfully, but none so devastating as the care of Alex. And if his daughter did not have enough with which to cope, Robin was aware of an unpleasant side effect of the daily baths. They would leave her smelling of musty dead skin.

"It was unpleasant and when we were out with her you could sense and see passers-by sniffing the air. Young as she was, sitting in her little buggy, Alex was sufficiently astute enough to know she was the object of their curiosity. But she ignored them and just moved on. Sometimes though it was difficult not to just go up and hold and cuddle her. But that would have caused her agony."

It was small incidents such as these that had ultimately convinced Robin to steam full on into the task of raising sufficient money to allow researchers to concentrate on finding a cure for EB. He knew from the reaction of his friends and family just how the plight of the disease's tiny victims pulled at heartstrings and opened purses and wallets. An example of that was when Robin announced to colleagues in the TA in March 1994 that he intended pushing Alex around the course during a local marathon event to raise money for Debra. Not only did seven other part time soldiers instantly offer to accompany him but his good friend Paul Middlemiss, a regular army Colonel volunteered to attract extra attention by roller blading his way around. These were gestures that would be repeated many thousand times over in the years that lay ahead.

His mind made up on his astonishing career change, Robin wound down his thriving business and rang John Dart at Debra. "I said to John, 'I'm coming to work for you. I don't want any money but I want you to pay my expenses'. And that was it. They did." Virginia, her initial acceptance now coloured by a natural concern as to how the family would pay their bills, had asked her husband, 'How long are you going to do this for?' His response was, 'Give me two years and I'll raise enough money to find a cure for this. I can't go on seeing Alex and all the other children suffer. Two years, that's all I need.'

He had blurted out his reaction without stopping to find out just how steep and expensive was the road that lay ahead.

Now he admits, "Had I any idea at that stage how much a cure would cost? I kept making things up.

I talked to a researcher who said, 'Seven million pounds will do it.' Another told me, 'Four million, that's what we need.' Everybody I discussed this with gave a different figure and a different timescale. 'The project will cost this, cost that', the fact was nobody knew." Not only was he about to enter the dark as far as his own finances were concerned, he would be working blind when it came to Debra's needs. He realised that if he was to talk about Debra and EB then he needed to know more about the condition, what the funds were needed for, what was being done to find a cure, what progress, if any, was being made and whether there was in fact any realistic hope of ending the misery of EB. And so he journeyed to Dundee to meet the distinguished geneticist Professor McLean. The Professor, now regarded as one of the world's leading researchers into EB, gave this brash, determined pupil a short lecture on the disease. But when Robin asked, 'And how is the research going?' he was disappointed to be told, 'We are shooting into the dark. We do not know which way to go.' Robin felt like a man who, having volunteered to climb Mount Everest, now found himself standing at the foot having been issued with a pair of training shoes, a walking stick and a compass.

"I knew Virginia wanted me to go ahead but she didn't realise, indeed neither of us knew, just what was involved. Now I was beginning to get an indication of the enormity of the job. Debra sent a fundraising expert to meet me in Scotland, a very nice guy and very experienced. I met him at Glasgow airport and spent two hours listening to what he had to say. Then I went off and did it my own way. "To me, from the reaction of my TA colleagues and friends locally, telling them about

EB through the story of Alex was the best, the only way, of getting their attention. My initial thoughts were quite simply that the more people who knew about EB the quicker it would be to raise whatever money was needed."

A problem that had raised its head from the very first days of Alex living at Lochside Cottage now towered over the Hood family. There had never been any freedom for the youngster from the sweat that every night of her life soaked and saturated her bandages, worsening the friction against her butterfly skin. The answer was air conditioning. The house had neither gas nor electricity. An open fire supplied heat. Power came via the generator, but as time went on that was beginning to tire with the extensive use to which it was put. The family then discovered it was not capable of powering an air conditioning unit twenty four hours a day. What was required, urgently and desperately, was for Lochside Cottage to be connected to the mains electricity supply. And that was around two miles away. Robin and Virginia delved into their savings and emerged with £29,000, the figure quoted by Scottish Power for linking them into its mains system. But a cable had first to actually reach their home and that involved crossing property owned by others. Getting permission for that could potentially bankrupt the family.

"I recalled Virginia asking me when I first said I wanted to work for Debra for no pay, 'How we were going to live?' and my assuring her, 'Oh, something will turn up'. But then the monthly bills started dropping through the letterbox. They kept coming and we began dipping into our savings. The need for a very costly power link could not have come at a worse time."

What happened next was a remarkable fight by the Hood family led by Robin, and it was one that would teach him an invaluable lesson, even providing the key to his opening the door to a treasure chest.

"The particular type of EB, dystrophic, that affected Alex necessitated her bedroom being kept at a constant temperature. Because she was covered in bandages it was like anyone without the disease going to bed in all our winter clothing including an overcoat and having the heaviest blankets and a duvet on top. As she grew older and the area of bandages bigger, the problem of her sweating increased until it reached a crisis point. Each time she woke up and wiped away the sweat from her face, her skin would tear off. In the mornings her face would be a mass of raw, red flesh. We just had to somehow link our home to the mains electricity supply.

"I contacted a local housing association and said I desperately needed to get mains electricity into the house and explained why there was the pressing need. I was asked where the nearest supply was and had to say it was around two miles off and would need to come across fields and forested terrain. The association promised to investigate. After a while I contacted the Association again and was told it had looked into the situation and discovered a cable would need to cross fields owned by a number of farmers and also the final mile or so would be over Forestry Commission territory.

"A very helpful lady at the Association told me, 'I've got all the farmers to agree, but the Forestry Commission is asking where you will get the money from to pay for this. And why do you need mains electricity anyway?' When I heard that, I just flipped. Who were these pathetic white collar workers demanding to know where I was getting the money from and why did I need it? They were looking for an obstacle to stop us."

Desperate and angry he took the fight to his local newspaper. From there the story of the fight to free a little girl of never ending pain was spotted by national newspapers in Scotland who suddenly wanted to know about Alex and her family. The Times and Daily Telegraph told their readers of the Butterfly Child. Sky Television became interested, the power struggle was featured on breakfast television and now the plight of Alex and the Hoods was being beamed into homes throughout Britain, homes where the occupants needed only to press a switch to bring on instant and powerful lighting, to power their deep freeze and multiple electrical gadgets. The battle, through the Media, was one-sided. Newspapers, radio stations and television channels made it clear that their sympathies lay with Alex. Robin had set out his stall by announcing, 'I am fighting for my daughter's future. If we do not get electricity it will shorten Alex's life'.

Now the Forestry Commission was being portrayed as the big bad wolf. It countered with a statement that clearing a path for a power line through its trees and over its acres would involve considerable disruption and cost at least £100,000. 'In view of the existing woodland cover, size of trees and topography, an effective line would require the felling of a substantial wayleave. On steep ground this will be expensive and time consuming. The resulting corridor would have a serious landscape impact beside Loch Ken, which is designated by the regional council as an important scenic area.' In addition, said the Commission, the work would put a quarry out of action.

Government bodies are always an easy target, often inviting criticism as a result of their inflexibility and reluctance to be frank. One newspaper declared: 'The Hoods are not looking for hand outs. The Forestry Commission should reverse its decision – and fast. The quicker it finds a cheap and sensible way of helping the Hoods get their electricity the better it will be for its distinctly tarnished image.' The News of the World conducted an investigation and a reporter examined the route the Commission said it would require to clear to create a path for the cable, only to find much of the land had already been subject to tree felling. The pressure on the Commission and its management arm, Scottish Enterprise, increased when Robin sent off a video of Alex showing her horrific blisters traumatised skin condition to Diana, Princess of Wales and pleading for her backing.

There were, inevitably, those who felt little or no sympathy for the family, as Robin conceded. "People were stopping me in the street and asking, 'Well, why don't you just move?' I told them, 'We specially adapted Alex's bedroom to cope with her condition and needs, it has cost us thousands of pounds, this is our home, why should we move, I'm not asking for anything for which we are not prepared to pay. All we want is electricity, just like those who criticise us doubtless have in their own homes. Why can't we have it? More importantly, why can't Alex have it and be given the chance to live nearer to some semblance of normality?' It was hard to argue against the needs of a lovely little girl living out her life in extreme pain."

Throughout the fight, Scottish Power had never wavered from its willingness to connect Lochside Cottage to its mains lines. Now it began being tarred with same brush, accused of the same inflexibility as the Forestry Commission and yet it had at no time placed any stumbling block in the way of keeping little Alex cool and comfortable. Clearly Scottish Power rightly felt it was being unfairly treated. Were moves made behind the scenes in an effort to call a truce in the Battle of Lochside Cottage? Scottish Enterprise was government controlled and word of Alex's predicament reached the then Secretary of State for Scotland, likeable Conservative politician Ian Lang, later to become Baron Lang of Monkton. One day the Hoods heard a knock at the door of their home and a representative of Scottish Power stood there. Robin said, "He looked at me, said, 'Do not get any more negative press as we're going to put your electricity in for nothing'. And I went along with that." Suddenly the Forestry Commission had agreed to help out.

That was not the end of the story by any means. Public sympathy was overwhelmingly with Alex, so much so that around 60 Scottish Power workers including office staff, linesmen and electricians volunteered to give up a series of week-ends in order to install the power line. Part of it would run on pylons, part underground depending on the topography of the terrain. Now the good publicity that had been enjoyed by the Hoods was being extended to the one-time villains. The Commission, ably seizing an opportunity for plaudits, even made a reserve generator available to the Hoods in case of their own breaking down. It was a kindly gesture and one well received even beyond the local community. One of the volunteers admitted, 'It makes you really humble when you see an effort like this. Everyone is helping. It really is tremendous. Firms have given materials and donations and dozens of people have been involved in this effort. Everyone is mucking in.'

The plight of the little girl had spread far beyond Scotland. In Spain a manufacturer of air conditioning units offered to supply one for free. A major company in Kent generously provided help and equipment. Scottish Power and the Forestry Commission were seen as heroes who galloped to the side of a child in distress, For Virginia, the installation of mains electricity meant an end to having to drag herself out of her home in the middle of the night and into the building housing the generator to wearily crank it to life when her daughter needed light. 'No one knows what a difference just being able to flick a switch will make to all of us,' said Robin, when he was interviewed by a television station. He had learned an astonishing lesson, one that would affect the lives of many thousands.

CHAPTER THIRTEEN

Robin Hood had discovered a new weapon in his fight to fund a cure for his daughter's terrible illness – the Media. Newspapers, radio programmes, television shows clamoured for stories about the little girl who felt she was on fire. That weapon was one he would ceaselessly abuse in the years ahead and lead to accusations that he used his daughter in his campaign to raise money. The initial involvement of the Media had been, he realised, a major factor in shaming the authorities into cutting through red tape and agreeing to provide the Hoods with mains power. He did not realise just how important that involvement had been, but now he was about to see the full potential of the Media in his cause.

While he waited for workmen to make the link up, Robin had given a lengthy interview to the Daily Record newspaper. The subsequent article was spread over two pages of the tabloid and in it Alex's predicament was reported extensively. The well written piece was intended to play on the feelings of the newspaper's readers. It included such quotations from Robin as. 'Alex is battling bravely. We can only hope that a cure is found soon. She's had a miserable five years. Alex was completely normal at birth. Her brother Robin was eight and healthy, so we had no reason to think Alex would be any different.' The article went on to record Robin's feelings when it was discovered Alex was a victim not of the fatal junctional type of EB. 'I was ecstatic. I could have thrown a party when they told me Alex would live. But then it gradually sank in how ill she'd always be and as time's gone on it's become harder and harder for the whole family. We'd never have knowingly put Alex through this – she's had a terrible life. You have no idea what it feels like to listen to your child screaming in agony for hours every day. When Virginia changes her dressings and gets the needles out, she screams: "Please don't hurt me any more, mummy, I hate you, you're wicked." Sometimes I sit downstairs and sob, but there's nothing we can do. I just put my arm around Virginia and try to comfort her. If every working man in the UK was to donate the price of a newspaper, my girl's life could be saved. Five years ago we were told there would be a cure in five years. Now we're told it'll be another five years because the cash isn't available. If they don't find a cure, Alex will die from skin cancer or infection and probably before she's a teenager. But we have to live in hope.'

The article, headlined, 'Even a cuddle could kill my wee girl', and illustrated with dramatic, eye-catching colour photographs of father and daughter, ended with details of how donations to Debra could be made. It was the first fully public appeal he had made for money for the charity. Many hundreds of stories about Alex and her family have appeared in all forms of the Media since, but this was the most significant because of what happened next. It subsequently brought home to Robin the remarkable value of publicity.

"I was away with the TA when the article went in and during a phone call home to Virginia she told me, 'There are lots of letters arriving with money inside.' After that I was ringing her every day. 'It's raining money,' said Virginia. It was incredibly exciting. Within a few days of that article appearing, £36,000 was raised for Debra, more than one third of the charity's annual income at that time. What was my reaction? I thought, 'This is easy.' I hadn't expected anything like this and was absolutely blown away. I'd had a chat with a reporter, posed with Alex for a few photographs and suddenly there was £36,000. Dead easy. A month later, when we wrote a short follow up piece thanking everybody for their generosity, they donated another £9,000. I could not believe it, could not grasp just how easy it could be to raise money once you grabbed the sympathy of the public.

"When you are at the bottom, as Debra was financially, then the only way is up. And I knew that we were going to climb, get enough money to tell the scientists, 'Go ahead, spend what you need, we'll get it, just find a cure.' Because that what this was all about.

"I soon found out, particularly in regard to the Press, that newspapers need hundreds of human interest stories every day. If there's nothing in the papers to attract readers, then people won't buy them. Suddenly I knew I had what newspapers wanted, a great human interest story about a little girl with the most terrible condition imaginable and what was being done to bring an end to not just her suffering but that of all the other little victims of EB. The way I saw the whole Debra situation was simple: This is the problem, this much money will make the difference. The problem was EB but the difficulty came in trying to find out just how much money was needed to successfully research a cure. The general public can be hugely generous if a cause moves them. But there are so many causes appealing for help. Give them a cause that really distresses them and they will readily respond. Give them a cause that distresses them and tell them exactly how much money is needed to provide a cure and they will rally round even more magnificently and try to reach that target. It is far easier to raise money by telling potential donors, 'Look we need one million pounds' or 'We need one hundred million pounds'. If people have a target towards which they can aim then they feel more eager to get involved. I desperately wanted to be able to say 'This is how much money we need' but the goalposts kept changing. So I simply told them what I believed the target to be.

"I just had no idea at that stage how much a cure would require so I simply kept making things up. And the truth was that nobody else knew either. Everyone I spoke to, quoted a different figure. I'd already heard about seven million and four million. Now I was being told anything from half a million to ten million, but no matter what the figure the common factor was that I knew, enormous though they might sound, they were all perfectly achievable."

The public loves newspapers. At the time Robin made his Press debut, in 1994, newspaper sales accounted for the equivalent of around one third of the population. Some, of course, bought none; most one; others two or more. He reasoned that here were probably a potential fifteen million people waiting to be milked of the money in their pockets and purses. All it needed was the drive and determination to tell them about his daughter and how they could help.

There had been an extra bonus from the publicity about Robin's plea for electricity and the Daily Record article. Now all over Britain, people moved by Alex's plight were getting in on the fundraising act. They ran races, took part in darts contests, golf competitions, held raffles, played dominoes, swam lakes, climbed mountains. Schools allowed pupils to leave their uniforms behind and turn up for classes in jeans and sweatshirts provided they chipped into the Debra coffers. Stars from Aston Villa, the famous Midlands soccer side, turned out for a match against the King's Own Scottish Borderers. Money poured in. In between cheques for £20 or even one of £100 that dropped through the letterbox of the Hood home came an envelope containing a one pound note and the simple message, 'God Bless'. At times the family were moved to tears by the generosity of those who mostly they did not know.

A few days before Christmas 1994 workmen finally connected the heavy cable that would carry electricity from the national grid to Alex's bedroom. Robin was learning fast. Here was a heaven sent opportunity to put his daughter in the news once again and by doing so attract money. A celebrity publicist would have been proud of the manner in which he made the most of the event. Television cameras, their spotlights dazzling, radio station reporters with tapes turning and journalists their pens and pencils busily filling pages of notebooks were all there as Alex pulled a switch that turned on the gaily coloured lights on a Christmas tree in her garden.

The spirit of the season of goodwill extended to all, even to the Forestry Commission which had admitted, in its defence, 'Alexandra's very special circumstances were not made known to us. Once we realised the situation we pulled out all the stops.' Robin joined in. 'Since coming round to our side the Commission has been marvellous.' There was, he rightly reasoned, no point in making enemies. After all, each friend was a potential donor. As if to give reassurance of how own confidence in the Debra cause, he told the crowds who had gathered to watch, 'I have to be optimistic about the prospects of a cure. Otherwise I would walk into the loch and simply keep on walking.'

The switch on confirmed him as a more than capable apostle of the Debra message. "Suddenly I realised that not only did I have the gift of translating Alex's story into a form of emotional blackmail, but I was enjoying talking about my daughter. It wasn't an ego trip for me, my only motive was helping to spread the word about EB and making a difference."

His determination to raise the Debra profile by telling the world about Alex quickly grew into an obsession. He had a knack for knowing what would make news. He remembered the impact of watching Alex write a letter to Santa had under such stress , and Robin made a plea to the heads of 500 companies throughout Scotland asking them to donate £100 each to Debra. 'What will your child or grandchild be asking for from Santa this year? With normal skin and hands' he wrote. 'My daughter wants only something we all take for granted, a few minutes free of pain. Will you help her wish come true?'

He made sure the appeal was picked up by the Media. 'Every MD of every company is probably a father or grandfather,' he told a reporter. 'I bet their children will be asking for a lot more than new skin.'

He began an incredible and gruelling programme of visiting anyone willing to listen. It was largely disorganised, frequently spur of the moment, but always the message was delivered with an honesty of passion that his listeners never doubted. Here was a man speaking from the heart, a man begging for the life of his daughter and he made them feel that they had the power to give he and her that life.

"I used emotional blackmail to get into establishments. Once you began speaking about a little girl and her terrible suffering, people felt guilty about being healthy. I'd tell them about the sort of things Alex would say. Once when I had spoken about a trip she and I would take when she reached her teens she had said, 'But Daddy I won't be able to go will I? I won't be alive then.' I told them, 'I've promised my daughter we will raise enough to find a cure for EB so she won't die. I am here because I want to put this condition into the history books. It's something I genuinely believe. No father wants to bury his own child.' Every time I spoke, I learned more about how to persuade audiences to part with their money.

"I'd go anywhere, talk to anyone no matter how big or small the audience. I spoke to all sorts of organisations, Rotary Clubs, Ladies' Clubs, Probus Clubs, schools, social clubs, you name it. I refused nobody who asked me to speak. I once went up to the north of Scotland and only two people turned up. But I still talked to them for almost an hour. I felt that if they had made the effort to be there I owed it to them to spend time telling them about Alex and EB. That first winter I often discovered that although I'd driven 100 or 200 miles to a function, hardly anybody had turned out because the weather was bad. But that should not prevent those who had attended from hearing what I had to say. I owed it to them because I believed they were making that effort on behalf of Alex and all the other EB victims."

But as the flow of money grew, the strands of his sometimes taut relationship with Virginia began to snap. In the first year of his mercy mission he spent 100 nights away from home. Sometimes he would be missing four or five nights in a week. "I had talked over with Virginia what it would mean if I began working for Debra and she wanted me to do it. But she didn't realise, neither of us did, what was involved. I was trying to be in a dozen places at the same time. Virginia said, 'You'll never keep this up, it will kill you'. But I was like a man running downhill hoping to find a pot of gold at the bottom. I couldn't stop."

The installation of electricity had been a help to Virginia. But whereas in the past although Robin had been heavily tied up with his business, he had at least been at home or around home each day. Now he hardly ever seemed to be there. She still had the twice daily bandaging sessions, the feeds of vital nutrients through the gastrostomy tube to keep infection at bay needed to be carefully supervised, there were morning and afternoon journeys to and from school with Robin junior to be made.

The fusing of the skin over Alex's hands was a never ending nightmare despite trips to hospital for operations to open up her fingers. Similar webbing on her feet added to the difficulty of her walking because putting pressure on her heels caused blistering and the loss of skin. The solution was to put her heels in splints. Regular check-ups on Alex had shown she had an iron deficiency and these required blood transfusions that needed to be carried out with extra care because of her condition.

A friend of the Hoods, watching Virginia fighting fatigue and struggling to cope with the role of what was now practically that of a single mother, saw the first signs of disintegration in the relationship between her and Robin.

"It was desperately sad. Virginia was doing an incredible job raising young Robin and nursing Alex while running a home. Robin genuinely believed that if he could raise sufficient money he could save Alex's life and what parent would not want to go down that road given the opportunity? Once he had set his mind on working for the charity there was no turning back, he was a very strong willed man. But the strain was beginning to tell and it was made worse through no wages coming in. If Virginia complained, then she did so to her husband. She kept her thoughts to herself but her friends wondered whether it was simply a case of her being too busy or too tired to moan about her lot. One of the jokes that went around the circle of their friends was that you didn't need to call on the Hoods to see how they were managing, you just had to read the newspapers or watch television. Robin and Alex seemed to be there every other day."

Alex's christening in Lillington in 1989

Alex with Barbara and Dennis Hood in 1992

Alex and Robin outside No 10 in April 1999

Tony Blair with Robin Hood

Robin talking to the Prime Minister April 1999

Alex sitting in the PM chair in the cabinet office

Alex and Robin Jnr at 1st reception at No 10 1999

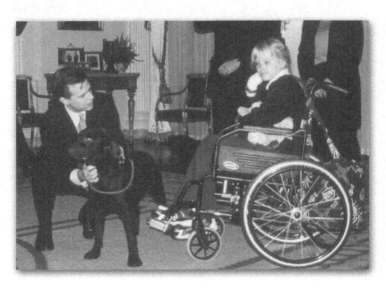

Alex doing PR at American Embassy in 2000

Alex and Robin in London Marathon in 2001

Robin had a small pot of Alex's ashes when he ran this.

Robin Jnr spreading the word in Jordan

Alex on holiday
in Paris 2005

Alex's graduation party

CHAPTER FOURTEEN

He had promised half a year of his year to Debra but long before the six months was up, it had become clear to Virginia that Robin had no intention of sticking to his half year deadline. He was too engrossed in his money raising campaign to give up while a cure had not been found. Gradually but painfully she came to accept the likelihood that their bizarre life would only get even more difficult. When he told her, 'Virginia I need two years, give me two more years', she did not argue against her husband.

To save money during his sometimes marathon journeys, he drew on his Army training, by living rough. He drove with his lightweight waterproof Bivouac sack in the boot of his car and if the weather was reasonable would simply pull up at the side of the road, put a sleeping bag inside his 'bivvy bag' and climb inside. Sometimes he sweated profusely and woke up damp, a condition that instantly made him think how his daughter, swathed in her bandages, had been similarly discomforted until the advent of air conditioning. But for him it was a minor unpleasantness when compared with the distress constantly faced by Alex. At other times he would simply curl up in the back seat of his motor.

"I'd gone into the Debra job with my eyes open. I knew it wasn't going to be easy, that there would be lots and lots of sacrifices. And sometimes I'd wake up in the morning in the middle of nowhere, look out of the car window and tell myself, 'This isn't real. If I close my eyes it will go away. Why me? Why us?' But of course until someone discovered how to isolate the rogue genes and find a way of replacing them, the nightmare was never going to go away. Not for Alex, not for us, not for the hundreds, the thousands of other parents of EB children. I was determined I wasn't going to carry Alex's coffin."

His confidence in his speaking ability grew. He found he could vary his talks from the strictly factual to bringing tears to his audiences. Often before beginning he would ask organisers of a meeting how emotional they wanted his address to be. "I always based what I had to say on Alex. I'd talk about being in a race against time where losing was not an option. I'd ask them to try putting themselves in Virginia's place and say, 'How would you feel if you had to stick a needle into your daughter thirty or forty times and day and hear her squeal in agony with each prick? Could you do that? My wife has to, there is no alternative and she and all the other mothers of children with EB will have to go on doing it until either a cure is found or the child dies'.

"I would go back to the days before Alex was born, how we'd had an idyllic life with our son and had moved to what we saw as a little bit of heaven in Scotland. How we'd looked forward to the birth of a daughter and of being told she had EB and what that meant.

"Sometimes I would be asked whether I was doing the right thing for my family by leaving Virginia to cope while I travelled around raising money. I'd say, 'If you saw your son or daughter drowning in a loch, would you go off and have your tea before coming back to try to rescue them? Dystrophic EB is fatal. I have to do something now. I am a great believer and my daughter, young as she is, is the same. We believe that if something is wrong, you should get off your backside and do something about it. It's no use just sitting about moping and crying. If I sit at home on my wife's lap crying, is that going to help raise money for Debra? I don't have the skill or expertise to actually find a cure. I am not a scientist but what I do have is the determination and willingness to make sure those who do have the technical know how to resolve this can have the funds they need for their work. I know that given enough money they are going to find a treatment for EB, a cure for this most terrible, this most horrendous disease and the day that treatment becomes available I want Alex to be the first to get it. That's how I feel and it's how the parent of every EB child feels.'

"I would tell anybody who would listen, 'EB is not infectious, it is inherited. So those of us who don't have it will never know what it feels like to be a victim. But if we who are lucky enough to lead normal lives were to somehow fall victim to EB for just a few hours we would know the true meaning of pain and beg to be free of this, the most awful condition known to mankind. These children who suffer the disease live in the constant hope of there being a cure before they die. Because die they will. In my daughter's case her heart is continually weakening through it having to pump faster and faster to get blood to the areas of her body where her skin has peeled away. Every minute of every day and night her heart races as if she had just climbed a very steep flight of stairs. That extra workload will ultimate cause her heart to fail. There are so many other ways in which having EB could cause her to die. Cancer is another. And yet children such as my lovely daughter constantly apologise for having the condition because they know just how distressing are their screams from the pain of bandaging to those doing this work. Alex is forever telling Virginia how sorry she is for crying'.

"The trouble was that I became so obsessed with publicising Debra through telling everyone about Alex, that I forgot to behave like a father. Alex became a tool in the quest to raise money, but it would be years before I realised that. At the time, when I set out on my fundraising campaign, I just didn't see it that way. I thought that what I was doing was for my daughter's benefit, it was my way of dealing with the distress of her condition. There were tears from me, but maybe there should have been more. At least one day a week or a couple of afternoons each week I ought to have said, 'Right Alex, here we go. Come on, what do you want to do darling?'

"There was no point in my going to the Media and telling the world, 'My daughter has the most terrible condition in the world and there's no hope, she's going to die'. Had I done that people would have felt there was no point in giving money. So I had to give them hope that there would be a cure. Right from the start I knew the best way of fundraising was to promise there was light at the end of the tunnel, there was hope. What would we have achieved if I'd gone about with a message of doom and gloom, that there was nothing new on the horizon? I had to be positive and positive towards Alex by giving her hope that a cure was out there somewhere in the distance.

"I once turned up at Lochside Cottage after being away for days, with a radio reporter wanting an interview with Virginia and Alex, and Virginia was upset. She told me, 'Don't you think I'm already coping with enough, looking after the family, looking after the house, looking after your dogs? Yet you turn up out of the blue with a stranger and a pile of dirty clothes'. Of course it was unfair, but I thought Virginia should support me because I was doing so much on my own. I saw nothing wrong in walking in off the streets and asking her, 'Can you do this?' or 'Can you do that?' and expecting her to agree. I just did not respect what an amazing job Virginia was doing. As I saw it, she and I had made a pact in which she would keep Alex alive while I raised enough money to let the experts work on developing a cure. Maybe I was arrogant, maybe too confident in my own ability, but I'd told her at the outset, 'Virginia, give me time and I'll have this job done.'

"I never did the bandaging. When I'd been at home before I worked for Debra, Virginia always did them and I never took my turn. I wasn't running away from it, but I'd walk in, have a little look and then walk out because I considered this to be Virginia's job. But at least what I did worked, because in the first six months as a fundraiser I almost doubled Debra's income. The trouble was I was away from home so much, so often, that sometimes when I came back I felt a stranger. I knew Virginia was growing increasingly unhappy at my not being there, but what else could I do? Give up, sit back and watch my daughter fade away and die? No way.

"Frankly, I developed into an inconsiderate bastard. If I came home and Virginia told me about something happening to Alex I'd be right on the phone to the Media, encouraging them to hot foot it to the house with a photographer. Alex knew incidents such as her losing the skin of her hand while out with her mother upset me. She was a wonderful kid who thought more of how these things upset others. 'Never mind daddy, it'll be better in the morning,' she'd say while I was trying to publicise her suffering.

"I don't think I was being a bad father. I wanted Alex to live. But I was conscious of the effect on Virginia. One day she said to me, 'The only time I see you is a photograph of you in a newspaper and the only time I hear your voice is on the radio talking about Alex and Debra. I don't know how much more I should be expected to take. If you don't give this up, I'm going to leave you'. I told her, 'But if I give this up and Alex dies, I will never know whether my input would have made a difference'. I was actually quite arrogant because I thought she would never leave me."

The problems were exacerbated by his continued membership of the Territorial Army, his duties still requiring him to spend time away from his family.

Virginia has never before spoken at any length about her role in Alex's story. A calm, thoughtful and reserved woman who does not enjoy publicity but values her privacy, she never sought to be pushed into the spotlight and chose to remain in the background. However she agreed to be interviewed for the story of her daughter and her ex husband and was remarkably candid about her relationship with Robin. She admitted that what added to the pressure on their marriage was that on occasions the frequency of his absences led to her having doubts over whether these were solely to do the work of Debra. Just as he, following his accident, began doubting her fidelity, now she had suspicions over his.

"He was just never there," she said. "It wasn't only Debra, once they gave him the job of fundraising. He had the TA but also still liked to go shooting.

"So he would be away all the time and I'd be on my own with the children. He'd be away four or five nights a week, but that was not all Debra. Then I'd say, 'Right Rob, I need you to be home more.' I said that to him so many times that I lost count and the fact was I didn't actually know what he was doing. Once he said he was going to Portugal with the TA to do some walking. He said, 'I have got to do that but then when I'm back, I will be home more, I won't be doing it so often.'

"When he said that 'I'm going to raise money full time to get a cure for Alex'. I was fine, absolutely fine. I never thought he was opting out of anything, such as the bandaging, because I could not have done what he did. But when we were fundraising people kept asking about Alex and I couldn't cope with constantly having to tell them about her, I didn't want to do that and I'm sure that Robin didn't really enjoy doing that either. But whenever there was an opportunity to be with Alex he would make it a newspaper opportunity which isn't fair and he shouldn't have done that. He used Alex.

"He would tell her, 'We'll have found a cure by the time you are twelve', and while they might even have discovered a cure the next day, I knew the truth was it would more likely take a long time. But I knew too that finding a cure by the time she was twelve was what

Robin wanted, what he worked for. But the fact was because our home was three miles from the nearest village and we didn't see many people, we needed him to be there. I didn't marry somebody for them not to be there for me and for the children. I married somebody because I wanted to be with them. And that's the way I look at it.

"I think marriage, or at least a part of marriage is a friendship and if one partner isn't there, then it isn't a relationship. But Robin was dreadful. I'd go away with Alex and with Rob junior to my parents' home which was the only place where we went on holiday because we just didn't have the funding, and stay with them. We needed to take a huge amount of equipment for Alex, the bath chair, wheel chair, all the dressings and so many bags full of stuff that you need for a child with EB.

Sometimes when he came back it was as if he wasn't pleased to see us and no sooner had he arrived than he was planning his next campaign instead of devoting time to the children. If Alex came home from school I'd say to Robin senior, 'Will you listen to Alex read?' but he would tell our son to do it. Alex missed her father. She wanted him to be there with her but he became totally obsessed with the whole thing. But that's the way he is. And whatever he was, what he did was brilliant. He did a wonderful job."

It was not just Virginia's patience that was running out, the Hood financial reserves were dwindling. But Robin was determined his money worries would not spread to Virginia and detract her from the task of keeping their daughter alive. "Money was tight but I left it to Robin to sort that out. He told me, 'If you can do it better, you do it' and I thought, 'Oh God no, I've got

enough on my plate without doing that as well.' Once
when I had complained about his being away so much
he said, 'Well, swap jobs with me' and I thought, 'that
would be interesting'. I said, 'No' but should have just
said 'Yes.' Was I conscious of our funds going down?
I never even thought about it. I had too much on my
plate with Alex. And we weren't spending very much.
I wasn't spending anything. If I bought anything I'd
buy it in the second hand shop."

Throughout all the worries of the family, Robin
junior is often overlooked. At the time his father began
working full time and unpaid for Debra, his son was
approaching his fourteenth birthday and beginning to
nurture ambitions to become a vet. All too often he was
left in the background. This was not a deliberately
unkind act by either parent. His father was absent for
much of the time while, understandably, Virginia needed
to devote the bulk of her resources to Alex.

However unfairly Robin's magnificent obsession
may have rebounded on those he loved most dearly, his
wife and children, he never doubted his was the right
course, a view backed up by the increasing flow of
nationwide support for Debra. Each time he returned
home it would be to a pile of envelopes containing
money and he used up much of the little home time there
was ensuring each writer who identified themselves was
sent a response outlining how their money was being
spent. There were, too, times when he would return
tired, hungry and exhausted from a long and weary
fundraising mission, depressed about the prospects of
saving Alex, knowing he must show a brave face. Never
could he allow his own despair to infect his daughter's
hopes.

Occasionally he wondered about the families and individuals who sent money? Almost certainly few, if any, had ever met or seen an EB victim. But then with just one in every 217 humans carrying the defective gene, the odds against two carriers meeting, falling in love and conceiving were huge. And even then the one-in-four ratio had to be taken into the account. Every day thousands of EB free babies were coming into the world. Babies such as Cody Forsyth, a brother to Tanis. Cody was born to Dianne and Peter in 1995. They named their son after the city in Wyoming, which took its name from William Frederick Cody, Buffalo Bill. They had never heard of EB. And no wonder, Tanis and Cody were, happily, wholly healthy and normal.

CHAPTER FIFTEEN

By the summer of 1995 Robin had been working for Debra for just over a year. His campaign and the plight of Alex had been the subject of scores of news items and the profile of Debra and its consequent ability to attract donations, was climbing dramatically.

Never afraid to push himself under the spotlight, knowing a combination of his name and the cause for which he worked always created sympathy and brought in cash, he decided to try for a place in the highly popular London Weekend Television series Gladiators. He envisioned himself battling before the cameras with Alex in the audience. He spoke to a friend in Birmingham who advised him he would need to be supremely fit, one of the tasks being set would-be contenders being to complete ten chin-ups and another to run 800 metres in two minutes.

Robin threw himself with gusto into a tortuous training routine in preparation for his audition. At the same time he was continuing his exhausting schedule on behalf of Debra. Preparing for a meeting of the charity in London, he realised he needed documents from his home. It meant driving from Birmingham to Scotland then overnight to London. During the journey he stopped briefly at a service station at Tebay in Cumbria. While in the washroom trying to clear the weariness from his tired eyes, he was mugged by two yobs, one of them armed with a knife. Robin's karate technique left the cowardly pair fleeing, but then he realised he had been slashed and the injury required stitching.

When he next tried exercising, the stitches burst and his arm had to be put in plaster meaning his inevitable withdrawal from the Gladiators' audition. Later he was given a second opportunity, but his efforts for Debra had seriously curtailed his training routine and he failed to come up to the required mark. However London Weekend Television came up with a £10,000 donation to Debra.

It was clear a generous spirit of goodwill towards the charity had sprung up, but not everyone wished the Hoods well. The marriage, already on rocky ground due to Robin's constant absences, now came under fire from an anonymous sniper who seemed intent on preying on Virginia's vulnerability and misgivings, determined to smash the remaining threads binding the couple.

"I cried all the time and trying to make a decision as to what to do was the worst thing in the world," she said. "I'd be driving along in floods of tears all the time and the tears weren't about Alex, they were about the fact that I didn't know what to do and how unhappy I was. I didn't know if Robin was having an affair. He has always sworn he was faithful. But different people began telling me different things.

"One week-end when he was meant to be with the TA I telephoned for him and was told he wasn't there. But the explanation could simply have been that I'd spoken to the wrong person. In the end though it all boiled down to my feeling that there was no point in staying with someone who wasn't there for you, especially when you needed them to be there. Robin was selfish and perhaps I should have put my foot down more firmly about things.

Her continual pleadings with Robin to stay at home more, to cut down his astonishing itinerary of visits had not fallen on deaf ears. He knew she was right, but then he reasoned that his bizarre lifestyle gave the only hope for Alex to stay alive. He knew fate had dealt the family an appalling hand; he was in a no win situation; continue and lose his marriage, give up and lose his daughter. He had to gamble on the latter. As a result when Virginia, nearing the end of her tether, told him in July that year, 'If you carry on then I'm going to leave' his reply had been, 'Then you've got to go.' And so she had.

"I left because he wasn't there for us. I warned him so many times. I'd say, 'Look, Rob, if you're not here more than I'm going'. We even talked to the children and told them I was going back to my parents. Robin couldn't see that I meant I was going for good. 'Oh, you'll be back,' he said. I couldn't sleep for worrying. I'd tell myself, 'This isn't normal. We're meant to be together'.

"I knew I had to do something and so a friend offered to look after Alex for a short time while I went to meet up with a friend who lived in the Lake District. We couldn't stay there long because we didn't have much money but I talked through with her how things were. 'That's not how a relationship should be,' she told me. She was one of my oldest and dearest friends; I had known her since we were at college together and while I would never act on what somebody else told me, I did listen to what she said.

"After seeing her I returned home to the children and then went to stay with my parents. I hadn't said a word to anybody other than my friend about how I felt and about how things were. But somehow my dad sensed something was not well. He said to me one day, 'You know Virginia, if you want to come back you can stay here'. That came as a real shock to me, realising he could have known things were not well.

"His saying that helped make my decision, because with Alex there was so much involved. It meant making so many new arrangements. Where to get the bandages, where to get her medication. At Lochside Cottage I'd trained somebody to look after Alex overnight. It was a helluva thing to learn to do and in addition I had quite a good network of friends. The local doctors were very supportive and knew all about Alex. I know all about there being a higher rate of divorce among couples who have children with disabilities and it's usually the mum who is left holding the baby so to speak. Yes I'd complain to Robin about his not being at home, but the truth is that even if he had been there, he would not have done anything.

"He was off on one of his trips when I decided enough was enough and I was leaving him. Our son Robin was already in the Midlands, having a holiday with Robin's parents, so I started making arrangements to go off with Alex. I organised removal people to come and take the furniture that I'd need to my parents' home at Leamington Spa. But as Alex and I were getting ready to go Robin's mother rang. She asked if Robin knew we were going and when I told her, 'No' she asked me to wait for him to get back home. She must have telephoned him because he rang. 'Please wait until I get back,' he asked and I felt, out of decency, I should do that.

"When he arrived we were ready to go but Robin asked if he could come with us to Carlisle. Because of the amount of stuff I had in the car there was nowhere else for Robin to sit, except in the well of the motor, in front of the front passenger seat. During the whole of the journey he was trying to persuade me to stay, telling me things about him I'd never known including how he had been abused by his stepfather. Nothing he said altered what I'd decided to do. We left Robin at Carlisle and Alex and I drove off. Oh God, it was dreadful."

Although the break up was on July 20, 1995, Robin remembers it as though it were yesterday. "I'd been off fundraising and in the time I'd been away from the house she'd packed up everything, furniture, clothes, all the kids' stuff, Alex's equipment and medication. I rang her and begged her not to go until I made it home and she was actually waiting for me when I arrived. She'd promised to stay until then at least. My car had broken down and I had arranged to collect a hire vehicle from Carlisle so she gave me a lift. The journey down there was horrible. I was pleading with her to stay. I'm quite a persuasive character and did everything I could to try and get her to change her mind, but she made it clear she had had enough and was going. I kept looking at Alex knowing that my life was being ripped apart because of a freak of nature, because of something that neither Virginia nor I had any control over. When it was obvious that as far as Virginia was concerned there was literally no turning back, I got her to drop me off in Carlisle and I waved her and Alex off. I was gutted, totally, absolutely gutted. All I'd wanted was a happy and healthy family.

"I thought of our cottage at Lochside, the cottage where we'd lived with Robin and Alex. It was just a tiny, poxy little cottage that had once been a gunpowder factory which was why it was so remote. In my mind came memories of nights when the kids were in bed and Virginia and I would just cuddle up in front of the log fire. Okay the place was a bit damp at times, but it had been such a great adventure. Sometimes there would be water pouring in through holes in the roof but Virginia had been simply fantastic.

"It was in the moments after her car disappeared around a bend in the road at Carlisle that I realised not only was I surprised at how long she had actually stayed, but just how much she must have loved me. But I'd pushed and pushed and finally gone too far and lost her."

Robin drove home from Carlisle that night, distressed and depressed to a house almost bare of furnishings and fittings. It was empty and miserable and the only sign of life was from one of his Labradors. He spent the next couple of days in torment, unable to sleep or eat; missing the family he had rarely seen for a year and more.

"I had some dark days on my own and one night very nearly shot myself. My very best Labrador was a dog I'd named Zeiss, after the world famous binoculars. He was my soul mate. He used to travel everywhere with me in the car to meetings. After Virginia left, Zeiss would come up to the bedroom with me where I now slept alone and curl up at the side of the bed, as if he knew I was desperately unhappy and wanted to tell me he realised what I was going through. About this time I used to drink a lot of spirits, although I haven't touched them for something like 15 years now. My big favourite was Southern Comfort, the American liqueur. I was also a big fan of the band Pink Floyd. Some of their music can be quite morose. It tends to bring you down and then lift you back up again, a sort of musical roller coaster.

"After Virginia walked out taking Alex and Robin, everything just seemed to be a waste of time. All the work I'd done for Debra meant nothing. All it had achieved for me personally was the loss of my family. I still had the gun at the cottage, the gun I used for shooting. I wasn't falling over drunk, but I was drunk on

Southern Comfort and I'd been listening to Pink Floyd. I don't know what came over me, but I went up to the bedroom and got the gun out and loaded it with cartridges because I was going to shoot myself. I remember looking down at Zeiss and the dog just looked up at me and in my mind it was as if the dog was saying, 'What are you doing? Get a grip.' I stared at Zeiss for what seemed a long time and thought, 'You fool.' Then I put the gun away and that was the end of it. I'd never done anything like that before, and never since. Would I have actually had the balls to really go through with it? I think the answer is 'No' because I'm still here.

"At the time when Virginia said, 'I'm going to leave', knowing that Alex was going to die anyway even though I was promising her there would be a cure in two years or so, I thought, 'Well, at least I'll still have my wife and my son'. The promise of them always being there if I needed them kept me going. But the truth of the matter was that I was so obsessed by this time with fundraising that I took the view Alex would just have to put up with her father not being there. And that may have been one of, if not the, most difficult decisions of my life, not only to take but to put into effect. I had passed the stage where giving up would have been easy; now giving up was out of the question.

"The cottage had given us such hope and promise when we'd first gone to live there. Now it was empty and desolate. There was very little left inside. I had some dark times, was lonely and sad. Our savings had been getting lower and lower and I believe Virginia's father had advised her to start divorce proceedings while there was at least still something left, before I had to put the house up for sale to get in enough money to live on. I was determined to hold on to Lochside Cottage and stay there, and the fact I did both were major factors in my carrying on. There was a wonderful therapy in simply gazing out over the waters of Loch Ken, at wandering around over the superb countryside, drinking in the scenery, climbing hills and watching the wildlife. From a young age I'd had an affinity with nature and now I started appreciating what I had even more with the result that in a short while I felt rejuvenated."

There were occasions when as he approached Mossdale after a long mission he realised he would be returning to a Cottage that was empty, lonely and he would be fearful of what the future held for Alex. Faith in the ability of the researchers was the antidote with which he prevented self pity seeping into his thinking.

Robin quickly climbed out of depression. There wasn't time to feel sorry for himself. He went back to work and began the task of rebuilding his relationship with his family. During a visit to Leamington Spa to see Alex, Virginia taught him how to bandage his daughter. "I told him he would need to do the bandages if she was going to be able to spend time with him at Lochside Cottage. He was understandably slow and very conscious of hurting Alex, but it was impossible to treat her without causing some pain."

Realizing their son was broke, his parents began helping out. He had no means of heating the house. "One day the coalman turned up and when I had to tell him, 'I can't afford to buy coal' and he said, 'Don't worry, it's paid for'. It turned out my father, my lovely, lovely father Dennis had got in touch with the local coalman and sent him a cheque with the result that he dropped off a ton of coal that saw me through that winter." There was still, however, the problem of where to get money for food and clothing. It came from a most unusual source.

CHAPTER SIXTEEN

In the spring of 1996 panic gripped Britain with an outbreak of bovine spongiform encephalophathy, better known as Mad Cow Disease. A handful of people were diagnosed with dangerous and invariably fatal Creutzfeldt-Jakob disease, effectively the human form of BSE. It was widely believed they had caught the disease as a result of eating meat or drinking milk from infected farm animals. Outbreaks of Mad Cow disease occurred from time to time despite efforts to eradicate it. The effect on sales of meat and the farming industry was severe as households began shunning meat eating despite reassurances that what was being offered to them was perfectly safe. Others suffered too. Off the coast of Wales, 16 Cistercian monks dependent for their existence on visitors calling at their island home to see, among other sights, their farm, broke a vow of silence to make a television appeal for callers scared off by the disease to return. A survey showed that almost half the teenage population was refusing to eat British beef. One alternative was venison. Suddenly Robin saw a means of extracting himself from near economic ruin, at least temporarily.

"I'd never really thought about my financial situation because we'd always had money. Once I started work for

Debra that changed. I hadn't asked for a salary at the start because the charity didn't have funds, and while I wasn't a millionaire I was just able to cope. But by the time Virginia left me I was on my uppers and knew there was worse to come. Virginia would be entitled to her share of the equity on the house, for example.

"I still had shooting rights to land over at Newton Stewart which had deer on it and I was going out three or four times a week and getting up to £1000 a week which got me through my immediate crisis. I knew it wouldn't go on for ever, but while it lasted it was a Godsend."

Not long after settling in Leamington Spa, Virginia arranged to see a lawyer to begin divorce proceedings. She knew there was no hope of Robin giving up his work with Debra; no chance of having a husband who would be at home for her and the children seven nights a week. Fighting her divorce petition, Robin knew, would cost thousands of pounds, money he simply didn't have and in any case he resolved not to cause Virginia any problem that might threaten to side-track her from her role as a mother to Robin and full time carer to Alex. So he agreed to a divorce although the law worked at its customary slow pace and it would be some time before the sad break up of the marriage was formally finalised. And throughout his costs continued to be a drain.

He would also discover his reputation as an honest hard worker devoted to saving his daughter had not gone unnoticed. "I was so lucky in having a very, very supportive bank manager in Drew Machin. He allowed me an open ended overdraft and watched me go further and further into the red. He'd ring up and say, 'Sorry to mention this Robin but your overdraft is up to £8,000' and a few weeks later it would be, 'Sorry to mention this Robin but it's now £10,000.' I'd tell him, 'I really mean this, it won't be long before I settle it'. Fortunately he was a very patient and trusting man."

Robin knew that at some time matters would come to a head and they did with the arrival of documents from Virginia's lawyers asking what he intended doing about her equity. At the heart was the house, the matrimonial home that had increased dramatically in value from the original buying price of £60,000 by the addition of the extension and, more crucially, the installation of mains electricity.

"My parents helped me get a mortgage and Lochside was transferred into my name and Virginia had her equity out of it.

Clearly, friends knew Virginia had walked out on her husband. Yet, remarkably, despite his high Media profile, news of the break up did not appear and it would be almost two years before Robin confirmed his marriage had ended.

"Because I was educated in Birmingham and had many business contacts it had been my home area for so many years I knew lots of people in the area and one morning did a radio interview in the city, on the Malcolm Boyden show on radio WM. I was allowed to read out the head office telephone number for Debra and for two days their phones didn't stop ringing with offers of money. Many of the callers said they had been in tears after listening to me talk about Alex and all the other children who were victims of EB. 'What a great guy, what a great job he does' they said and so for a while I shuttled between Birmingham and Scotland, fundraising in both locations. But Scotland remained my home and it was always to Lochside Cottage that I returned whenever I could.'

His money raising pleas, his letters begging for help to celebrities, businessmen, anyone he felt look sympathetically on the charity, continued to bear fruit. He knew there were those who, while not telling him directly, believed the obvious solution to the devastation to his personal life and the horrendous difficulties he faced financially, was to go back to a more normal existence, resume his highly prosperous business and work in a part time capacity for Debra. That would have been the advice from anyone not knowing the real Robin Hood. Those closest to him knew that having set out to achieve a goal he was not going to renege on the promises he had made to his daughter. He was not a man who backed down. Virginia knew that and realised the hopelessness of her task in trying to plead then cajole then threaten him into staying at home. That was why she had left.

There could be no doubt that his incredible and tireless efforts to raise money were paying dividends for Debra. His mind was a constant buzz of ideas. He would talk to anyone about Alex and EB. "I had the view that the stranger I was sitting next to in a plane or on a train might be a future lottery winner who would remember us. It was a case of trying to make everybody aware of EB and that given enough money a cure would be discovered.

Robin had made a plea for cash help to the National Lottery Charities Board, confident that after hearing his case Debra would receive part of the vast millions of pounds it had in its coffers. He hoped to win funding to encourage the dedicated team of experts at Dundee investigating the genetic defects that caused EB and at the same time pointed out to the Board that the 300 families of children with EB living in Scotland needed on the spot practical and skilled nursing assistance, pointing to the immense task that faced Virginia 24 hours a day.

Robin knew just how potentially lucrative could be the business sector. Many companies, including hotel chains, would select a charity each year and sponsor it. Guests would arrive in their rooms to find a leaflet telling them about the work of the chosen charity together with a small envelope into which they were invited to consider making a donation. For a charity the potential was huge, considering that the majority of those staying in hotels were relatively well off. Debra was a comparative latecomer to the highly competitive fundraising sector, but the pace of Robin soon made up lost ground. He fired off letters by the hundred, appealing for help. If there was no response, further pleas would follow until many executives, maybe worn down by the never ending flow of paper to their 'In' trays and headed 'Debra' simply caved in and coughed up.

The generosity of others was spontaneous. A firm of career consultants organising a series of annual charity events on behalf of clients, chose Debra to benefit from a charity soccer match featuring television personalities and even former internationalists. An added bonus from events such as these was that frequently those taking part wanted to know more about the charity concerned. They were then likely to pass information on to others. Robin made sure nobody was left in the dark.

Always though in his thoughts was the condition of his daughter. At every opportunity he quizzed researchers and scientists on what, if any, progress was being made in the search for a solution to the nightmare that was EB. Too often the responses were not encouraging despite superhuman efforts by the most brilliant minds. Often too few resources was quoted as a prime stumbling block and that merely drove him on to even greater efforts. So too did occasional dips in Alex's condition.

After her gastrostomy operation she had, despite the side effects of reflux, gained weight and now in Leamington Spa had been able to begin her schooling. But then her weight stalled and her health deteriorated. Robin wondered whether this was as the result of a delayed reaction to her gastrostomy, or to her frail body finally objecting to one of the numerous medicines fed into her each day. He had total confidence in Virginia. Their marriage might have ended, but his love for her and for the care she gave his daughter never diminished.

CHAPTER SEVENTEEN

Virginia too had her share of headaches after the split from Robin. Walking out had not been a decision she took lightly because while the relationship had never run smoothly, and few do, more than a decade and a half of marriage had left her with many happy memories and two children on whom she doted. She had fought to prevent her tears showing to Alex during the journey south after leaving Robin at Carlisle that grey day in July 1995, but the thirteen months following Robin's announcement that he would work full time for Debra had at times been hell. Alex was aged six and her son approaching his sixteenth birthday when mother and children began trying to re-organise their lives in the home of Virginia's parents.

She had held on until July, when schools in Scotland had begun their annual lengthy summer holidays in order to minimise the inevitable disruption to Robin's schooling. "I brought him to live with Alex and me at my parents at the right time to start his GCSE studies. I just couldn't move when he was in the middle of his courses but moving and staying with my parents was very difficult for him. He was still a child really. In Scotland he had been able to get off the school bus when lessons

134

for the day were over, come home, get into his old clothes, go into the loch with the dogs, walk around with them, really do whatever he wanted. He had so much freedom there and now he was discovering a very different lifestyle.

"My father was really ill, my mother was unwell and although we didn't know it at the time she had the start of Parkinson's Disease. It was really, really difficult for all of us because my parents very kindly let us stay there and anyone knows how awkward it can often be when people, even close family, come to stay in your home with you. I don't think Robin appreciated that, although he did his best. Alex and I were in the bedroom next to my father's bedroom and that meant having to keep the fan on to prevent her getting too hot. When you are older you often don't realise how hot you keep your home and that wasn't suitable for Alex. Then when I was doing her dressings my parents would hear her screaming out. How is that for grandparents? It's upsetting of course. It was dreadful, really, really hard on them.

"Robin was in the downstairs room which had been my father's study. He wasn't allowed friends in. I think he felt he was being organised; it was so different from what he had grown up to in Scotland and he would get upset. When we had moved there it had meant him changing schools. Now he asked, 'Why have we moved? Why have you moved me to another school again?' I promised him, 'You're not going to have to move again. This is it. 'I honestly meant it."

The teenager stuck to his studies for a year. But he missed the wildness of Scotland. At times he felt caged, but when school term ended the following year and his GCSE course had been completed, he asked his mother if he could go back to live with his father. It would, of course, mean him reverting to his old school in Scotland. And he knew he would miss Alex. Brother and sister had always been close, they were best friends, he felt protective towards her not just because she suffered so dreadfully from a condition of which he himself could easily have been a victim, but because of a genuine liking for Alex. His father welcomed his son back, and the teenager was enrolled at Kirkcudbright Academy, eighteen miles from Lochside Cottage.

Left alone without his family, Robin had been lonely and sought to escape from that solitude by working harder than ever for Debra. There was no doubt his efforts were continuing to pay off big style. Sometimes the returns were relatively small, but they were as important as any to the huge fundraising picture. Every gift was a personal indictment of Robin's work. More and more individuals were becoming aware of EB and Debra as Media coverage continued. A keen horticulturalist opened his garden to the public; a gifted artist laid on an exhibition of his work and invited donations. The two efforts raised £230. Just as the mystery letter writer who sent a one pound note to Robin every week helped close the funding gap towards the day when a cure would be discovered, and would go on doing so for a decade, so did these kindly efforts. Alcan, the international aluminium producer, offered to give Debra a penny for every drinks can handed in for recycling. Runners continued to sweat and strain over marathon courses; children sold their toys at pavement stalls watched over by parents grateful that their offspring were not EB victims; elderly ladies ran raffles and sold cakes.

In December 1996 Christmas came early for Robin and the Debra team with an announcement from the National Lotteries Charity Board, better known as The Community Fund. The Board gives its aim as, 'To give grants mainly to groups that help meet the needs of those at greatest disadvantage in society and also to improve the quality of life in the community'. That includes bringing, 'Research within the reach of the voluntary sector and to support it to develop effective and innovative responses to present and future challenges'. In presenting Debra's case Robin had clearly not only shown the charity met the Board's requirements.

It awarded a grant of £155,000 to allow the team of scientists at Dundee to press on with their work. And it gave another grant of £96,000 so that Debra could appoint a welfare worker in Scotland to provide on the spot help to the parents of the 300 EB victims in the country. Prior to this, sufferers and their families had had to rely on nursing help and advice from Debra's head office in England. Sometimes that meant an inevitable wait until the nurse became available.

Just how crucial was the role played by Robin in the applications for the grants was demonstrated by this statement from Graham Bowie, chairman of the National Lotteries Charity Board Scotland. 'We have been highly impressed by his strength of character and motivation,' he said. And how other members of the Board had been stimulated by Alex's plight was revealed by director John Rafferty who said, 'When we learned about EB through Alexandra's father Robin's application on behalf of Debra, we were all very moved by the horrific nature of this condition and the pain and trauma that the sufferers, especially young children and their families, have to go through. We were also highly impressed by the strength of character and motivation shown by Mr Hood in his personal mission to help find a cure for his daughter.'

It was glowing praise and richly deserved. Just how important was the larger grant was emphasised by Professor Birgit Lane, at the time holder of the Cox Chair of Anatomy and Cell Biology in the College of Life at Dundee University. Her contribution to research into EB has been enormous. Among her many present posts, she is an Adjunct Professor at the Karolinska Institute, Sweden and Emeritus Professor at the University of Dundee. She is an elected Fellow of the Royal Society of Edinburgh and of the UK's Academy of Medical Sciences. The money, she said, would be used to buy sequencing equipment and so allow researchers to investigate and research genes five times faster. 'It is an absolutely vital tool and we are delighted that it will be sited at Dundee,' she said. The fact was, though, that the University team believed at least £2.5million was needed for further research. The figure would ultimately turn out to be but a relative drop in the ocean when estimates of the real need would show it to be many, many times greater. However, no matter what the ultimate requirement, nothing would deter Robin from his mission.

Since his wife had left him he had thrown himself into the task of fundraising with an extraordinary abandon. Close friends wondered for just how long he could continue at such a pace. Virginia herself recalled her warning that if he carried on. 'You'll kill yourself.' But there was another terrible motive behind his frantic forays around Britain. That spring and summer, Alex's condition had begun to deteriorate to the extent where the prognosis of her living until mid adult live looked decidedly over optimistic. Her weight had at first stabilised and then reduced until she weighed just under three stones. A minor operation had helped her recover weight, but the worry about her only served to remind Robin that he was racing against time. He had promised her a cure within two years and that time span was rapidly slipping past. To add to the family's fears, they were now becoming ever more conscious of the dangers of Alex contracting skin cancer due to the constant open sores that increasingly littered her body as wounds left by blistering and skin loss struggled to heal.

'She will die if we cannot find a cure, but there is no way, while I have breath in me, that I will allow that to happen,' Robin told a journalist. 'Her courage is an inspiration to everybody around her. Those of us without EB have no concept of the pain the disease means. Eating is the equivalent of swallowing broken glass.'

However EB was threatening, indirectly, to claim another victim. Robin junior had never complained about having to take a back seat while attention was focussed on his sister. Even at the outset, when she arrived on the scene red raw and screaming, he had adored her and accepted with remarkable maturity for his eight years that her needs took precedence. Feeling restricted, hemmed in even, at the home of his grandparents he had longed for a return to the wideness and openness of Scotland. But, back with his father, he now realised he had gone from one extreme to the other. In short, he was lonely, an emotion for which his father accepts blame.

"Naturally all the concentration had been on Alex. Was I conscious that maybe Robin had not been given the attention he should have had? Well I was delighted when he came back to live with me and we got on really well. But then I did to him what I'd done to Virginia, sometimes going off for weeks at a time on fundraising trips.

"So there he was at sixteen years of age left to fend for himself. Before going away I'd leave him a stock of food and some cash, an emergency fund of maybe £50 so he could buy anything else needed and tell him, 'Right, see you soon son.' Then it might be a fortnight before I'd be back. So Robin would get the bus to the Academy each morning and come back at night to an empty house with a meal to make for himself, watch television and look after the dogs then go to bed. It must have been a miserable existence. But I was determined that nothing had to get in the way of my fundraising.

"Once I came back from a trip and he fell into my arms. He was crying and said, 'Dad, I'm sick of being on my own.' I thought, 'This isn't fair, what I did to my wife I've now done to my son' and told him, 'Pick a holiday and we'll go away' and we went off for a week. We had a great time but even on holiday abroad I found it impossible to switch off.

"After a couple of days the hotel receptionist said the manager would like to see me. I asked why and she said, 'There's been a complaint about you'. I was sure I hadn't done anything wrong and when I met the manager told him, 'I drink but I don't get drunk and I don't shout or make a nuisance of myself'. He told me, 'Oh I'm afraid you do. We've had complaints from other guests in the hotel that you are forever telling them about the charity you are with and your daughter's disease. It's upsetting them and spoiling their holiday'. Then he said, 'I'm going to give a donation to your charity on condition you don't talk about your work or the illness any more'. And he handed over a cheque for five hundred dollars.

"I'd actually been sitting at the hotel pool giving talks about Debra and Alex, but the problem was that I found it really hard to go away anywhere knowing that wherever she was she was in pain. Once on a train journey with a colleague I lectured a fellow passenger, a total stranger, about EB. It emerged he worked for a big company in Carlisle and before we arrived gave me a sizeable cheque. My colleague told me afterwards, 'I wouldn't like to be sat on a train going anywhere next to you Robin.'

"Fundraising was a total consuming passion to the exclusion of everything else, even those I loved most dearly. I just could not see the darkness of the tunnel into which my work was taking me. But there was never a time when I thought of packing it all in. I was good at spreading the word, good at raising money, my work was the blood that kept me alive."

That work had claimed him his wife. Now his son was about to follow her. "I was so proud when Robin told us he wanted to be a vet. We knew he was clever enough to study and succeed. Once during a rare visit home I went to a parents' evening at his Academy and one of his masters sought me out. 'In 20 years of teaching I've never had such a capable pupil as your son Mr Hood,' he said. Once Robin came home with one of the papers from a maths exam. He handed me three pages of A4 paper covered in script and what to me were hieroglyphics. I'm as thick as mince and couldn't understand a word of it so I told him, 'I'll have the sweet and sour pork'. His mother was doing her best with Alex, but I let Robin down because I was never there for him."

Finally teenage Robin decided enough was enough. He had enjoyed the Academy where he made lots of friends. Most of his fellow students and teachers were aware of the heartache he hid daily over the suffering of his sister. They were keen to help and at one stage organised a non uniform day, paying £1 each to turn up in their jeans and gaily coloured tops. A photograph in a local newspaper showed smiling young people handing over a cheque to Robin, the only member of the little group not to wear a broad smile. Virginia knew from conversations by telephone with him that he was increasingly unhappy. "He was left to do everything, make meals, do his washing, chop kindling to light the fire. The only contact he had with others was through the school bus. He was so lonely and it was so very, very hard for him. Throughout all of it he worried about Alex and finally he rang one day and asked, 'Can I come back'. I told him, 'Of course'.

Robin had once told himself that if Alex died he would still have the solace of his wife and son. But now, his son too having left him, they were gone. That spurred him on to even greater efforts to try and ensure his daughter was not lost to him too. In Dundee the installation of the sequencer had hugely encouraged scientists at the University and heightened their optimism. Experts were trying to resolve, through research, whether the best way of dealing with EB was to find a cure or somehow to bypass the faulty genes altogether, to merely create a link between sound genes. To this end, teams were comparing normal skin cells with samples of the defective cells taken from nearly 100 EB victims. The equipment meant vastly less waiting time for results. 'We are making steady progress,' said Professor Lane. 'There is a lot of consolidation work going on round Britain now on new pieces of information which we have been able to identify in this past year. Finding out about one weak link in the chain leads us to the next stage. If we can obtain significant amounts of research money then we can do the work more quickly, because much of the process is quite straightforward and only requires an increase in the number of people working on it. Making a breakthrough is not a question of if, but when.' Ultimately, three separate groups would be carrying out different areas of research, but all with a dedicated common aim of ending the EB misery, bringing relief to the many thousands of little victims worldwide.

Robin's visits to see his daughter were infrequent, his time mostly taken up by fundraising. When he did arrive, Virginia again insisted he bandaged his daughter in order to prepare for the holidays she was determined Alex would spend with her father at Lochside, a spot she loved. Robin found the procedure difficult and even distressing. "I knew there had been times before we split up when I could have helped Virginia, especially in winter. But I hadn't. I'm not sure whether I simply saw bandaging as her job or if I just didn't like doing it. Virginia was very good. When it was obviously hurting Alex she'd say, 'Alex, chin up, I can't do anything about it. You've got EB' whereas I'd say, 'Oh Alex I'm sorry'. But she didn't want a drooling, drivelling woosy like me; she just wanted somebody to get on with it. And I just wanted to get on with raising money so there would be no longer a need for bandaging." Help was about to come from two vastly different sources.

CHAPTER EIGHTEEN

Mohammed Abdel Moneim Al-Fayed, well known as simply Mohammed Al Fayed, was an enormously successful Egyptian-born businessman. He owned the world renowned Knightsbridge department store Harrods, the Hotel Ritz in Paris and Balnagown Castle with its vast estates in the north of Scotland. He was also a most generous benefactor. In 1987 he had established the Al Fayed Charitable Foundation with the aim of helping children with life limiting conditions and kiddies forced to live in poverty. There were many who believed his kindness and generosity had been deliberately overlooked by the United Kingdom authorities.

The profile of the multi millionaire had been raised even higher by the fact that his son Dodi, a film producer whose credits included Oscar-winning Chariots of Fire, was regularly seen with much beloved Diana, Princess of Wales, former wife to the heir to the English throne and mother of Princes William and Harry. Newspapers grabbed every opportunity to photograph the Princess and Dodi together and openly speculated about a possible marriage. Among a host of good causes supported by the Princess was Great Ormond Street Hospital, of which she was President and after reading about the plight of a child with EB she had willingly agreed to become a Patron of Debra.

Mohammed Al Fayed had bought much of the estate in France, including jewellery, of the Duchess of Windsor who, as American-born divorcee Wallis Simpson, had married Edward Duke of Windsor in 1936 causing a constitutional crisis and resulting in his abdication. The Duke had died in 1972 and his wife in 1986. In July 1997, Dennis Hood pointed out to his son a newspaper item reporting that Mohammed was to auction many items from the estate and give the proceeds to charity. Robin wrote to the businessman telling him about EB, Debra and Alex and asking if he would consider making a donation to the charity. His letter would, in fact, ultimately not just result in a generous donation but win the friendship of Mohammed Al Fayed.

Later Mohammed would reply, as Robin remembers, he confirmed a most generous donation to Debra of many tens of thousands of pounds and in his most humble letter to me added, 'Thank you for giving me the opportunity to help'. Here was one of the world's richest men, humbly expressing gratitude at being allowed to help others. I was so moved when I read his words." It was the first of many contacts the two men would have. There was similar generosity from the Memorial Fund set up in Princess Diana's name. Mindful of her close and long links to Debra, the trustees of the Fund gave the charity £60,000.

Robin's own personal sacrifices had not been in vain. It was clear that Debra, symbolised by its' butterfly emblem, was clearly benefitting from his work. From an income of just £90,000 in 1989, the figure had rocketed to a staggering one million pounds in 1996 and he constantly set himself even higher targets. Money came from unexpected sources. As 1997 drew to a close Robin opened his mail and there was a cheque for £25,000. The windfall had come from a man he had never met or even heard of. William Fisher Wilson had died in Edinburgh in July that year leaving £100,000. In his will he had directed that the executor should give the proceeds of his estate, 'to such charities and in such proportions as he in his sole discretion may decide'. Robin would never learn the identity of the executor. But the executor had heard of him and Debra and decided the organisation would be one of four to share in William Fisher Wilson's fortune.

Others were equally kind. In 1937 Arthur Kimmond Bell, whose father Arthur had founded the world famous Bell's whisky business, set up the Gannochy Trust to help worthy causes in the Perth area of Scotland. Later the Trust spread its' wings over the whole of Scotland and gave £31,000 to pay for research into pre-natal tests for EB. Punters at Ayr Racecourse came up with another £1,000 and pledged a further £7,000 while a charity ball at Edinburgh Botanical Gardens raised £6,000.

These were good news items, but all was not plain sailing for the Hoods. Alex bravely tried coping with the problem of her webbed fingers. From time to time surgeons operated to separate her fingers, but their efforts were not always successful and she was frequently reduced to just having the full use for a time of one hand. There were problems too with her getting about. The simple everyday task of walking could turn into an appalling ordeal. It was not only that the skin on her heels could be rubbed off; the mere act of an accidental brush against someone else could result in blistering and skin loss.

Virginia was surprised one day when her father asked her, 'What about getting Alex a motorised scooter?' He had always been so protective towards her, even worrying when she told him of using an electric drill or performing simple DIY tasks at Lochside Cottage during Robin's frequent absences. "So we bought Alex a scooter and although it wasn't very far from where we lived to her school, she would use it to get there. Other parents would be dropping off their children from cars but there would be Alex, off on her own and coming home on her own on her little scooter. It meant that at last she could feel she had a degree of independence."

The sight of the gallant little blonde haired girl chugging her way through the busy streets around her home became familiar to neighbours and her school friends. If it took considerable courage to venture out, her body swathed in bandages, her face sometimes marked where the skin had snared off as she turned in her sleep, one and sometimes both of her hands in splints, then Alex gave no sign of nerves on her expeditions. But for a youngster who endured daily suffering and at times excruciating pain, an occasional bump was small beer. Like so many afflicted with EB, Alex was determined to live as normal an existence as possible. She did not want to be regarded by her friends as freakish or out of the ordinary. Her happiest times during her schooling were when she was looked on as simply another pupil. But of course the truth was she was not. Nor was any EB child. In Scotland she had had a pony, but was never able to ride so the dream of tearing across a field, leaping high in the saddle as her mount soared over a five bar gate had never been within her compass.

She longingly looked forward to the visits from her father who, despite on-going divorce proceedings, was on friendly terms with Virginia. Both parents knew their children were suffering, in their individual ways, sufficient traumas without having a mother and father at war. Robin continued to assure Alex a cure would be found that would allow her to live a long if not normal life. Sometimes he had to convince himself when he told Alex, 'There'll definitely be a cure found within four years' that he truly believed what he was telling her. But what would have been the effect on her had he admitted that researchers were still struggling to discover the answers to key, even basic, questions as to why genes became effective and how the rogues could be treated. Everywhere, parents of EB youngsters were asking themselves the same questions. And the fact was that no matter how hard the scientists worked, EB children were still entering the world.

Two hundred miles to the north and east of Lochside Cottage, Dianne Forsyth lay in Montrose Royal Infirmary waiting to give birth. Just a few miles to the south scientists were frantically searching for a means of curing EB. Dianne's was an ordinary, comfortable happy family and, not one ever expecting to make headlines. She and her husband Peter harboured the same hopes for their children as any other parents, success at school, sound careers, marriage and families of their own to bring happiness to Dianne and Peter as they grew old together. Should they need advice along the way they knew they could always turn for help to the children's uncle Michael Forsyth, Conservative Member of Parliament for Stirling, Scotland from 1983 until the previous year and during his tenure his abilities had been recognised by Prime Minister John Major who appointed him Secretary of State for Scotland, a post he held until leaving government at the 1997 General Election. Knighted that same year, he took the title of Baron Forsyth of Drumlean, the town near Stirling. A keen climber, the father-of-three often raised prodigious amounts of money for charities.

Dianne had undergone all the standard pre natal checks. Testing for EB was not among them and with two healthy children already there was no reason to expect anything other than a third. She and Peter did not know whether to expect a boy or girl so each chose a name. Peter looked at a world atlas and spotted the city of Adana in Turkey, famous as being near the spot where in 1943 Prime Minister Winston Churchill has tried to persuade the Turks to enter the Second World War on behalf of the Allies. "That's it, if it's a girl we'll name her Adana," he told his wife and she smiled her agreement.

Tests had indicated little movement by the as yet unborn baby leaving doctors to wonder about the cause. "I had no inkling at all when I was carrying my third child that there might be anything wrong," said Dianne. "We looked for everything to be normal." She entered hospital in early January and then went into a long labour, eventually giving birth to a six pounds one ounce baby.

"There was actually no amniotic fluid when she was born so it was a really horrible birth for me. After the birth we realised that she had obviously been in pain inside me as well. Pretty much right away after she arrived she was taken away. They were tidying me up and I could hear her screaming in the next room, but

I was just relieved it was all over. Then someone said, 'We're getting a doctor in' and when I asked why was told, 'Didn't you notice the strawberry coloured marks on her legs?' I said, 'No.' The midwife was trying to be as kind as she could just chatting to me and I said, 'No. Are they big?' She said, 'They are right down the fronts of her legs,' and I said, 'Oh well, it's not a big deal, she could wear tights.'

"And then they brought her through, wrapped, really swaddled up. Usually they put the baby right on your stomach but she looked as though she was in total agony. And of course she would have been in agony because she had raw skin that was getting rubbed by these really coarse blankets. They gave me a bottle to feed her so I put the bottle in her mouth and the skin came off her lips. So I was, 'Ohhh, what's going on here?' and I still didn't know what was happening.

"Then they tried to put a plastic wrist bracelet on her with her details on it and when the nurse pulled it on it took the skin off her arm. So then they took her away and I was really apprehensive. The staff came back and said they were taking the baby to Ninewells Hospital. We'd just actually phoned everybody to tell them, 'We have a little girl. She's lovely.' And so then we had to basically phone my mum back and tell her, 'There's something wrong'. An ambulance arrived and they made me have a quick, quick shower and then a little sip of tea while they got her in the ambulance. It wasn't a long journey to Ninewells, but all the way there you could see her curling up in the incubator. She was screaming all the way through, so obviously she was in a lot of pain. When we arrived they took her away. I was shown to my room and then taken to see her.

"At this point we didn't know it was EB. But luckily a doctor remembered the birth of the baby there with EB a few years previously and so he recognised that what Adana was suffering from was the same. He told me 'Epidermolysis Bullosa' but those words meant nothing to me. I'd never heard of the disease. He mentioned there were various strains but at that stage we did not know what the type was of which she was a victim. Poor little Adana was lying there with no bandages on, she was obviously exhausted and her skin must have been so sore, but somehow she had managed to sleep and I got to see her. I had so many tears, 'Why me, why is this happening, why my baby? What's going on? Surely they can cure this?' But nobody had answers."

By an awful irony deep under the layers of rock on which the town of Adana had been founded many millennia earlier, came the first faint rumblings that all was not well below ground. But the concern of geologists there was as nothing compared with the distress of the Forsyths.

CHAPTER NINETEEN

Dianne and Peter were about to live the nightmare of being EB parents. Unknowingly, each had carried the defective gene that led to an absence of Collagen VII and now they would reap the consequences. Dianne would be put to the same test that every EB family must face. Could she, as a mother, cope? Could Peter face the daily trauma of watching his child not only suffer but slowly die? Those first hours were a mirror of the ordeal Virginia and Robin had endured. Like Virginia, though, there could be not a moment's escape for Dianne of living with the reality of the illness.

"I didn't sleep very much, but when I was half sleeping the words Epidermolysis Bullosa kept going around my head. I still thought that maybe we could get some answers and perhaps find it was something they could fix. It was like a bad dream only when I woke up there was no one to tell me it was going to be all right. Talking now, years after, the memory feels as fresh as it did then, the feelings and what we went through. One minute I was crying. The next moment Peter was crying. We were trying to stay strong. The people at Ninewells Hospital were great. They had met the other little girl who had been born with EB. Although it didn't feel very positive to me, the staff kept trying to be so kind. They were saying, 'She'll be okay. The family of the other child have coped and she's a lovely little girl now.'

"On the second day we were told Adana was being transferred to a specialist unit at Edinburgh and we went there with her to see a consultant, a dermatologist who explained there were different strains of EB and to find out which one Adana was suffering from would need a biopsy. While we were there, we'd managed to get our hands on a textbook, a guide for hospital staff about EB. It seems it was not something we were meant to see but Peter had read it and told me, 'She's either going to live and be like the other little girl, I can handle that one; she's going to have a very short life with the junctional type of EB and I can handle that one; or she's going to be disabled and I don't know if I can handle the disabled side'.

"Every hour that went by seemed to be making everything even more awful. We wanted to know all we could about Adana and EB, but no matter what we read it seemed to be all bad. I was feeling tired. I'd just had a baby and I wandered around like a zombie, unable to sleep. I was meant to have regular checks with the midwife but couldn't face them and just meandered up and down trying to see Adana.

"While we were at Edinburgh, the staff tried to do Adana's dressings. There was blood everywhere but the nurses were so brave, And, no fault of theirs', but they were using the wrong dressings on her and so, because we didn't have more information about what type of EB Adana had, and how to deal with it, they were ripping her skin off when they were removing her dressings. Nor was Adana on any proper pain relief at this point. It was all so new and strange and we didn't know enough about this disease.

"We were transferred back to Ninewells and basically up to this point I hadn't had to do her dressings. But the nurses put Adana on to morphine and other pain relieving medication for the changes of the dressings. I had decided I would go and help, even if it meant simply soothing her while they did the dressings, but I went in and, again, there was blood everywhere and I couldn't watch it. I had to step back. I couldn't even stay and watch, which I'm angry about now. But I just couldn't handle it and so I walked out of the room. I didn't think I was ever going to be able to bandage my own daughter.

"It was dreadful watching this happening to my new born baby. I'd just had her. It's bad enough when they put a needle into your little baby to take blood, but they were ripping skin away and she was in absolute agony. All I could do was to let them get on with it at that point and I asked that when they had finished I'd be called through so I could sit and feed Adana. And I did. I fed her, comforted her and got some nice moments with her and bonded with her. But all the time, 'Why, why, why?' was going through my head. 'What's happened?' I kept asking myself. I thought maybe it was because of something I'd done. Things were in such a blur, nothing had really sunk in.

"I was pretty distraught. I had two young kids at home who were missing me and their grandparents were struggling to cope with them. But when Tanis and Cody were brought to hospital to see their sister and me, they were trying to push all the buttons on the incubator, just being kids. I spent two weeks at hospital learning how to look after Adana and then I began going home, spending time with Tanis and Cody during the day and going back to hospital at night. But I'd find different nurses had been caring for her; her lips might be black and blue simply because a nurse hadn't known to use a different teat and to put special liquid stuff on the teat when she was being fed, so it would go in her mouth comfortably without ripping skin and hurting her.

"It was really, really hard. Peter found it tough going too. Each night he would drive me back to hospital and one night we were stopped by the police and accused of speeding. I sat crying in the car while we tried to explain, 'We're in a hurry. Our kiddie's in hospital.' But there was no sympathy. Obviously we shouldn't have been speeding, but being accused of going too fast was the last of our worries and frankly at the end of the day I just didn't care. But they must surely have wondered why I was sitting blubbing my eyes out. These were really difficult times.

"A lady who had been a midwife approached me and asked if I'd like to be put in touch with the mother of the child who had been born with EB a few years previously at Dundee and I leapt at the chance to meet her. When we got together, she was just incredible, popping in to help re-bandage Adana's hands, taking a real, full on interest. Until then I had been trailing around hospital corridors, miserable, my legs dragging. I had no flowers, no cards in the hospital unlike the other mums, but meeting this lady was as if suddenly a light had been turned on at the end of the tunnel.

"Her daughter had the simplex form of EB and I was sure Adana's strain was simplex too. I didn't think it was junctional, but one day at the hospital Peter and I were taken into a private room and told the biopsy had shown she had dystrophic EB. I couldn't believe it. We had so many tears. And when we asked, 'Will she have a shortened life?' they told us, 'Yes, she probably won't live past 30'. This was our newborn baby and we were being told when she'd probably die. That night, we drove home in total silence.

"We wanted to bring Adana home. But just as we were about to do so, her temperature shot up, she had an allergic reaction to morphine and then contracted an infection in hospital due to a little cut that meant suddenly her legs went all mushy, the whole of the front of her legs was raw. So it was a month before we could get her home. I was frightened for her, us, everybody. But then she was such a little cutie.

"By the time we'd had her home for a few weeks she was the talk of the town. Word had got about there was something seriously wrong with Adana. People would even run across the street, look into her pram and say, 'Oh, she looks fine'. They just didn't grasp this was as serious as it was. Having her was like a grieving. I was grieving for my life change, it was as if I was being bombed up for life. I no longer had this feeling of freedom in the sense that if you have three kids there's not much freedom anyway but now there would be none. Yet, after that initial grieving for having lost my life the way it was, and having a different child to the child I expected to have, I learned not to be a 'Poor me'. Because Adana was the 'Poor me'.

"There was so much to learn. I was quite a 'ring' person, but with the need to put so much surgical spirit on my hands, and not to catch Adana's skin when doing her bandaging, I just threw my rings out. But you get used to not having stupid things on your hands. I'd have a lump in my throat all the time I was bandaging her. Initially I was going to keep a diary, write a book about it for other parents because I was learning new things every day."

The mother of the simplex victim told the Forsyths about Debra and from her first contact with the charity Dianne came to look upon it as a lifeline. She was able to learn from the unique knowledge of nurses wholly proficient in the treatment of EB. Then one day her telephone rang and Robin Hood introduced himself.

He was still going through a difficult time himself. Once again his debts had reached crisis point. Rumours about his private life had begun sprouting arms and legs with talk of an affair and finally, to set the record straight, he agreed to be interviewed by the News of the World in March 1998. Robin admitted, 'There was a huge burden on Virginia and when she needed a shoulder to cry on I wasn't there. She's gone. I'm tortured by guilt and blame my obsession for the collapse of the marriage. I was devastated totally but now I realise it wouldn't have been fair to expect her to carry on so much. What started for me as a job has become a mission. I'm doing what any father would do. That's meant sacrifice and the loss of my marriage.'

Then came more sorrowful news that hurt him deeply. He had always felt close to his son, conscious that Robin had unselfishly taken a back seat as far as attention from his parents was concerned in order that the greater share of their affection could be lavished on Alex. As a schoolboy he had frequently had to fend for himself. The move to stay with Virginia's parents had meant he was unable to invite in friends; his move back to Scotland left him lonely and back in the Midlands he was no happier. And so he announced he would be entering the Army. Through his relationship with the King's Own Scottish Borderers, Robin wanted his son to join as an Officer Cadet, but his initial Assessment was not promising. At that stage many, keen to become officer material, might have opted to return to civilian life for a spell to gain experience and maturity. But Robin went ahead and joined as a private. "I think he just got sick of being left on his own and he had a shitty time," said his father. Joining up meant Robin faced the probability of duty tours in major trouble spots around the world. In time these would heap further worries on his parents and his sister. But never would he shirk his duty either to his country or to Alex.

Robin knew what Dianne and Peter Forsyth were going through. He'd been there and already paid a high price. But he saw in them an opportunity to use Adana's misfortune. At their first meeting Dianne realised he found it difficult to switch off being a fundraiser to just being a parent. "Robin talked a lot about his own experiences. I could see he was passionate about what he was doing and while he may have run away from caring for his daughter, maybe that was a little bit because he and Virginia would be biting at one another. Certainly Peter and I never used to argue before we had Adana. Robin had been able to block off the emotion of being the parent of an EB child by thinking in terms of fundraising and I would come to learn that, and that annoyed some of the other mothers," she said. "His total dedication wasn't everybody's cup of tea. But I understood him.

"That very first time Robin told me, 'If you go to the newspapers, and my ex-wife didn't particularly want to, you get all that comes with that but you actually open peoples' eyes to the condition and to some degrees it paves the way for Adana's future because people know more about EB and therefore are willing to adjust things for her. If people are aware of it then they aren't so likely to ask, "What's wrong with you?"'

"I had been warned that Robin could be quite brutal and it was obvious his whole focus was on raising money for the charity. But he and I clicked with one another from the start. I knew there was good sense in what he said and decided I should talk about Adana. He talked about a cure and from that I felt some sort of hope because he was so positive. Sometimes I'd cry because I hadn't realised how kind people could be. I wanted them to know what EB was like so they would understand. If I could have somehow got film cameras into the hospital when my daughter was lying in that incubator, just a tiny little six pound newborn in agony, then I would have done that."

Dianne's first move was to contact a local newspaper and arrange for Adana's story to be told. It would be the first of many articles and each brought with it vital donations to Debra. But it was impossible to explain to members of the public, seated comfortably in an armchair or riding a bus to work, the real horror of EB. Robin had warned Dianne of the devastation the disease would wreak on her family and as time passed she came to realise the true extent of the trauma it caused.

"Initially nurses did Adana's dressings and Peter and me would just do the patch up in between, but we knew we'd have to do it all ourselves sooner rather than later. If she had an accident you couldn't call out the nurses and wait, you had to get the dressings on right away, take away the bloodied dressing, stop the blood flow and get her bandaged up again. It was so stressful."

The stress, coupled with the continual need to use medications, caused outbreaks of eczema on Dianne's hands. At first, remembering her thoughts of a book, she kept a record of her daughter's condition. "I'd write down things like, 'She had five blisters on her right leg' but writing about it just made me sad because I knew she was never going to heal. I'd bandage her, make her clean and fresh, but the next day there would be another batch of blisters, blisters on her body, arms, legs, mouth, eyes even. They were absolute agony for her and she would be in so much pain that it ripped your heart out. Yet always the hope was hearing Robin talking about raising money and finding a cure."

That summer, as the Forsyths struggled to come to terms with EB, newspapers and television stations around the world reported on a horrific earthquake in southern Turkey that had cost the lives of more than 150 people. The name of the city on which it had been centred? Adana. Peter and Dianne hoped it was not an omen.

Weeks earlier Robin had run the London Marathon, pushing Alex around the course in a supermarket trolley packed with padding to try lessening the friction and blistering and subsequent pain. "Three quarters of the way around the heavens opened. Alex looked wet, anaemic and very miserable and so I stopped running and asked her if she wanted to stop. She told me, 'No way Daddy. If we're going to save my life we have to raise more money'.

He found her selfless attitude was often typical of those most in need of sympathy and succour. Just over two years earlier, on March 13, 1996, , madman Thomas Hamilton caused carnage at Dunblane primary school shooting dead 16 children and teacher Gwen Mayor. Now Robin contacted the fathers of one of the victims because here was a loving dad who had lost a child; a predicament that Robin himself was desperately trying to avoid.

The dad told a newspaper, 'He telephoned me and said his child was going to die unless a cure was found and you can't help but feel your heart is breaking when he talks about Alex. I can understand why he is so motivated, because any parent would be the same if they had the chance to save their child from a painful life and probable death. It doesn't matter whether your child is killed in an accident or through illness. It is still agonising when it happens and nothing can prepare you for the shock.'

The outcome was a donation from one of the funds set up to help victims of the Dunblane tragedy; but just as important was the encouragement from a father who knew the ramifications of losing a child. There was encouragement too from one of the three scientific teams at Dundee University working towards a solution to EB. Using a £300,000 grant, Professor Seth Schor and his wife Ana were researching molecules that affected the healing process on wounds. Normally dormant cells would come to life when a victim's brain notified them of a wound. They would repair the damage then effectively go back to sleep until needed again. But if the process went wrong, as a result for instance of poor blood circulation as in the case of many EB victims, then the wound might not heal and lead to scarring, again a feature of EB.

The scientists were optimistic that they had discovered a molecule called Migration Stimulation Factor (MSF) that might stimulate healing. The research was in its early stages but might lead to the development of dressings impregnated with medication that would rush MSF into life. If successful, it could have a major effect on the treatment of some aspects of EB. However, there was a potentially terrible side effect that the scientists had to recognise. In some cases MSF contributed to the growth of cancerous tumours.

American Seth, and Spanish-born Ana, who had met and fallen in love while students at Cambridge University, had spent 15 years researching wounds and were, naturally cautious about their discovery. Not unnaturally, there was enormous interest in their work and to satisfy a Media eager for any hopeful news, the University issued a statement saying, 'To develop this properly the right commercial partners have to be found. Patients become upset when there is news of a scientific breakthrough which could help their condition. They are hailed as miracles. But the reality is that it will take several years to develop the discovery into a useable product.'

Robin wondered not just if the product would help Alex, but if it would come in time to give her the chance of life.

CHAPTER TWENTY

Dianne Forsyth was about to follow Virginia along the path to loneliness. At first she and Peter had performed together the heart piercing task of bandaging their daughter daily, trying not to run from the incessant shrieks of pain. "Peter was really good at doing the dressings. Sometimes Adana preferred her dad, but he took forever. Whereas my theory was, 'If the bandage is going to catch on the skin it's only going to be a little sting so long as it doesn't tear the skin off'. But Peter would take so long it used to frustrate me and we would argue.

"Initially we'd had two nurses helping us; that was cut down to one but because Adana's arms were flailing about she was doing herself damage and we needed somebody to hold her leg so it wouldn't blister while the dressings were put on her tiny little feet. We tried to stop her toes fusing together but eventually just gave up on that. It was an inevitability, and ultimately all her toenails and fingernails fell off. My mum had tried to help, but one day she accidentally blistered Adana's hand and after that didn't want to do it again. It wasn't something a granny should have to do anyway. It became so stressful that I'd do the dressings myself.

"Probably the toughest thing I ever had to do was to try and bandage her hand myself. I basically had to just let it be raw and comfort her until she calmed down enough to get her to keep her hand still enough for me to cut dressings and put them on her hand just, to get the air with all the germs floating around in it off the raw area. At first I'd get angry at people who hurt her, Peter among them, but as time wore on other people were more upset than I was if they hurt Adana while I realised that sort of thing was bound to happen. One day she had been sitting in her bouncy chair and I heard her screaming. Cody had tried to give her a toy and it had taken the skin off her face.

"Adana was about a year old when Peter went away to work. He changed because now he was away from home, living a normal life. He was abroad and for tax reasons only able to come home for 90 days a year. But I think he just couldn't handle the invasion of his privacy by nurses and social workers when he was at home. So he bought a camper van, loaded it up with all Adana's dressings and medication and we all went off to Ireland. We found a camp site with a pool and decided to take Adana swimming. We had rubber coverings to put over her bandages and legs to keep them dry, but the water got in and as her dressings began slipping off she started screaming."

Once, while left alone with the children at their home in the country village of St Cyrus, twenty five miles from Dundee, Dianne realised Adana had contracted an infection. "She was ill, I was in such a panic I couldn't remember the doctor's telephone number. My mind had just gone blank. I rang a friend who came out and we called the doctor, but when he arrived I made my friend hide. If it was thought I had help with me I would have been told to take Adana to the surgery and I couldn't move her because her bandages were soaked with poison.

"When the doctor handed me a prescription I went mental asking how I was supposed to get to a pharmacy with two kids in bed and a really ill baby to take care of. I think because I'd yelled he gave me a sachet of antibiotic. It was a constant battle to get understanding of the situation I was in. Once, to try and draw attention to the need for specialist care, I was actually going to leave Adana in her car seat outside the doctor's surgery, but then I thought, 'I can't do this, they'll hurt her'. All of it meant Tanis and Cody having to grow up so quickly. They were never jealous of the attention given to Adana. They were aware of her condition, saw the horrors for themselves. Sometimes they'd hurt her by accident but they loved their sister and never pestered me if they knew I was busy bandaging her."

Robin knew just what Dianne meant. His own son had acted with astonishing maturity towards Alex, but now he had gone off to soldier and increasingly newspapers began talking about Afghanistan and Iraq as likely spots where British troops might eventually find themselves in danger, under fire and facing death and terrible injury. Whether they were, of course, was largely in the hands of Prime Minister Tony Blair. As the leader of the revitalised Labour Party and its 'New Labour' policies, he had crushed opposition parties by winning a huge majority in the 1997 General Election. At that stage, the Prime Minister and his barrister wife Cherie, daughter of the BBC television comedy actor Tony Booth, had three children, their youngest, a daughter, Kathryn, barely a year older than Alex. Robin reasoned the Blairs might be sympathetic to the plight of parents of children wracked by an agony from which there was little, if any, hope of freedom.

"My constant media attention was helping the income of Debra grow, but I knew that if I could enlist the support of the Prime Minister or his family it could have a potentially huge beneficial effect. My attitude was always, 'What have I got to lose?' and so I wrote off to him. Plenty of people were sceptical, but I felt if I could somehow communicate as one father to another, he would understand. In my first letter to Tony Blair I told him about Alex, what life was like for her and said, 'I've never voted for you in my life. Do you think you could do your job as well as you think you are doing it if you had a child like my child in your family? Would you allow me to come to number 10 Downing Street to create some awareness for Debra and EB?'

"A polite reply came back saying the Prime Minister was too heavily committed for a meeting. There was no way I was going to be put off. When I set my sights on doing something I didn't give up at the first fence and so started firing off letter after letter. After six or seven knockbacks, Downing Street eventually said the Prime Minister couldn't see me, but would I like to see Cherie? It was a wonderful opportunity to well and truly put the campaign on behalf of Debra on the map."

Robin was asked to call a telephone number to arrange an appointment and the meeting with Cherie was set for early April 1999, a couple of months after Alex's eleventh birthday. A letter from Tony Blair confirming the date said, 'No one can fail to be moved by the stories of children who have this condition'. Swathed in her bandages, Alex chatted to Cherie Blair, an experience that left a deep impression on the wife of the Prime Minister. She was allowed to sit in the Prime Minister's chair in the Cabinet Office and presented Cherie with one of the paintings she had so skilfully completed, ignoring the pain that came with every brush stroke.

"Cherie was so taken with what Alex and I told her that she said she wanted Tony to meet me and dragged him out of a meeting. I had five minutes with him. He was a wonderful man and that day wasn't a politician or the leader of a country, he was just a dad. I knew we'd get great publicity but there was more. The Prime Minister asked, 'What else can I do for you?' and I said, 'I don't know, what else can you do for us?' He said 'How about a reception?' I told him, 'Great.' I had no idea what a reception would mean to us. Before we parted I gave him a letter addressed to Donald Dewar, then the Secretary of State for Scotland and when he asked, 'What's this for?' I said, 'It's a letter asking for money'. The elections for the new Scottish Parliament were just a couple of months away and this was the start of my relationship with the Scottish Executive."

Politicians have a reputation for uttering empty words. Tony and Cherie Blair would come to demonstrate the sincerity of their concern. For Robin, striving to gain the type of profile recognition that would guarantee a major fillip in terms of fundraising, the promise of being treated to a reception by the Prime Minister and his wife was the equivalent of winning the National Lottery. It was a remarkable achievement, not just because of the inevitable publicity that would result but because it brought with it the opportunity to mingle with those seeking the ear of the nation's most powerful and influential. The reception would well and truly put Debra on the map.

Yet no end of excitement could wipe out the personal tragedy that was EB or the sadness, much of that brought on by ignorance that came with the disease. Like all victims, Alex had to endure a multitude of hurts. One incident that Robin came to use in many of his speeches was especially distressing. "Alex had a great perspective on putting things in order, prioritising things and some of her friends used to be quite horrible to her but she just let it go. She had been off to Great Ormond Street to have her fingers separated and it meant being away from school. The operation hadn't gone well, but as the school was on the verge of breaking up for a holiday she was determined to go back and tell everybody she hoped they would have a good time, knowing she wouldn't be seeing her friends for many weeks.

"While she was there, three of her girl schoolmates came up and each handed her a letter. Because of the bandages on her hands Alex had been unable to make the trip with her scooter and had gone along in a wheelchair. She usually had a carer, a minder with her when she was at school to help her. The carer looked over her shoulder when Alex opened the first letter. It said, 'Dear Alex, please keep away from us, you smell, you can't run round the playground, you can't eat your lunch, we don't want to be friends with you any more'. The two other letters were more or less identical, saying pretty much the same thing. Alex kept hold of the letters for a time and then stuffed them down the side of her wheelchair but said nothing. When the minder went home with Alex, she told Virginia about the notes and what was in them. Virginia never asked Alex about the notes, but that night found them still in the wheelchair and threw them away. It was so sad. What was going on in the poor child's mind when people were treating her like that? Kids were horrible to me at school, and there was nothing wrong with me, but I just can't imagine how it would have been if they were doing it and I had EB. Alex couldn't do anything about it, she couldn't run after them. She just had to take it."

Despite their parting and divorce, he and Virginia were still on good terms. 'I love and admire Virginia so much, sometimes I just don't know how she manages to carry on,' he told a close friend. Of course the answer was simple; Virginia had no alternative. Alex was totally dependent upon her mother, as was Adana Forsyth to Dianne. The mothers were on their own.

Robin on the other hand was not a man who dealt well with loneliness. He struggled to overcome the darkness that on occasions flooded into his mind by simply working flat out, driven on by his obsession. But there was no way out; the harder he worked to stave off loneliness, the less he saw of Alex, Virginia and Robin and the less he saw of them the lonelier he was.

CHAPTER TWENTY ONE

In October 1999 Alex and her father went back to London as principal guests of Cherie Blair who had kept her promise of raising awareness of EB by arranging an early evening reception. It was an exciting time for Alex because the following morning with her father and brother she would be going to France for a long promised visit to EuroDisney. The trip had the dual purpose of hopefully helping Alex recover from the recent disappointment of an operation on her hand failing to be the total success for which surgeons had hoped. With the Downing Street occasion just hours off, Robin and his children, accompanied by long time family friends, were meandering through the capital, admiring the sights when they found themselves in Knightsbridge and passing the giant Harrods store.

"On the spur of the moment I said, 'Come on, we'll call in here.' We literally went in off the street up to one of the security personnel and I asked if I could speak to Belinda White, Mohammed Al Fayed's Personal Assistant. I'd dealt with her during the previous request for help for Debra and found her extremely charming. He dialled an extension, handed me the phone and I heard her voice at the other end of the line. 'Hello

Belinda, it's Robin Hood here, I'm here with Alex', I said and she invited us into the Harrods restaurant. Belinda met us then disappeared briefly and returned, giving Alex a huge cuddly teddy bear. With her was Mohammed Al Fayed.

"He was being so polite to everybody listening to them and nodding when they spoke to him, but it was obvious he was really only interested in Alex. 'What are you doing in London Alex?' he asked and she told him we were going to a Downing Street reception that night. He said, 'Well it's no good going there, he's got no money' obviously meaning Tony Blair and laughed. Then he asked what she was doing next and she told him, 'Dad's taking me to EuroDisney tomorrow'. Immediately he pulled out an envelope and gave it to Alex. I didn't like to open it then but did so later that night after the reception and inside was one thousand pounds. Before we left Mr Al Fayed told me he was heading off to the USA for a convention of plastic surgeons in Baltimore. He said he would see whether any of them might be able to help Alex and if the prognosis was good would even pay for her treatment."

It was a kind offer, but in America, in every other country of the world, were children, some as badly affected as Alex, others worse, with EB. Plastic surgery would not help replace the devil genes that caused such mayhem and suffering.

The Hoods could tell the plight of Alex had moved the wife of the Prime Minister; her sorrow and concern showed. Others invited to the reception included representatives of the Media, Parliamentarians and members of the Sainsbury supermarket family, all important if the message about the work of Debra was to reach a wider audience. That, indeed, was what Downing Street receptions were all about; nevertheless when Robin said his farewells that evening he had with him two cheques for £1,000 made out to his charity. During the evening the guests were briefly joined by the Prime Minister who interrupted a round of discussions with aides and colleagues to meet the Hoods. The opportunity to again talk to the Premier, business people and leaders in the communications industry was an opportunity of which Robin made good use and he would come to call on the contacts he made that evening.

The next morning the two Robins gently guided Alex in her wheelchair to a train that would take them to Paris and EuroDisney. It would be a wonderful experience for the ten-year-old. To keep down the cost, and because they felt they needed to be right on hand should Alex need help, all three shared a hotel room. But it turned into one of the most horrific experiences of their lives. "The first night we were there I hadn't put enough protective bandages in Alex's pants. When she woke up the next morning her pants were stuck to her vagina. I had to soak water on to her crotch to try to ease them away from her body and the noise of her screams coming out of the bedroom was horrendous, so appalling that someone called the hotel manager who came to the bedroom door demanding to know what was going on. It was dreadful trying to explain to him that my child's underpants were stuck to her vagina and I was trying to free them without ripping off her skin. That incident ruined the holiday for me. I'd wanted to take Alex away to give her a good time and I didn't. She forgave me, but I knew the memory of that would never, ever leave me."

The incident showed just how severe could be the result of the slightest error in treating any EB victim. It had a traumatic effect on Robin. He was unable to put her screams out of his mind and years later would still recount them during fundraising talks. More immediately it made him even more determined to do whatever was needed to put an end to the misery of the condition. He threw himself into his work for Debra with even greater gusto and recalled his short conversation with Tony Blair at Downing Street.

"I had seen the President of the United States, Bill Clinton, on television accompanied by a chocolate Labrador dog and was naturally interested because I'd been breeding them as a hobby since 1984. So I brought up the subject with the Prime Minister and told him, 'Alex and I saw you at the White House with Bill Clinton and he had a chocolate Labrador'. He told me, 'Oh yes, that dog's called Buddy'. When I got back home to Scotland I wrote to President Clinton saying, 'Dear President Clinton please see the enclosed photograph of me talking with our Prime Minister Tony Blair about my daughter's condition.' I went on to explain that Alex suffered from EB and told him something about the horrors of the condition. 'Did you know there are at least 46,000 Americans, mostly children, with EB?'

"Then I wrote, 'Alex is concerned that your chocolate Labrador Buddy is on his own a lot while you are away on your Presidential duties. This gives her some concern. I happen to breed chocolate Labradors as a hobby. Would you allow Alex and me to come across to the White House? We will give you a puppy to be a companion to Buddy. This will put my daughter's mind at rest knowing your dog has a companion and this will create awareness on both sides of the Atlantic for Debra UK and Debra America, because my name is Robin Hood.'

"I sent the letter off and within two weeks received this huge envelope from the White House, photographs of Bill Clinton with his dog, his life story and so on. At the time I was working for Debra from my home and remember the postman saying, 'Oh aye you're moving up in the world now aren't we Robin?' Inside was a letter obviously written by one of Bill Clinton's assistants, saying, 'Dear Mr Hood, can't help at the moment but please get in touch in the future.' So I immediately got on to the phone to the American Embassy in London and said, 'Look, does this mean "Thanks but no Thanks?" What does it mean?' The man at the other end of the telephone said, 'Unlike you Brits, when we say something, we mean something. But in this case I should take it that that's all you are going to get because the White House receives 40,000 items of mail a day. Why don't you try and get in touch with some high profile people in your own country?' I said, 'Well I've already met the Prime Minister, I've got negotiations going on with The Queen, who do you suggest?' And he said, 'What's your name man?' and I said, 'Robin Hood'. He put the phone down."

America had reckoned without his dogged persistence. Clinton, still trying to recover lost political ground after a failed attempt the previous year to impeach him over an alleged sexual liaison with White House worker Monica Lewinsky, became a prime target for the Hood treatment. Dozens of letters were sent every week to the President and his wife Hilary asking for a meeting. Eventually, after four months, a message was left on Robin's answering machine at his Lochside

Cottage home. 'Please stop sending letters to the President,' a voice begged. Robin sat down at his kitchen table and began writing.

His relationship with a girlfriend, Samantha had developed to the extent where they contemplated marriage. It was a bizarre arrangement in that Robin first sought the views on his potential nuptials from Virginia and Alex. The fact was that he still loved Virginia. "Sam would not have known but I knew he always wanted me to go back to him," said Virginia. "Before he married Sam he said he wanted to come to see me to ask if he was happy for him to marry her. He might have been bullshitting me, because that was the sort of thing he'd do, might have just said that to me for effect. But, in any case, why should he have to stay on his own? When he asked how I felt about his marrying her I told him, 'Well, this is nothing to do with me. I'm the person who came away from you', and he went upstairs saying he was going to ask Alex if she was happy for him to re-marry. Alex said, 'Yes' and so he married Sam. But he should have married not because we said he should but because he himself wanted to marry. Robin junior and Alex couldn't stick Sam. And yet I was continually taking Sam's side. She was a nice girl, but she and Robin senior didn't get on. The children would tell me, 'They're always arguing,' but that was the nature of their relationship."

By the time the couple married in June 2000, Robin's cash situation had become so critical he knew he could not continue working without pay. His family had done their best to help, but he was heavily in debt and so he sought a meeting with his friend John Dart, his boss at Debra. Robin had performed extraordinary feats and made incredible sacrifices for Debra. To many he was Debra, and the outcome was never in doubt. He was formally appointed Debra's Scottish fundraiser and given a salary.

It was no more than he deserved, but despite his herculean efforts the task he and Debra faced remained mountainous. Occasionally there was good news. In Dundee the Schors were pressing ahead with their research into wound healing; elsewhere, even as far off as Italy, scientists were experimenting with parts of cells known as fibroblasts in their efforts to produce a dressing or an injection that would both encourage the healing process, but at the same time avoid irritating the skin. Tests carried out on chickens and mice were encouraging, but the reality was that the best that might be hoped for, at least initially, was the development of help for those EB children not so severely affected as Alex.

Seth and Ana Schor were anxious to keep the feet of everyone concerned with finding an antidote to EB firmly on the ground. 'Patients with EB suffer pain and agony every day,' the couple told the News of the World. 'They can lose their fingers through scarring and internal scarring can make it impossible for them to eat properly. Developing the discovery will take several years.' Birgit Lane was more specific. 'Our research is moving forwards really quickly at the moment, and five years ago we never dreamt we would now know so much about the disease,' she said. 'But there is still quite a long way to go and for families like Robin's, time is absolutely critical.'

These were not the words victims wanted to hear and it was hard for her father to tell Alex the truth. As she had grown older and her weight had increased, the simple act of sitting down could tear the skin from her backside. He longed to be able to tell her of a definite end to her ordeal being in sight. But there was none. Instead he was forced into a white lie. 'There'll be a cure in three years darling,' he told his daughter. But he suspected she did not believe him and that his predictions were beginning to wear thin. The fact was that Alex was wearying of the constant spotlight. She longed only to be a normal little girl. It was an impossible dream.

Once when he called to see her at Leamington Spa, she told him, 'One day, when I'm better, I'm going to relive my childhood, do all the things I've missed.' She had already tried following the example of her friends and it had left her in horrendous pain. "Alex couldn't walk far before the skin would be rubbed off her heels," said Robin. "One day the children at her school were being sponsored to run around the playground for charity. Alex felt isolated. She wasn't expected to run and so had no sponsors. But as she sat in her wheelchair she saw what all her friends were doing and only wanted to join in. So she climbed out, got to her feet and did a complete circuit. When she arrived back at her wheelchair she had no skin on her feet or heels, they had literally been rubbed red raw. I was shattered, distraught, when I found out. She was my little girl and only wanted to be like the others. But what a terrible price to pay."

He had been upset on the way back to their hotel following the Cherie Blair reception. Outside the famous door of number ten Downing Street Robin had spoken to waiting television cameras and newspaper reporters, posing for photographs with his daughter. In the relative privacy of a taxi Alex had turned to her father and asked, 'Daddy, can we be a normal father and daughter now.

Can we not talk to any more newspapers, I've had enough.'

He knew he was using her in his quest. And having shattered one marriage his obsession had remarkably not altered the way he saw married life the second time around.

Within weeks of the wedding Robin had admitted to the News of the World, 'Sam and I don't live together. She knew when we married that I wouldn't be easing back or giving up fundraising and because that means her being on her own most of the time she doesn't want to be living in isolation. So she has a home near her family close to London and I call in to see her when I can. It's not ideal, but there's no way I could give up on Alex now having come so far.'

CHAPTER TWENTY TWO

Kirsteen Gardiner looked forward to motherhood. She and her husband Sam were well known in their Ayrshire, Scotland community as always happy to offer a helping hand at local activities such as galas and fundraising events. Bright, attractive, intelligent Kirsteen listened to other mothers at her pre-natal sessions and the more she heard from them the greater was her excitement. She knew she would be a good mother and at 30 was sure the time had been right for her and Sam to begin a family. She did her exercises with enthusiasm; with family and friends began collecting the many items a baby would need and with Sam drew up a short list of names for their first child. They did not know if that was to be boy or girl. If it was a girl, she would be called Georgia, a name both liked, Sam in particular. Kirsteen had undergone all the routine tests, enjoying them as part of the experience of pregnancy, constantly questioning the need for each, and all of them indicating she could expect a healthy baby. It was a wonderful time.

She had never met or heard of Robin Hood, Debra or Epidermolysis Bullosa. Kirsteen and Sam were oblivious to the fact that some incredibly unlucky couples each carried a defective gene that might result in a child whose skin was as fragile as that of a butterfly. Nor had she heard or read about little Adana Forsyth, now just over two-and-a-half. The only minor cloud on the horizon was the fact that the baby did not arrive on the due date but that was hardly a pointer to instigate undue alarm or concern. "I was having a completely normal baby. As far as I was concerned everything was absolutely fine. There was no indication whatsoever that there was anything at all wrong," said Kirsteen. In September 2000 she and Sam went to Ayrshire Central Hospital at Irvine, North Ayrshire.

"When I was a week late it was decided to induce the birth and I went into labour. I was longing to hold my baby and it was only when she was being delivered that the nurses and midwife realised she was starting to struggle. The labour became difficult and when she was finally born it was obvious Georgia had problems because she had skin missing from her scalp and from different areas of her face and body. We didn't know she had EB. As far as Epidermolysis Bullosa was concerned we knew nothing about it, nor did the nurses. It all happened too quickly, too suddenly and to be honest it was devastating. All we knew was that something was wrong." The atmosphere in the delivery room had become strangely tense; there was a silence that hinted all was not well; whispers, sympathetic glances at the newborn, bloody red baby and then at her mother lying helpless and unsure, her moment of great joy turned to fear. In fact something was terribly wrong.

"Georgia stopped breathing and so they had to resuscitate her. So she had a terrible entry into her life. It was frightening, terrifying and nobody knew what to do. "As I lay there she was immediately taken away and so

I knew something wasn't right. I didn't know what. All sorts of things were coming into my mind, was the breathing difficulty caused by the umbilical cord somehow wrapping itself around her neck?"

Fate had struck twice at the tiny child. It would emerge that Georgia had been born not just a victim of EB but suffering from Edwards syndrome, sometimes known as Trisomy 18, a genetic disorder resulting from the presence of an extra chromosome, the microscopic vivid red particles that are part of the structure of a cell and help pass on hereditary characteristics. Normally these form a pattern from which the baby is formed in the womb. But the appearance of an extra chromosome causes confusion as the embryo develops into a baby and can lead to appalling abnormalities and defects. Most foetuses die before birth. Those babies that are born with the syndrome are given little hope for survival because of the severity of the problems they innocently bring with them into the world. In the case of Georgia Gardiner that problem was a severe breathing difficulty.

"She was taken off straight away and so I knew there was something wrong. I was desperate to know what was happening. I could tell she wasn't breathing and so many things go through your mind. But everyone was concentrating so hard on the baby that there wasn't time to tell me what was going on. It was dreadful. Then the staff said they would let me nurse her for a few minutes and when they added, 'Then we have to take her away to special care', I feared the worst.

"I could see blood and other marks on her, but I was full of drugs and other medication I'd been given for the birth, so it was very difficult to understand what was taking place around me. It became even worse when, just after they took Georgia off to be weighed – she was five pounds and thirteen ounces – and then to the special care unit, they returned with a Polaroid photograph of my baby. Then I knew it was really serious because I remembered a friend who had previously had a stillbirth and they'd given her a Polaroid of her baby.

"As soon as they handed it to me I told myself, 'My baby is going to die and all I'll end up with is a photograph'. Then they came and said, 'If you want to go down to special care and see her, you can.' They took me to the special care unit in a wheelchair because I couldn't walk. I'd had an epidural and was still feeling the effects. But by the time I arrived to see her in the incubator they had lots of plugs and monitors on her.

"She was a mess because when they'd tried to clean her up they hadn't known that as well as Edwards syndrome she had EB and so her face had come out in blisters with skin missing. In the special care unit, the staff told me they'd kept her alive so I could see her and have some time with her. They said, 'You have a choice. Your baby is going to die really. You can watch her die in the incubator or take her out and unplug it all and just nurse her until the end.' I said, 'Just give her to me' and so Georgia was lifted from the incubator while everything was switched off. They wheeled me into a family room so I could sit and hold her until she died.

"Every so often she turned blue and I'd blow on her and she'd come back to me. The midwife told me, 'The first time she has breathed properly on her own was when you held her' and as you can imagine that was a huge thing for me. I'd really given life to my baby. 'Just stay with her, nurse her until she goes', they said and I did. I think the nurses telephoned my parents, even though it was four o'clock in the morning and said, 'Come up, the baby is here but she's sick.' And so my mum and dad came to join Sam and me and so we sat with Georgia. We were still sitting there two or three hours later when it had got to seven or eight in the morning and I said to the nurse, 'Shouldn't we feed her? She's still here.' So, that's what we did. They said, 'Okay. She's obviously not going in a hurry but she's still very sick'. And so we fed her.

"When Sam and me had been told the baby was only going to last a few hours I said, 'We have to name her. I'm not having my baby die without a name'. We liked Georgia and told each other, 'Somehow the name suits her. Let's just name here' and the chaplain came into the hospital and baptized her. It was something I felt had to be done. I'm not a religious person, but it seemed important to do that.

"Up to that point I hadn't known what was wrong with Georgia and it was then that one of the midwives came in to see me and said she had seen Edward's Syndrome before at Ayrshire Central Hospital and recognised that Georgia had features that were similar. But she also said, 'There's something else wrong and it's with her skin. About ten years ago I was present when a mother gave birth to twins and they had this similar problem to Georgia. I think they were diagnosed as having a disease called EB. It affected their skin and what's wrong with Georgia's skin looks to be the same. I think they went off with their parents to live abroad. We had no more contact with them after that and nobody since has been aware of an EB baby born here because it is so rare. Some maternity hospitals never come across a case of EB.

"The midwife went off to look up hospital records, found the birth of the twins, read the notes and read a reference to an organisation called Debra. She said, 'We need to get it confirmed first that it is EB'. And so tests were done and it was. It was sheer luck that the same midwife had been on duty then and when Georgia was born and had been struck by how familiar her skin was to that of those twins." In reality Kirsteen and Sam had been incredibly unlucky. Not only had they fallen to the dreadful odds of producing an EB child, but Edwards syndrome strikes just once in every 6,000 pregnancies.

Hospital authorities contacted Debra and were put in touch with EB specialist nurse Jackie Denyar at Great Ormond Street who was quick to point out that EB was more than a mere skin disorder, telling nursing staff, 'It affects every cell in the body.' She passed on expert advice on how to deal with the blisters on the face and body of tiny Georgia, the need to burst them before they worsened the damage to her skin, how to handle her correctly and how and when to bandage her. She promised to get to Georgia as soon as possible.

"Jackie sent leaflets and pamphlets trying to explain to the hospital what they could do in the meantime until she got there," said Kirsteen. "We remained in hospital for the best part of a week with Georgia. We had to stay there because they needed to get all the information they could about the condition. Then I had to learn how to pass tubes down into her stomach to feed her. There were lots and lots of different things that they needed me to be comfortable with by the time we took her out of hospital. But really of course, when we did take her home after a week, we were taking her home to die. The staff said, 'Get out of the hospital. Go home. Go to your own surroundings and have her there with you for a few days.' And that's what we did."

A nursing team arrived from Ayrshire Central having been given intensive guidance from Jackie Denyar and other nurses at Great Ormond Street Hospital to see what help they could give Kirsteen who, even though she knew her time with Georgia was limited, was thrilled to have her baby at home with her. It was confirmed, after tests, that the child had the most severe form of the disease, junctional EB. Her love for her baby was infectious. If visitors to the home of the Gardiners feared they were intruding on a gloom shrouded tragedy, they were instantly aware of the enormous pride Kirsteen took in her daughter. She cared for the baby knowing that care would be limited by time but determined to ensure every hour that Georgia survived was an hour filled with love and joy.

She was so absorbed in looking after the infant that she had no time for, or inclination, to be sorry for herself over the appalling treatment luck had dished out to her and her husband. Instead she was grateful for the support and kindness that filled the lives of the family. Her GP was caught up by the swirl of goodwill. "He was simply great. He had never seen EB before and was trying to root out as much information as possible for us because we wondered what had caused this, was it genetic, was it my fault, how did it happen? There was so much I wanted to know."

Georgia died the following month. Her few weeks of life left a lasting impression on all who saw her. Her courage and that of Kirsteen shone through the sorrow of her loss. "When Georgia died I had a visit from the village minister and I remember her saying to me, 'Are you angry? Do you want to say anything? Is there anything you want to say to me? A lot of people get angry with God, especially when someone dies, and most especially when a child dies'. I could understand that, but I wasn't angry with anybody really. Maybe that's just my nature. At the time I felt it was quite a strange thing for her to have asked me, but then I thought, 'Maybe a lot of people do feel that way'. She said some people vented their grief and anger at the church and some found religion because of a death. On occasions the circumstances were such that people thought they needed more faith in order to try to understand what had happened. I'm a bit of a common sense person and told myself, 'Well, it wasn't God's fault, it's genetics. At the end of the day it's down to genetics, I understand that'. Had it been a condition for which there was no explanation then maybe I would have felt differently."

Just over a week after Kirsteen and Sam said goodbye to their daughter, Jackie Denyar arrived from London. They were grateful to her for making such an effort, knowing the enormous demands on her time and for her expertise. "Georgia was dead but Jackie still went to a lot of trouble to come to us. She felt it was important to explain to us what EB was, and we needed to know why our daughter had died. She was so sorry not to have come earlier, but there would not have been anything she could do to save our baby. Jackie gave us leaflets and pamphlets describing EB and the various forms of the condition and sat with us for a very long time talking about the disease and Georgia. She told us about Debra and discussed what the options were for us for the future, for having other children." When Jackie left, Kirsteen and Sam knew what the chances had been for them of having an EB child. One in four. They'd had their one.

The following Spring Kirsteen was told of a conference being held in Glasgow by Debra. "I went up with my mum to see what it was all about, especially to discover whether we could get more information about EB, knowing Sam and me were both carriers of the defective gene. As we sat in the audience listening to the speakers, Robin approached. He'd obviously spotted that we were new faces and introduced himself, at the same time asking what our connection was to Debra and wondering why we were at the conference.

"I told him about Georgia. How she had been our first baby and how she had died and had been diagnosed as having EB. He asked, 'What type of EB did your daughter have?' and when I told him she suffered from the junctional form he asked how old she had been when she died. 'Four weeks', I said and he looked at me and said simply, 'You're perhaps one of the lucky ones.'

"For an instant I sat there speechless, open mouthed, aghast. Up until a moment earlier he had been a total stranger, someone I'd never met or seen. I thought, 'How dare you say that to me'. Then he began explaining about Alex and what he had been through, how she was then coming up to being a young teenager. But what was important was his telling us more about the disease, about some of the children who suffered from the different forms, about the other strains, dystrophic and simplex and the lives the victims had. It was then that I understood where he was coming from.

"Yes I had lost my daughter and I was grieving, however at least I didn't need to watch her suffering for years and years and years for the inevitable to happen.

''You're perhaps one of the lucky ones' was how he had put it, but I soon realised that was the way Robin was. Straight to the point. And as I came to know him, the more I knew exactly what he meant. I didn't feel particularly lucky, but after that and since then, when I see and hear of other families whose babies die within a few hours or days, then I realise that at least I got to know my daughter, albeit only for a few weeks."

Kirsteen drew from that short time with Georgia every scrap of happy memory she could extract. Friends told her, 'It can't happen again. Nobody is so unlucky'. In fact her nightmare was far from over.

CHAPTER TWENTY THREE

Robin could do nothing to prevent the death of little Georgia Gardiner. Until a cure was found many, many more children would die, their short lives a miserable ordeal of pain. He feared that among them would be his own daughter. He did not have the skills of the scientists working tirelessly for the EB youngsters and their families; his talent lay in providing the researchers with the resources to continue their work. Publicity was the tool with which he turned the wheels of income. He felt no shame or embarrassment at using the plight of Alex, Adana, any other children who could raise Debra's awareness. His persistence had led him into the home of the Prime Minister. Now the President of the United States was about to capitulate.

In October 2000 Bill Clinton, finally worn down by the constant barrage of letters that had induced his staff to beg him to intervene, wrote to Alex. His letter, headed simply 'The White House, Washington' and signed 'Bill Clinton' read:

'Dear Alexandra,

Thank you for your offer of a chocolate Labrador puppy just like Buddy. I have asked Ambassador Lader to accept the puppy on my behalf. I am sending to the ambassador to give to you my favourite picture of Buddy, which was taken here at the White House.

'Your generosity confirms your father's description of you as someone who has great affection for animals and tells me that you are a very caring person. I hope that this special gift will help you with the challenges you face, and raise awareness and understanding of Epidermolysis Bullosa.

'Please know that your thoughtfulness means a great deal to me, the First Lady, Chelsea, and Buddy, too. '

The puppy that Alex was giving to the Clintons was 16-months-old Dash, one of eight chocolate Labradors with the family. The fact that the most powerful man in the world had corresponded with a sick girl 3,000 miles away was a huge publicity coup for Robin. He knew it and made sure the world's media knew it too. Television cameras and newspaper photographers were there when Alex and her father travelled to London and formally handed over Dash to Philip Lader, United States Ambassador to the Court of St James's who told the News of the World, 'This is a wonderful gesture from a little girl who put her own agony behind her to bring happiness to others.'

Bringing happiness was what Robin's frantic money raising campaign was all about. The happiness of parents being told their children would be finally spared the misery of EB. Literally hundreds of charities scrambled to persuade the public to part with their pounds and pennies. Robin had always known that the visual impact of children with torn faces and webbed hands was more likely to attract donations and for that reason encouraged the mothers and fathers of EB children to publicise their plight. Dianne Forsyth had agreed with his reasoning. So did many others. Often going public and telling the world just what EB was, that it wasn't infectious, wouldn't spread like an epidemic through a school or a community, brought about a greater understanding and sympathy. Neighbours who might have politely shied away from a pram or push chair holding a tiny victim or approached reluctantly, became more willing to offer involvement and help. The devoted parents of a six-year-old schoolgirl in the north of England saw the good sense in trying to spread the message and told ten million readers of the News of the World what caring for a youngster born with the same strain of EB as Alex meant.

The child's mother told the newspaper, 'Opening her Christmas presents brought tears of pain to her eyes. We barely wrapped them for her so she could get to her toys easily. But even pulling off the bit of paper that was on them hurt her. It is as if she has 100 per cent burns all over her. But she is so strong. The pain she endures every minute would destroy most people. If she falls over she cries and needs a cuddle but I have to be very careful not to make matters worse.' And her father said, 'She just gets on and copes with life but it is a heart rending illness. When she was a baby she fell off the settee and my natural reaction was to grab her hand but it literally stripped the skin from her fingers.' That incident reminded Robin of the day Virginia was left holding a glove of Alex's skin.

"I knew exactly what this family was going through," said Robin. "The pattern was nearly always the same. Parents having no inkling that when their child was born something would be wrong; the first shock at the point of birth when skin peeled away; hospital staff initially baffled by the cause; parents afraid; eventually Debra coming in and explaining how their lives would change; frequent hospital visits; operations. And throughout, the constant and piteous cries of the child and the prayers of everyone for a cure to be discovered to end the misery. I didn't want this to be how Alex, or any child, would spend the rest of their lives and if manipulating individuals, including my daughter, and the Media to bring about progress then I was prepared to do that."

Occasionally there were lighter moments as he kept up his hectic schedule of meetings and speeches interspersed with occasional visits to see his daughter and his new wife. "One day I picked up the telephone at Lochside Cottage and a voice said, 'This is Cherie Blair.' I replied, 'This is a wind up isn't it?' because I was convinced it was one of my pals and started running through loads of names but each time the caller just said, 'No'. Then the penny finally dropped and I recognised her voice from the meetings at Downing Street. I felt terrible, embarrassed but thankfully Cherie saw the funny side and started giggling. She had called to talk about another reception for us. She was a tremendous supporter."

Even more hilarious was a bizarre incident during a fundraising trip across the Jordanian Desert, although the omens at the start of the adventure were far from promising. On September 11, 2001 terrorists belonging to the Islamist militant group al-Qaeda hijacked four civilian passenger jets. Two were flown into the North and South Towers of the World Trade Centre complex in New York; a third into the Pentagon at Arlington, Virginia while passengers on the fourth gallantly struggled with the hijackers forcing it to crash land in a field near Shanksville, Pennsylvania. Altogether almost 3,000 lives were lost, including those of 343 firefighters and paramedics. The outrage, which became known by the month and day as 9/11, led to worldwide condemnation of al-Qaeda and the invasion of Afghanistan where numerous militant training camps and bases were thought to be.

"One of the American banks, which had a major base in London, had promised Debra £100,000. But following 9/11 the bank wrote to one of my colleagues and said, 'We're sure you'll understand that we have now decided to give this money to the New York Police and Fire Widows' and Children's Benefit Fund so that dependents of those who were killed in the line of duty can benefit. It meant we were £100,000 down."

Things threatened to get even worse. A group of 20 volunteers had offered to spend six days trekking 80 miles across dangerous desert and through mountainous terrain, sometimes climbing to 2,000 feet, starting at the south east corner of the Dead Sea and through the Jordanian Desert south to Petra, the famous tourist attraction famous for its rock cut architecture. It could be a hazardous journey and needed an expert guide to lead the party, each of who had encouraged friends, family and workmates to sponsor them, the proceeds going to Debra.

"The guy who was going to be the guide was worried over the increasing unrest in the Middle East following the 9/11 attacks and the threatening response of the United States and Britain in particular. He thought it over and with the trip just a couple of weeks away said, 'Sorry, but I'm not going. I'm too concerned about the state of things where you'll be'. That meant the whole expedition having to be called off and with the volunteers having done brilliantly already raised £80,000 in sponsorship Debra would lose that too.

"John Dart knew I was a guy who loved the outdoors life, knew I was still in the Territorial Army, knew I had been attached to the regular Army, had map reading and outdoor skills and was confident when it came to leadership. He called me up, explained the situation and said, 'Robin, you'll lead the party across the desert!' And so off we went, just a couple of months after 9/11 with the world still reeling from the enormity of it and with the Middle East being a no-go area for many. It was a real challenge for me. But I thrive on challenges. I knew I'd need all my wits about me, but I reckoned the trip could both let me recharge my batteries and maybe allow me to think up more money raising ideas.

"We had such good fun on that adventure. Each evening we'd sleep in a big Bedouin tent where the group would tell stories and share a few laughs. One of the girls in the party was the wife of a very well known television personality. I won't say who she was for fear of embarrassing her but will call her 'Mary', which isn't her real name. She was a wonderful member of the group, who did a fantastic job on behalf of Debra. She was also very attractive and unlike a lot of people continually in the public eye, got on really well with everybody.

"Most of the party had done some training in preparation for the trek, but you can't really prepare yourself in Britain to walk across a desert and in mountains in blazing heat. During the day everyone walked as best as he and she could. I was forever telling them how to look after their feet and to change their socks regularly so they didn't get blisters, the dos and don'ts. I'd be walking up and down, encouraging them, giving them moral support and making sure they were motivated, but by the end of the evening I just wanted a break to do my own thing.

"A Jordanian back-up team accompanied us, putting up the tent at the end of each day, cooking our meals for us and also providing alcohol although anybody wanting alcohol had to buy it. One night I was sitting with the back-up team around their camp fire and they were smoking a shisha pipe. We know this as a hubbly bubbly pipe or a hookah. They've been used by desert tribes in particular for thousands of years. They guys in the team asked if I wanted to smoke it but I'd never try anything like that because I didn't know what they were smoking. 'Go on, it's not a drug just flavoured tobacco', they said but I politely turned them down.

"I was talking to the eldest team member. He was aged about forty and whenever we looked at someone he'd say, 'There's my brother' and then at another, 'There's my brother' and yet another, 'There's my youngest brother'. The youngest brother was about ten. I said, 'Hang on a minute, are you all brothers? There's a big age gap here.' He said, 'Well under Jordanian law, a Jordanian man is allowed four wives. I'm from Mother One, that brother there is from Mother Two and the youngest is from Mother Three. Dad hasn't got a Mother Four yet but we all count each other as brothers. The fact we have different mothers that doesn't mean anything to us. We have the same father and we are brothers'. I was bemused but told him, 'That's fine.'

"Then just as if by magic the old man appeared from out of the blue. It was like something out of Lawrence of Arabia, He had a wizened old face, features that meant he must have been sixty plus but he just sat down cross legged. He was a very agile guy. I said to the lads, 'How does he manage to get out of the house when he's got three wives at home?' and they went through the motions as if to indicate that he'd given them all a good seeing to in the bedroom. They translated this to the old man and we all sat down laughing, and then all of a sudden I noticed over my left hand shoulder 'Mary' passing. She'd had a couple of glasses of wine, it might even have been more, and was staggering across to the loo these guys had erected for the ladies. As she was heading back to the others in the tent I called her over.

"Now while it was very hot during the day, the evenings could get pretty cold and she had on a great big thick woollen cardigan. She said, 'I wondered where you'd been all night. What have you been up to?' So I said, 'These men are all brothers, this man here is the father. He's allowed four wives but he's only got three and they all count themselves as brothers.' She said, 'Why hasn't he got four wives?' and I told her, 'I don't know.' And then she said to the eldest, 'Ask your dad if he wants me to be his fourth wife. How many camels am I worth?' The eldest brother whispered in the ear of his father who cackled and said something back. His son said, 'One.' And she said, 'What? One camel?' and then she took her cardigan off and with the cold night air in the desert in Jordan her nipples just went, 'Ping' through her tee shirt and the old man's eyes opened and he said, 'All right, four.' We all laughed and that was the end of it.

"The next morning 'Mary' woke up with a really shocking headache and asked, 'What did I do with that drink last night?' So getting her through the walk that day was really hard work. At the end of it, the brothers had set up the tent at next staging post and as we sat around there was the old guy coming across the desert towing four camels behind him. I said to 'Mary', 'You're in big trouble now.' She said, 'Tell him I was only joking. I'm married.' That night the old man was dancing around the camp fire like some dervish, trying his best to impress 'Mary' but in the end went sadly off to his three wives pulling his four camels. At least Debra scored. At the end of the trek we were £80,000 nearer a cure."

Robin had needed that trip. It had been a difficult year for him. Charity workers are not well paid. Robin was, in effect, a super salesman, selling the pain of EB to a public snowed under with appeals for money. Like so many of his colleagues in the charity industry, he could have boosted his income considerably by offering his undoubted talents to private enterprise. The vast majority of those like him carried on because of the satisfaction of knowing what they did was needed and worthwhile and compensated for low pay. In Robin's case he worked for Debra because he believed he simply had to. And what greater encouragement could there be than to have the target of saving the life of the daughter he loved?

Now his savings gone, he knew he would never be able to rebuild them. Although he now had a salary from the charity, there were still numerous financial commitments. When the chance to earn extra cash came along he felt obliged to take it although he would never enjoy the circumstances. In February that year foot and mouth disease was discovered on pigs in an abattoir in Essex. It was eventually traced back to a farm in Northumberland. The disease spread alarmingly and as the days turned into weeks and then months became an epidemic. Government scientists ruled there was no alternative but to destroy sheep and cattle within and around affected areas. By October, when the last outbreak was confirmed, 10,000,000 animals had been slaughtered at a cost of £8billion.

With so many to cull there were calls for those skilled in shooting wild life to offer their services. Robin's long experience in stalking and shooting dear made him an ideal candidate when he put his name forward. It was gruesome work, slaughtering innocent beasts, then dumping their bodies into huge pits where they were burned and the remains buried. But it had to be done and at least allowed him to earn some desperately needed funds.

CHAPTER TWENTY FOUR

As Alex grew older, her problems increased. When the time came for her to begin wearing a brassiere, the friction of the straps against her shoulders caused the skin to rub off. That left Virginia with the difficulty of trying to bandage her daughter's shoulders, a difficult task even for an experienced nurse. The burden on Virginia was immense and yet she somehow coped remarkably, caring for Alex, arranging appointments with doctors, encouraging her at school where she was one of the brightest pupils and frequently travelling to London for hospital appointments and stays. In between she encouraged Alex to have a busy social life.

"She needed supplements for iron, vitamins, calcium and zinc because her osteoporosis became more severe. She would need regular visits to hospital for a drug to help strengthen the bones and it was fed directly into her veins, by intravenous therapy. She needed three doses a day over a three day period and the dosage would last for three months then as the effects weakened she needed to repeat the process," said Virginia

"The normal person in the street has no idea what's going on inside their body, they only discover that if there's a need for a scan. When it came to Alex the doctors had to continually find out how her organs were reacting and so she was constantly having all sorts of tests, especially blood tests so they could pick up on problems that needed attention. Zinc helps with our skin healing processes and so she had to be monitored in case of a lowering in her zinc level. She had so many more supplements given to her and yet she never had an issue with that, never complained.

"Occasionally she would get upset, but that didn't happen often and when it did, it would be from the pain of the dressings when she would be screaming out. Among the drugs she needed to take was Midazolam which is normally given to patients to sedate them and bring on amnesia before hospital operations. Before bandaging Alex could have a mild dose of that so that she wouldn't remember how bad the pain was. At the beginning of her taking Midazolam it left her a little dozy but as she grew older and her body became more used to it, it was less effective. She needed that and morphine before having her bath and her bandaging."

Robin never doubted that he had made the right decision to work flat out for Debra. Occasionally he needed to gee himself up. For a reason he could never work out, he had felt oddly deflated following the success of his battle to have mains electricity installed at Lochside. Yet it was what many others regarded as failure, or news of it, that often motivated him to even greater effort. He was in regular touch with scientists asking about progress so he could pass on news to potential donors. "I'd gone to visit Professor Irwin McLean and he told me, 'Look Robin, we're firing blanks into the dark, we don't really know where we are going at the moment.'

"There would have been no point in my going to the Media for instance and saying, 'My daughter has the most horrific condition in the world and there's no hope, she's going to die'. In that case people would not give money. So I needed to put some spin on what the experts said by giving out the message that there really was hope. That's why I would tell Alex, 'There'll be a cure in two years' or 'Four years Alex, hang on'. I could see her condition slowly worsening though. There came a stage where she was even unable to wear one of her favourite sweaters, because the weight of it caused friction against her skin which simply slid off leaving great red areas of bare flesh. Injuries like that made me all the more determined to get out there and fight for money."

Every now and again a glimmer of hope would appear. Phyllis Hilton had started it all off by setting up Debra. As word of what she had done slowly spread, other Debras, each independent of one another, began springing up. Mostly they were run quietly, almost apologetically, asking the public to give them cash. Robin had brought with him a dynamic, aggressive, "in-your-face" attitude, challenging everyone to see for themselves what having EB meant to victims and those around them. His technique was direct, not always welcomed or appreciated, but it got results and gradually his methods began to be copied. Soon after he began his work, parents of victims in Ireland formed Debra (Ireland) and gradually as word of the success of Debra UK was spread, other branches, each independent of one another, started to spring up. It was from them that the Media began picking up tales of incredible courage in the face of terrible suffering.

Typical was the story of Australian Robyn Perham who had been born on a pineapple farm in a remote area of north Queensland in 1952 with EB. Robyn, who has successfully campaigned to raise the profile of the condition, kindly sent a full account of her own story. This is a much condensed version of how she has dealt with the condition which also affects her daughter Julia and grandson Zach.

"Even as a very small child I was aware that there must be something different about me as people would whisper to Mum about me, in front of me, as if I was unaware of what they were saying. It made me uncomfortable, even then. I was the youngest within a very large, extended family. I was born with my skin coming off all over the place and no one knew what it was. Nor did they know what to do about it, so the doctor told Mum that she was the only one to touch me. I was five before the doctors took a large chunk out of my knee, without anaesthetic, and sent it off to England for diagnosis, and the eventual diagnosis was epidermolysis bullosa. It meant very little as there was no treatment and no cure, so it had been a painful exercise for little gain and nothing much was understood about it all anyway.

"At the age of six, I clearly remember trying to fathom out why the kids at school would happily play with me on a one-on-one basis when we were away from the school, but the same kids would shun me at school when we were all there together. 'Don't step on the cracks' someone would shout as I came to join in, 'Cos if she steps on the cracks her germs will be in there and YOU"LL get it! You'll have sores like she does'; teachers did little to stop this kind of bullying.

"What with living in close proximity to animals and farm life, in the heat, mosquitoes and the biting flies of the tropics, without ready access to antibiotics, I was often a mess of infected sores. In those days, doctors weren't sought out unless death was imminent. We handled things ourselves, with salted water bathing and dressings made from old torn up bed sheets. Wounds would stick to dressings and be pulled free. Sometimes the dressings were massive and that was embarrassing in itself, but sometimes after wounding I hadn't yet reached an adult who could dress my wounds, so I just went about with big, bleeding, or yellow-puss-filled wounds on display, with flies in attendance, the smell involved with rotting flesh and tried not to show that I was suffering pain.

"EB was not known and certainly not understood in our circles up until I did the 'awareness raising' myself as an adult. My 'condition' was considered to have been about anything and everything other than what it actually was.

As a result, everyone would come to us with the latest cure they'd read or heard about and they now swore by. At one stage I spent a lot of time eating molasses and sulphur, and mercifully, what hadn't cured me didn't kill me.

Another example was our flirtation with Colour Therapy. For eight months I 'underwent colour therapy' after a Dr Pro maintained that germs could not stand the sight of their own colour. Ones' arm or ankle was fitted with a circular, stretchy type of bicycle clip. Attached to this clip were several different coloured wires that disappeared into the end of an old sewing machine drawer. Inside this heavy drawer were several six volt batteries. Across the top of these, over a metal plate of some kind, the 'nurses' laid different skeins of coloured embroidery cotton. What colour they were to be was 'divined' by Dr Pro. The idea then was that these particular colours were transmitted throughout my body via a low voltage electrical impulse and these impulses carried the colours of the cottons with them. My parents, in their desperation for a cure for me, believed it and we all persisted by trial and error.

"The 'germs' would apparently eventually see enough of a concentration of these colours in my body and would run for the hills. Well, my skin was showing some signs of improvement every so often, but that was because I was lying in a bed with this ridiculous thing attached to me for hours each and every day instead of being outside playing like any normal kid would be doing.

"At a school sports day some of the parents saw my scars and had apparently asked Sister why I was allowed in the pool, transferring germs that their little girl could, quite possibly, catch. I was ordered out of the pool from that point onwards. The result was that I was more or less expected to just 'sit over there and play the disabled one', which has always made me so angry. I refused to wear the label of 'disabled' in any way, shape or form, and have striven to lead a life in which I have denied being 'disabled'.

"When my daughter Julia was born, after eighteen hours of second stage labour, three weeks overdue, 24 inches long, weighing ten and a half pounds, she was totally gorgeous. At three days old she looked as if she was three months old and had skin like a porcelain doll. My heart was bursting with love. Then Mum dissolved into tears. 'She has your skin.' She said.

"By founding the first Debra-Australia in the 1980's, I not only managed to draw people's attention to the issues and educate them on what was needed, we also managed to begin medical research into EB for the first time in Australia in real terms. People readily knew our condition as 'cotton wool baby syndrome.' A few weeks into it all, I was contacted by Phyllis Hilton who sent photos of her daughter, Debra whose EB was shocking in the extreme. She was raw. I'd had no idea someone could live like that. New Zealand and Hong Kong were also trying to get going and I'd try to give them my best advice on what to do next, but I wasn't in their country.

"At 20 years of age Julia also found herself pregnant and she vehemently stated that she was having this baby, regardless of the risks. Zach was the outcome and his EB is, again, slightly worse than Julia's. But we wouldn't be without him. He is a wonderful young man, funny and articulate, with a hard-won wisdom far beyond his years. He's tall and handsome and, like the rest of us, he's had more than his fair share of life's challenges to deal with."

A Debra had been set up in the United States in 1980 by Arlene Pessar whose son Eric was born with EB. Eric worked hard with his mother to establish and publicise the charity to an American public unaware of the scale of the disease. He gave evidence to the US Congress on a series of occasions pleading for government help for research into the causes of his condition and eventually five centres were set up across the country to treat victims. Eric studied automotive engineering for a year at Brooklyn Polytechnic Institute and attended the College of Staten Island. He became a familiar sight on campus moving between classes in his wheelchair and electric scooter but died in 1994 aged 24 from kidney and liver failure, both consequences of EB. 'Eric had been wrapped in bandages since he was one month old,' said Arlene. 'He never, ever complained.'

New Zealanders too had their own Debra, set up by the parents of child victims in 1980. Now, through it, they were learning about the plight of Holly Gilshnan. 'If there is a league table of worst diseases a child could be born with, dystrophic epidermolysis bullosa would have to be pretty much the tops,' said one journalist who met the schoolgirl. 'The wounds are like those of burns victims. For your whole life. There is no cure. Holly cannot even eat crisps. Or any normal food, really. The lining of her mouth and throat are just as fragile. Scarring leads the lining to fuse, as it has with her fingers. Every six months, she has to have surgery so her throat does not completely close over. Head to toe, Holly is encased in bandages. A strapping under her chin has come slightly unstuck at one end. The hands grasping her drink bottle are red raw, the fingers fused.'

Holly's mother Kathy, keen to raise the profile of the condition by talking about her daughter, told a newspaper, 'Holly sometimes looks at other children swimming and wishes she could join in. Open wounds prevent that, but otherwise she accepts she cannot do all the running around and rough and tumble other children enjoy. She's never known any different which is a little bit sad, but better than if it came later in life. Last summer she got good at hitting a tennis ball against the wall and she really, really enjoyed that. And she's pretty amazing with the hoola-hoop.'

In Canada, the remarkable selflessness of Linda Pasula encouraged the establishment of a Debra. Linda had been a victim and when she was old enough began raising money for research into the disease that, according to newspapers in Edmonton, Alberta 'produced sores and scabs on her body and gave her web-like hands'. In 1981 Linda, desperate for life and relief from suffering, travelled to Michelbach, West Germany to a private clinic run by Romanian biochemist Pavel Kozak. Kozak, who was not a doctor, had suffered from eczema and said that while looking for a cure had stumbled across a treatment that appeared to help those with skin diseases including EB.

He used salves made from Vaseline jelly, steroids and antibiotics combined with a diet that included celery and parsley roots, rice, lettuce, freshly slaughtered meat, chamomile tea and vitamins. Linda returned home and like others who visited the clinic seemed to have an improved skin. She knew there would be doubters but, encouraged and wanting others to benefit through helping research into skin problems being carried on in her own country, started organising bingo sessions with the proceeds going into a fund that would contribute towards the cost of work being done at the University of Alberta.

Sadly Kozak's treatment did not stave off her seemingly inevitable fate and Linda died aged 30 in 1988 of complications caused by EB. The $20,000 in her fund was given to the University. 'This is what the money was raised for,' said her mother Mary. 'At the moment there is no research going on in Canada, as far as I know, into this particular disease. She worked so hard and she would have been so happy.' Linda's money was used for research and the training of residents in dermatology. Kozak, meantime, had wanted to set up a private clinic in Canada but the authorities would not agree. However Linda's ordeal was not in vain or forgotten and ten years after she died Debra Canada was established.

Robin had always known of the reputation for generosity of the people of Ireland. Typical of their kindness was reflected in the story of Olivia Bannon from Castlebellingham, County Louth who had died at the age of 13 in 1991, having spent the majority of her short life wrapped in bandages covering the ravages of EB. While she was alive, kindly sympathizers had managed to raise a sizeable sum in a fund with the aim of sending her to a clinic in Spain offering treatment for skin diseases including EB. Olivia had visited the clinic five times but specialists had told her parents there was no point in her returning because there was nothing further they could do to help for the youngster.

Olivia though, after her cruel death, would not be forgotten. When she died there was still almost £80,000 left in the fund which was given to the specialist clinic at Our Lady's Hospital for Sick Children, Crumlin, under Dr Rosemarie Watson, consultant dermatologist, assisted by specialists from Great Ormond Street Hospital, London. At a court hearing to formally distribute the money, representatives from Debra (Ireland) admitted that despite very extensive worldwide research, no cure or effective treatment had been found for 'this terrible disease'.

Robin knew that each and every article could bring about assistance in the guise of cash, cash that would buy the researchers and Alex time. Even in death, there was hope because the death of a child from the horrors of EB had the ability to reduce readers or television viewers to tears, tears that could often reform as cheques or banknotes. One such tragedy was the demise of Jonny Kennedy, born in the market town of Alnwick, Northumberland in 1966 and who died in September 2003 at the age of 36 sitting in his wheelchair in a train taking him home from a meeting with Cherie Blair in Downing Street. Jonny was often forthright to the point of being rude and it was sometimes difficult for those on the receiving end of his terseness to remember he was in continual agony. On that fatal day when Cherie had asked, 'Have you been here before?' he had replied, 'No, and I don't want to come again'. He had his wish.

Robin knew Jonny and his mother Edna, a typical Northumbrian housewife who showed extraordinary patience when dealing with her sometimes waspish son. Typically too, of EB families, had been Jonny's father Frank who was embarrassed by his son's condition and did his best to shield him from the wider public. Before he died a television team had been making a documentary about Jonny in which he spoke candidly about his inevitable passing and even set about fulfilling a series of long held ambitions, a form of Bucket List set down long before the highly emotional film of that name starring Jack Nicholson and Morgan Freeman. Robin realised the potential of screening a programme about EB and a severely ill EB victim on prime time television where many millions of viewers might watch it. The many arguments he had made in favour of publicising the disease and its victims would be vindicated when Jonny's story, 'The Boy Whose Skin Fell Off' was shown in 2004.

And so it was that when Robin was approached by the BBC and asked whether he would be willing to be the subject of a documentary about his own life and that of Alex he was happy to make himself available. It meant many hours of interviews, of travelling to be with Virginia and Alex and of meeting, talking with the distinguished scientists striving to find a cure and all the while journeying the length and breadth of Britain to talk, plead and at times cajole in the never ending quest for funds. But he enjoyed the spotlight knowing how the profile of his work would be raised. Despite the seriousness of the subject, one incident brought a smile to the faces of the BBC crew following him although not to his own.

"When they first started filming, with the excitement and the thought that I was going to get on TV and was going to get recognition and create publicity, I was just overwhelmed. The producer told me, 'Right Robin, it's quite a demanding task. It's a 30-minute programme but we are going to be filming most days and we'll need many hours of footage from which we edit down to the final version'. So I was prepared for it all to be fairly exhausting. It all meant a lot of travelling, but I had to wear the same clothes every day for the continuity in the film.

"Now I can't wear yesterday's shirt unless it's been washed so wherever I was, I was washing everything out that evening, drying it on radiators and ironing it the next morning to be ready for filming. I thought we were all done and dusted one Thursday night and motored home to Lochside Cottage. I was shattered. I'd been driving all around the country filming as well as trying to keep up my fundraising job. But I'd hardly walked in through the door when the telephone rang and the producer said, 'Robin we've been going through all the footage now. We need to come back and ask you three more key questions to make it work. We'll be there in the morning.' I said, 'Well don't make it too early because I'm shattered.' I put my shirt in the washing machine, overslept and the next thing I knew was there was banging at the door and the whole crew was waiting to come in. I dragged my shirt, still damp, out of the washing machine and was standing there in my boxer shorts ironing it, getting ready to be filmed answering the final three questions when the interviewer Kirsty Wark arrived. She said, 'You don't look very happy this morning Robin' and I said, 'I'm not. I bet Tom Cruise doesn't have to iron his own shirt'.

"It wasn't the only time filming of that documentary left me unhappy. On the first day we did about nine hours of interviewing. It was obvious Kirsty Wark had been told to make me upset, to see how I'd react and so she gave me a pretty hard time. When I eventually cracked she said, 'I wondered how long it would be before you broke' and I thought, 'Well, if making a grown man cry on television is going to work for you then just show it. If it's going to help the profile of Debra, so what?' But my tears were never screened."

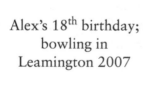
Prince Charles with Robin Hood

Robin talking to Prince Charles in Scotland in 2004

Alex's 18th birthday;
bowling in
Leamington 2007

Alex taking delivery of her car in July 2007

This is the last photo I took of my two
children together

This is the last photograph of Virginia, Robin, and their two children taken on Robin's birthday in 2008

This is the last photograph ever taken of Robin and his daughter the week before she died

CHAPTER TWENTY FIVE

The short, precious month that had been the lifespan of Georgia Gardiner had taught Kirsteen the true hideousness of EB. She remained in contact with Robin, attending Debra conferences where she discovered "a great network of people within that fantastic organisation." But the one dilemma that now posed such a quandary for her and Sam was whether to risk trying for another child.

"Did we ever tell ourselves, 'We're not going to have any more children in case it happens again?' Yes, we went back and forward through that all the time basically asking ourselves for ages, 'Should we? If we don't have any more children then what will we do?' It was so difficult, but the odds given to us were that statistically one in four children was affected. So we could have had three healthy children, stopped our family at that point and never known about EB or that we were both carriers because you only discovered that once you had a child with the condition. In the end we thought, 'Well the odds must be right, they have to be in our favour because if it's one in four then we've had our one and surely it won't happen again'. So we decided to try again. That was all we could do and if I fell pregnant then we knew, through

Robin, that Debra would arrange for me to undergo tests in London that would tell us whether the baby was EB."

In the summer of 2002 Kirsteen discovered she was pregnant. Specialists carried out a biopsy taking five miniscule skin samples from the growing embryo and then she and Sam waited to hear the outcome, whether or not there was evidence of EB. "Sadly there was," said Kirsteen. "Lightening striking twice I suppose. We thought, 'How could this happen again if it was only one in four?' We really thought our chances of having a healthy baby were quite good but, no, they weren't. I was continually in touch with Robin and Sam and I had been doing our bit for Debra, such as running a fundraising stall selling cakes and so on at our village gala. I suppose I was selling scones while he was knocking at the door of the Prime Minister. Robin was such a brilliant example of what could be done, that I'd wondered how I could do my wee bit to help.

"We knew through the tests that my baby was going to be a girl. The plan was for me to stay on in London for the outcome of the biopsy and if the tests confirmed she had junctional EB then it would be arranged for the pregnancy to be terminated in hospital in London. And that was the advice we were given, to have the pregnancy ended. However I didn't take up the booking in London for a termination, instead I came home because I wanted to be there when the results were made known and to think about what to do. And I did. And I was at home when I was told the EB was junctional.

"It was then arranged for me to go to Ayrshire Central, the same hospital where Georgia had been born, to have the termination but I decided I couldn't do it. I was going to keep the baby, have the whole of my pregnancy to look after her. I was determined to enjoy her from the moment I fell pregnant. I knew that she was safe inside me and knew that it was only going to be when she was born that the whole environment would change. It was only then that she'd be ill.

"Not only did we know the sex of our baby, we knew she would die as well. I chose the name 'Freya' after looking through name books. It was a name I loved and Freya was the Norse Goddess of Love and Fertility. My Freya would have all the love in the world. And it turned out she was born on a Friday, a pure coincidence but a very appropriate day for a Freya to arrive. My doctor signed me off because I'd gone back to working full time after I'd lost Georgia and so I didn't work throughout my pregnancy with Freya. And so I really enjoyed blooming and preparing for her, even though I knew what the outcome would be. And when it came to the delivery I was completely involved in the preparation for that.

"Evelyn Gilday, who was then the Debra nurse in Scotland, came to the hospital to train the group of midwives that were hopefully going to be on duty at the birth. She left supplies and dressings, everything Freya and I would need. I think it's obvious that I enjoyed carrying Freya and having her. To other people it must have been completely bizarre when I was showing off my bump and saying to them, 'I'm going to have my baby, but by the way she's going to die'. Perhaps people thought I was strange. But it was my choice to do that and being able to be honest about everything probably drove me on. Even at work, where everyone had been through everything with me with Georgia, it was probably more upsetting for my colleagues because they knew I was going to have another baby who, like Georgia, was going to die. I could handle all that and was fine with it. I'd made the decision to have her and I'd told everyone, 'Well, if she's here for a day, if she's here for a week, for a month, however long she is with us we are going to enjoy her'.

"I already had my box filled with all the medical stuff I'd need in hospital and being prepared was so nice. It was also comforting and reassuring to know that as soon as my name came up, as soon as Sam and I telephoned to say we were on our way to hospital, as soon as I was in the delivery room everyone knew what to do. It was great going into hospital, going into labour. They pretty much left it to me and were on hand to do medical intervention if that became necessary, but when it came to the point of Freya being born the staff simply said, 'You tell us what needs to happen here. How much physical contact do we have with your baby?'

"And the birth was great, a completely different experience to having Georgia. There was no pain, which was such a relief. Freya was delivered in her waters. I'd read about that and found it was the safest way to deliver her because she wasn't going to get damaged on the way out. And once she was there nurses were asking, 'Now what do we do?' I dealt with her, dressed her. Dealt with the parts of her body that needed to be treated. She weighed in at seven pounds nine ounces, almost two pounds heavier than Georgia. When the formalities had been completed, I got up and went home with her a couple of hours later. I didn't need a rest, the excitement carried me through. I was thoroughly enjoying her.

"EB is not a nice disease. It's distressing. It's not nice to see and I know how many people get quite upset by it. Even my own family were distressed and didn't want to see my own children without covers or bandages when their skin was at its' worst. Sometimes I'd be changing a nappy and I would leave the room because I could see my parents' faces and those of my family and knew it was heart-breaking, totally heart-breaking, for them. Here was their grandchild and the only word to describe their feelings was 'distressing'. But the thing about EB is that you must face up to its' existence, it's no good pretending children aren't born suffering from it.

"I knew before I took Freya home that I was not just her mum, but her full time carer, her nurse, everything, 24/7. I didn't sleep properly for the whole of the time she was alive because she could have died at any time. I ran on adrenalin for the 13 weeks she was with us but at one stage the nurses suggested we could have some respite. Freya, they said, could go to Rachel House, the wonderful children's hospice in Scotland, for a couple of days and nights to let us sleep. There would be carers there, but we'd be with her. At first I thought, 'No way, that's for other people' but then a very good friend and a nurse suggested we visited Rachel House. One of the hospice staff came to see us and described what it was like and so we agreed to go. To understand a hospice you need to go so see what amazing places they are. Sadly they are needed, but there should be more of them to accommodate more children because they provide a fantastic service. Having been once, we went there twice more, once a month to spend a couple of nights with Freya.

"Of course even there I didn't sleep fully because I worried that I might wake up in the morning only to find Freya was no longer with us. But all the same, I believe the only reason I coped was because of the help provided by the hospice.

"Freya's first weeks of life were great. She had junctional EB, but we managed really well. It was only after eight or nine weeks that she started to have wee dips and declines and you could tell that infection was setting in. 'Oh, no, this is going to be it', I used to think, but somehow she pulled back from it.

"But during the last four weeks, and the very last week in particular, I knew we were getting near the end. I had known when Georgia was going to die. And I knew when the end was coming with Freya too. Call it a mother's instinct. Both of them declined to a point where I knew death was imminent. I knew when it was her last night. And I'd phoned my mum and dad and Sam's parents too and all the family came. Was knowing that was to be her final evening a relief? Yes, I was letting her go and saying, 'You have to go, your suffering is over', and even in the minutes the next day before she died, when I knew she had gone and I could see her eyes had gone, her little heart would not stop pumping. It just kept going and so I put my hand on her chest and told her, 'You've gone now, stop'. And it stopped. So it was a relief for us and a relief for Freya.

"You don't want to see your child suffering any longer because we'd had such a good time with her. I knew she was only with us for a short time, but I could have missed those wonderful moments and days. I could have mis-carried that baby. But I didn't, and so I had to be thankful for all those weeks I had her. She knew her family. She knew who I was, and she had those weeks of life and of being loved. Knowing that is probably what gave me the strength to pull through. I'd think, 'It's been okay. It could have been worse, but it's been okay'. But

I had to let them both go in the end and that was a relief for them from the pain they endured."

"Like Georgia, Freya died at home with me and that was the way I wanted it to be. Death isn't something you want to plan, but when it happens the way you want it, then it gives you some comfort. It meant they weren't dying alone in hospital. There had been no intervention after Georgia left us and the fact both my babies had EB meant doctors were constantly visiting them. It meant that although Freya died quite suddenly, the doctors knew the cause and there was no need for her to be taken for a post mortem. Frankly, I'd have eaten any policeman who came to try and take my child away. It would have been devastating and the fact that it didn't happen was a comfort, but it made me think of those poor parents to whom this does happen. I knew I'd seen both my babies through, given them life, cared for them and loved them, they'd died the way we'd have chosen and neither of them left my house until they went to the cemetery. That was how I wanted it to be and I found that this way helped."

An indication of the impression Robin Hood made on the Gardiners came in the fact that Freya died on May 10 and at the beginning of June Kirsteen and Sam were already fundraising for Debra at their village gala. "It was three weeks after Freya died and I stood there with a board showing photographs of Georgia and Freya and their blisters. I was giving out leaflets, information about Debra and was astonished at how many people came to speak to me that day. Ours was a small village. Everyone knew I'd just buried my daughter but there were plenty of visitors there too who asked me to tell them about EB and Debra. 'What is the condition?

I've never heard of it', I'd be asked, and I'd tell them about blisters and bandages and what Debra was trying to do to find a cure. My parents were there that day and I remember my dad looking at me and wondering, 'Is she going to crumble?' I knew that's what he was thinking, waiting for me to go to pieces. But I got through that day, enjoying it in a strange way, probably because I felt I had done something to help.

"A lot of that was down to Robin. He'd stayed in touch, explaining about a lot of the research that was being carried out and I'd look it up for myself so I could follow everything. I knew he made promises about when a cure would be found, but never to me personally. I know what promises he made to Alex but I can understand why he did that and had I been in his shoes I'd tell my children the same. You want to make it right for them, reassure them, make them believe it's going to be okay. So I'd defend him for doing what he did.

"Was he obsessive? Probably, yes, although I'd use the word 'driven' to best describe him. In reality he was completely driven and probably obsessive, but for me that wasn't a bad thing. However I wasn't married to him although I was on his side because being driven was going to help people like me in the future."

Later that summer her doctor confirmed to Kirsteen she was pregnant for a third time. "Deciding to try for a third after my two babies had died was the hardest decision I ever made. But it was my last attempt and if it had gone wrong I wouldn't have tried again. It was my hankering to have a baby. My babies had died. I didn't have any other children. Had I had a couple of healthy children first and then had an EB baby it might have been different, but I had the maternal instinct.

Selfishly, I wanted to have a baby. It was very difficult to decide what to do because I knew, in my mind, that this was my last attempt. I couldn't go on burying babies. I had two lying in the cemetery and there had to be no more. If there had been a third with EB, I think that would have broken me.

"Lots of people tried to talk me out of getting pregnant. I'd made many great friends, nurses and midwives as you can imagine among them – they are still friends – and so they were very blunt with me saying, 'You know what can happen, do you really need to do this?' They were probably more practical than my family who were just scared for me. My mum and dad asked, 'Kirsteen, are you sure. Maybe there are other ways. Maybe you could adopt. Maybe you could foster'. They put forward so many options.

"Everyone had a wee bit of advice but, maybe knowing me, they realised I would make up my own mind anyway and do what I wanted to do. So, in the end, Sam and I decided to try for a third time. I'd say, 'Don't say third time lucky' and if anybody had said that to me I'd have told them, 'Don't be so insensitive'."

Her pregnancy confirmed, Kirsteen once more faced up to the ordeal of a skin biopsy on her foetus. It meant another nerve wracking trip to St Thomas' Hospital in London for a consultancy arranged by Debra with a specialist. She had the option of remaining in London to await the outcome but, once more, preferred to journey home so that in the event of more bad news she would at least have the consolation of her family around her to give comfort and courage. She had an anxious wait at home in Ayrshire but when the news finally came though her tears were of joy and relief. "When the phone rang and I was told my baby was going to be EB-free I shouted, cried and laughed all at the same time. I'd steeled myself for the news to be bad. When I'd calmed down and told Sam and our families, I said to myself, 'Thank God' and started looking at names. I chose 'Ava' because it was a derivative of the Hebrew word meaning 'Life' and because I knew she was going to be healthy. If Ava had died, if she'd had EB, I would never have put myself, Sam, my family and everybody through everything again. "

Ava was born in March 2004 at the same hospital as her sisters. She was healthy and beautiful.

CHAPTER TWENTY SIX

Virginia and Robin Hood knew, as the parents of the other young victims of the junctional and dystrophic strains of EB knew, that the only chance their offspring had of living to a reasonable age was the discovery of a cure. This was especially true of the severely debilitating junctional form. Doctors tried reassuring those with dystrophic that they had an expectancy of mid-adult life but the reality was most died before they reached the age of 20. Simplex EB sufferers often lived to normal old age.

So it was not surprising that any glimmer of hope became a straw to be grasped. Newspapers jumped to conclusions that were far too over-optimistic whenever a scientist wrote a paper about cell healing progress. Articles were written in good faith, but the reality was that healing burns was one matter; that of trying to discover a cure for the complex and deep rooted problem of inherited gene defects was something totally different.

Robin had constantly assured not just Alex, but others, that a cure would come. Everyone was certain it eventually would. The question was when. His regular efforts to boost Alex's morale were born of genuine and loving hope. But the time came when assertions of 'two years', 'three years', 'four years' began wearing thin, as Virginia remembers. "Robin's fundraising was brilliant. He was always telling Alex, 'Oh they'll have a cure in four years or five years or six years and then in the end Alex got so cross with him, not just over that but for the way in which he made every opportunity to be with Alex a newspaper opportunity at the same time. He shouldn't have done that."

It wasn't only her father who left his daughter at times sceptical. The distinguished scientist Dr. Michele de Luca along with colleagues at the Istituto Dermopatico dell'Immacolata in Rome had spent years investigating the make-up of genes and investigating how to isolate damaged or defective genes. They developed a technique whereby they would grow cells under laboratory conditions and add to these healthy copies of the faulty genes. A form of this procedure was used to treat two volunteers who had suffered massive burns damage to their eyes. The healthy samples were taken from the volunteers themselves so that when the new tissue was grafted on to the eyes of these two patients it was not rejected because it came from their own cells. Two years after the grafts were carried out, both volunteers reported a big improvement in their sight.

Dr De Luca had moved on to experiment with using a form of the technique to add healthy genes to the cells of EB sufferers. One newspaper report, in 2002, claimed Alex would be one of the first in the world to benefit from this gene therapy. Another that Robin had been promised that if the tests were successful a cure could be available in two years. Sadly this presupposed she would still be alive when, and if, clinical trials turned out to be successful. This was, in reality, a highly unlikely scenario bearing in mind the extensive testing that would be required on animals and under laboratory conditions before transferring the experiments to humans. Italian authorities had given the scientist permission to conduct tests on a volunteer patient suffering from a milder variety of junctional EB in which blistering was limited to the hands, feet, knees, and elbows. Early results showed considerable promise. But one worry for gene researchers generally, was that sometimes patients undergoing gene therapy developed leukaemia. Another was risk of skin cancer affecting the lips, mouth, oesophagus, urinary bladder, prostate, lung, vagina, and cervix, among other areas of the body. Progress had to be slow, careful and painstaking. The loss of a single human life during trials could set back an entire promising programme by years.

Medical research was inevitably a long, expensive and often frustrating process requiring extreme skill and resolve. These were qualities with which the teams at Dundee were blessed in abundance. They were given some well deserved reward when their experiments aimed at seeking a cure for EB unexpectedly turned up results that they were confident would help many thousands of sufferers from some forms of skin cancer and the often embarrassing and distressing condition, psoriasis where the body was left with ugly patches of scaly skin. It was encouraging for Irwin McLean because here was evidence that he and his colleagues were working along the right lines in trying to develop a therapy that replicated a natural feature of the human make up.

Many scientists preferred their work to be carried out quietly and without the continued attention of the

Media. However in the case of the Dundee teams, and others investigating EB, so much of their ability to even work depended on grants and the money Debra could provide. If the supply dried up then the chances of discovering a cure would be cruelly set back, probably by years. Robin believed it was therefore important not just to tell the public, who gave of their hard earned cash, that the money was being put to good use, but to let any benefactor see in what way it was being used. And so he was in frequent contact with Professor McLean and his colleagues, ensuring he could pass on information that was both accurate and up to date.

Researchers could find themselves walking a rocky path. There were so many projects seeking grants and government coffers were not bottomless, as ministers frequently pleaded. EB was just one of the numerous conditions for which no cure had yet been found. Just as charities themselves battled for money, so did the research teams. Giving politicians and taxpayers encouraging stories about progress was one form of pressurising those holding the national purse strings into continuing their support. Robin had not initially set out to take on the role of lobbyist, but many in the research fields were grateful for his continued use of Alex to promote the necessity of their work.

It was not always smooth going though. His forthright attitude was not to everyone's taste. Not everybody appreciated his regular appearances in the Media. Even he admitted, 'Some people have said that they're sick of seeing me in the local paper or on television banging on about EB. One guy asked me if I thought I was a big shot. I told him, "Swap your daughter's health for my daughter's and you can have all the Media coverage you want. I'll gladly stand aside because I never wanted any of this. I'm doing all of this for Alex. She's all I care about. I couldn't bear her to die knowing I hadn't pulled out every stop to help change things while she was alive. I don't do what I do for an ego trip. All I want is not to go to my daughter's funeral. I'm sure any other father would do the same.'

One letter did pay remarkable dividends. Robin had long been an admirer of Prince Charles, heir to the throne and a man for whom he had the utmost admiration. "I wrote to Prince Charles telling him about my daughter's condition, although I didn't tell him that my fundraising had cost my marriage to Virginia. I had a fantastically well-informed letter back from His Royal Highness, together with a generous donation to Debra from The Prince of Wales's Charitable Foundation which uses the income it earns from its commercial ventures to support charitable causes. I was delighted with that although I had hoped that there might be an opportunity for Alex to meet the Prince. Such a meeting would really heighten the profile of Debra and bring in more money.

"The Prince is well loved and if it is known he has given his support to a cause, then that cause can expect a very big increase in public awareness. And the publicity, the newspaper and television coverage that would accompany a meeting with him was bound give me and Debra the chance to get across just what EB was and what it meant for its victims and those looking after them. So I kept my fingers crossed and then one Thursday I received a telephone call from St James's Palace and one of the Prince's staff told me, 'Mr Hood, Prince Charles is coming to Scotland on Tuesday and would like to meet you and your daughter.' I was shaking with excitement when the call came, because the day before the Royal visit, Monday, was also Alex's birthday. So I was straight on the phone to her. 'Come on Alex,' I told her, 'Prince Charles wants to meet you on Tuesday, it'll be a fantastic birthday treat.'

Then I actually rang Mohammed Al Fayed's office to inquire whether there was any chance of Alex being flown from Leamington Spa to Scotland in his private helicopter in order to save her the discomfort of a long journey. I knew there had been differences between Mr Al Fayed and the Royal Family following the death of Princess Diana and Dodi and I didn't know what the situation was with Mohammed and the Prince. But whatever the position was, it was nothing to do with me or Alex. My focus was solely on my work for Debra and my desire to keep my daughter alive. I'm not interested in religion. I'm not interested in politics. But Alex said, 'Daddy I'm sorry I don't want to meet Prince Charles. For my birthday I'm going to Mackie's with my friends and I can't come.' Mackie's was a local club. I said, 'Would you write him a letter?' but she said, 'No, no.' So I was pretty disappointed. I called up St James's Palace and said, 'I'm afraid to tell you that as a result of my fundraising it broke up my marriage to Alex's mother. Alex now lives in Leamington Spa in Warwickshire and it would be too much for her to come up to Scotland to meet Prince Charles. Thank you very much for the offer.' And I thought that was it.

"The following day the Palace rang back and said, 'Prince Charles wants to meet you anyway', so I said, 'OK,' and got on the phone to Alex. I told her, 'Alex, I'm going to meet Prince Charles, can you write him a letter?' And bless her, she did. The letter she wrote was fantastic,

230

'Dear Prince Charles, sorry I can't be with you today as it is my birthday and I have plans with friends, love to catch up with you some time in the future, please give me a call.' And she gave him her mobile telephone number.

"When Tuesday came I was introduced to the Prince and I handed Alex's letter to him. It had taken a real effort on her part to write it because her hands were always a painful mess. And I have a photograph of this lovely, warm, caring man reading her letter and when he had finished he gave such a delightful smile. I was with him for about twenty minutes and he gave me a wonderful gift to pass on to Alex for her birthday."

CHAPTER TWENTY SEVEN

The airing on Channel 4 television of 'The Boy Whose Skin Fell Off' in March 2004 was hugely significant, not just for Debra but for every EB sufferer and their families. There had been countless Media references to the condition and to its meaning for those who, by a freak of nature, had fallen victim. But what five million viewers now saw for the first time in graphic colour and as though they were there in the same room, was a 36-year-old man screaming as his mother gently lifted bandages from his chest, arms and back and in doing so literally peeled off his skin. It was horrific, frightening, sickening and just what Robin and all of the others fighting to raise funds for Debra wanted. Here was what EB was all about. Here was what it meant for Jonny, his mother and his brother Simon.

Jonny Kennedy and Robin had spoken often when they met at fundraising events. Jonny, a man trapped in the body of a child, his throat so badly scarred that his speech was high pitched and juvenile and never having gone through puberty, had intended to write a diary detailing the story of his pain. Robin had encouraged him, but after discovering he was dying Jonny discussed the possibility of television cameras following him during the last months of his life. Robin, experienced in dealing with the Media, was already working with a BBC television crew filming the story of him and Alex, and urged him to go ahead. He liked Jonny because both were direct and positive in their attitude to EB, conscious of the effects of the condition on others and determined to do whatever they could for a cure. The difference was that while Jonny knew there was no hope for him, that he was going to die, Robin was desperate to avoid that fate for his daughter.

"Jonny was a great friend. Once you met him, you would never forget him. It was a remarkable testimony to him and to his mother Edna in particular that he survived to his mid-thirties."

Neither Edna nor her husband Frank had known they each carried the rogue gene when they met and fell in love. They had a son, Simon, who was born a robust, healthy child. When Jonny arrived, Edna did not see her son for two days. He had no skin on his right leg from the knee down. Hospital staff thought he would die and wanted to spare his mother the ordeal of watching his death. Virtually nothing was known then about EB, there were no pre-natal tests to determine whether there was a problem with an embryo. When she was handed her baby, Edna discovered to her horror that each time she picked him up to be fed or changed his body was left covered in blisters where she had made contact with her son.

His childhood contained, in many ways, remarkably similar experiences not just to that of Alex but of so many EB children. He spent lonely hours and days seated by himself watching Simon at play with his friends, because every attempt at boyhood antics left him hurt and blistered. Robin junior knew all about what it meant to be the sibling of an EB victim. There had been countless occasions when he heard his father's voice warning, 'Watch your sister' if he went anywhere near Alex. Too often Robin was banished to his room, the safe but unfair option as far as his parents were concerned.

Simon felt robbed of the fun of having a younger brother. He watched his pals roll around and fight with their siblings, the roughness of their antics having little effect apart from an occasional tear. Jonny on the other hand had to be treated with kid gloves.

Frank never managed to come to terms with his boy's condition. He was embarrassed by the sight of his son having to be continually wrapped in bandages and by the sound of his cries when Edna changed his dressings. He was upset when concerned neighbours would approach the baby's pram and ask Edna what was wrong with the infant and she was left to try explaining the meaning of a condition of which they had never heard. He had little faith in the treatment prescribed by doctors and set about experimenting with a series of home-made cures including immersing Jonny in stinging salt water baths and even stripping him of every bandage and standing him in the garden where flies, attracted by the red rawness of the child's flesh, had a day of feasting leaving him in torment.

In September 2002 Jonny had gone to St Thomas's Hospital in London where specialists confirmed that, almost inevitably for a victim of dystrophic EB, his body had finally given way to a cancerous tumour. Their prognosis, made with uncanny accuracy, was that he had a year to live. He spent a good deal of the remaining months in the company of the television crew who filmed him as he planned his own funeral. Robin had been closely involved in the early stages of the making of the documentary but took a backwards step after a dispute with the programme makers, although his loyalty to Jonny never diminished.

The dying man drew up a wish list of things he wanted to do before dying. Among them was to parachute, fly in a glider, move to his own house, have a huge housewarming party with a stunningly beautiful celebrity as his guest, call at 10 Downing Street, draw up his own funeral arrangements and help design his own coffin. He fulfilled them all. In the documentary he was seen visiting a workshop to order his coffin. It was an exercise carried out with astonishing detachment from the sorrow generally associated with bereavement. Jonny allowed his body to be measured, five feet three inches tall by eighteen inches wide, settled for a plain pine box and lid and asked for two adornments, the design of a tiger on one side and a portrayal of a tin of Heinz Baked beans on the other. The tiger was the favourite emblem of this gallant fighter, the creature a reference from a line in his much loved Queen song, 'Don't Stop Me Now'. The baked beans tin? 'No special reason,' said Jonny. 'I just want people sitting at my funeral nudging each other and asking, "What's the Heinz beans for?" It'll get them talking.'

He was forthright about his approaching end. 'Will it be painful? How long will it last? Am I going to drag on and be a dribbling old fart? I'd rather just go to bed, go to sleep, pop my clogs. I'm not a nut case. I have different ideas to different people and I can't say I've had many fears in my life. Cancer doesn't worry me. Even in this day and age we're still frightened to talk about death and it's such a shame because it's part of life so why not organise it like you would organise a birthday? Let's get it right.'

At one stage he reduced the lovely celebrity Nell McAndrew to tears after telling her what EB had meant for him. Nell, a wonderful supporter of Debra, made a 600-miles round trip to join Jonny at his housewarming party in Northumberland shortly before his death. 'I miss out on a lot, but that's life,' he told her. 'I am used to it. I have to take each day as it comes. I know that one day with the help you and others have given, this will be history and it will be in the archives and people won't have to suffer like this.

'When you are hurting, suffering, you don't know who to turn to. You just want to get away from it and say, "I've had enough". I believe we all come down to earth to learn lessons and that earth is a classroom. I feel I came down to understand what it was like to be in discomfort all your life, to learn about frustration and possibly overcome that. Do you know if you've learned your lesson or do you go to your Maker and he goes, "Ah you've boobed. You didn't learn that bit and you'll have to go down and do it all again". I feel I have learned my lessons. I have come to terms with it and come to terms with people around me. I think I'll be bored if the angels sit around on clouds plucking their harps all day. I'll be up there, getting them off their clouds.'

Jonny had rejected the offer of the medical team at St Thomas's Hospital to remove the tumour and so probably prolong his life. He knew an operation was simply delaying the inevitable. His last few days were spent in obvious decline. The end was approaching quickly. 'It's a part of death, leaving people. We all know that.

My mum knows that. My brother knows that. I'm emigrating, I'm leaving. I'm going to somewhere that they can't join me at this moment in time but for me it's a freedom, it's an escape and I accept I'm going to have to say goodbye.'

In his vast experience of speaking about EB, Robin had always been aware of the enormous variety in the emotional desires of listeners. There were those who were jerked into life and action by shocking descriptions of Alex's suffering; others preferred a gentler less gory version of her treatment. The makers of The Boy Whose Skin Fell Off went for the former; in tabloid newspaper terms the programme was sensational, even outrageous. The opening showed dead Jonny seated in his wheelchair while his mother discussed the clothing he was to wear in his coffin. Scenes in which his bandaging was removed and changed showed his ravaged back, a red jellied mass of skinless flesh. Jonny described what happened when he tried to sleep. 'If a bandage comes off you stick to the bed; then your head sticks to the bed.'

Robin had retained contact with Cherie Blair, a superb ambassador for EB victims. As a result, when a second Debra reception was arranged for Downing Street, he was able to ensure an invitation went to Jonny. Edna knew her son was simply not well enough to make the journey but he had over-ruled her protests. 'I'm going to Number Ten even if it kills me,' he said. 'It can bring in the charity a large sum of money and mean other children don't have to suffer this dreadful condition.' On the train journey home, seated in his wheelchair, he died. He had recorded his account of his life knowing it would only be screened after his death. 'I have told my story and I hope it's given you something to think about. Do not be sad, for I am free.'

If there was justified criticism of the programme, it was that insufficient detail was given to precisely what EB was. It was left to Jonny to give a brief explanation, and reference was made to experts having managed to re-grow healthy skin on a victim. The reality that a cure was years off and needed tens of millions of pounds was missing. The programme editors allowed a brief glimpse of Robin at Jonny's funeral where he had joined Simon and his childhood friend, the Liberal Democrat peer Lord Rupert Redesdale in giving orations.

Alex had been spending a brief holiday with her father at Lochside Cottage at the time. "She and I were sitting by the slipway at the side of the house and I said, 'Oh God, Alex, do you know what I have to do next week? I have to speak at Jonny Kennedy's funeral. How daunting is that?' I looked around and Alex was in tears. She asked, 'Daddy, does that mean I'm going to die as well?' I remembered all my promises and said to myself, 'What a prat you've been'. I had to hide my own tears. I told her, 'Alex, don't be so stupid. I'm going to get enough money to find a cure. You're not going to die'. But it showed just how carefully you needed to think when talking about death.

Just as Robin had known it would, the showing of The Boy Whose Skin Fell Off gave a massive injection of funds to Debra. In just a few months more than £500,000 in donations poured in with the result that later in the year a specialist EB laboratory and ward were opened at St Thomas's Hospital. It was a particularly proud time for Edna whose courage and devotion to her son had moved hundreds of viewers to write to newspapers and magazines in her praise. 'When Jonny was small, no one knew how to handle the condition,' she said, in a statement. 'I hope the laboratory will be able to give people some relief from the pain, something other than morphine. Jonny maintained that the drug didn't kill the pain, it was just that you didn't care that you were in pain. If they did find a cure it would be like winning the lottery.'

How would the new facility help? Professor Irwin McLean, who would head it, was asked. 'We are hoping we will be successful with ex-vivo gene therapy, where we take a small skin sample, grow it in the laboratory, add an artificial copy of the missing gene – in Jonny's case it was a gene called Collagen VII – then graft the skin back on like a patchwork quilt. With fine tuning we should be able to use this treatment in two and a half years.' It was work very much along the same lines as that being carried out in Italy by Michele De Luca, but the scientists would never feel they were involved in a competition to see who would be first to discover a cure or at least a highly significant development. This was a race against time, not one another.

Money was not the only side effect to come from the programme. Just as important was the educational factor as, for instance, Dianne Forsyth who knew Jonny, was to discover. She had followed Robin's advice and allowed Adana's condition to be publicised, a move that not everyone agreed with although Dianne and Robin know it was the right course and one vindicated by the showing of the Jonny Kennedy story. Dianne said, "I'd get a lot of people telling me, 'Oh, I saw you in the papers again', as though we were on a personal publicity quest or were attention seekers. That was never our motive,

239

but the showing of the Channel 4 documentary changed all that. I found myself getting so much support. People who had belittled Adana's condition in the past were crossing the street to give me a hug. It made such a difference and helped my confidence. I'm glad I'd met Jonny not long before he died and had thanked him for what he was doing."

Edna was not the only grieving mother who allowed television cameras to intrude into her mourning. A few weeks after the birth of Ava, an overjoyed Kirsteen Gardiner agreed to a request by Robin that she be interviewed by the News of the World and some days later for a BBC television series, 'Extraordinary Lives.' She told the newspaper, 'Sam and I consider ourselves fortunate to have shared wonderful moments with Georgia and Freya. Their short lives were happy. Every child is precious and we feel Ava to be especially so. Now our happiness is beyond belief. When we hold Ava, or change her nappy, it's wonderful to know it's not causing her dreadful pain.' It was a sentiment the mother of any EB child would have echoed. Robin admits he realised the potential of Kirsteen telling her story. "When I first met Kirsteen and Sam I felt true sorrow for them. I normally always had my fundraising hat on, but at that initial meeting, after the birth and then death of Georgia, I had my genuine caring hat on.

"As a sincere caring person, I'd known the death of Georgia to have been inevitable through her having junctional EB, but felt genuinely sad for them and cared for how I knew they'd have felt because I honestly believed my daughter was going to live. And I'd have understood if Kirsteen had looked at me and said, 'Well, it's okay for you because you've got there in the end, but we've lost our child.'

"When Kirsteen became pregnant for the second time and decided she was going to keep that second child I was amazed, I tried to support both of them as much as I could, but I really couldn't understand why Kirsteen took that decision, especially once she experienced the horrors of the prolonged agony of Freya. It was almost like someone saying, 'If I hit myself in the face with a hammer it's going to hurt, but I'm going to do it anyway'. But like them I felt a great sorrow when Freya died. However, when they had their third baby, Ava, and she was healthy, I put my fundraising hat back on again and used them to publicise Debra. But it was only possible with their agreement."

Kirsteen felt an obligation to help and the publicity would prove to be effective. "There were people who told me, 'Oh you don't really want to do that do you?' but I felt I had to. And I was actually happy to do the interviews. We weren't doing this for ourselves but for all the little children who were still suffering and all those yet to be born to suffer. If you don't get it out there and let people see what it's about, if you don't put EB into people's faces, then how do you raise awareness? The public can choose whether or not to watch a television programme, and if they find it distressing they can always turn their set off or watch something else. But don't try sweeping these things away. They are there and people should know about them.

"On the same morning the article appeared in the News of the World, a young girl who lived in the same village as us pushed a hand-written letter through the door. It said she had not known why our babies had died and how saddened she had been by our story. What was fantastic about that letter was it meant the girl would tell somebody else about EB and they would tell a friend and so on and the existence of the condition and information about it would spread.

"I never put my babies out there to say, 'Look at me'. Because this wasn't about me. It's not about, 'Poor me, poor me'. It's about my children and all the other children with EB. I was trying to say, 'My babies had this horrible condition and I don't want anybody else to suffer from it. So if we can get enough money to research it and cure it then thank God'. It may be there are those who felt uncomfortable when they read about this and who might wonder, 'Why are you doing this?' But I'd defend myself by saying, 'This isn't about me, it's about the children', and I would defend Robin with the same argument."

Now Ava brings her mother supreme pride and joy. A happy girl, she lovingly helps her mother tend the graves of her sisters. Sadly, though, the marriage of Kirsteen and Sam has not survived.

CHAPTER TWENTY EIGHT

A lex's courage was the inspiration that drove Robin on. And her bravery shone through in his own television documentary. So did his honesty as to the promises he had made his daughter of a cure being found by her twelfth birthday, in time to save her life, admitting he had failed in his pledge of ending her ordeal within three years. His predictions had never been welcomed by Virginia. "The first time he said that, Alex got really upset about it. But I know he wouldn't say it if he didn't really want it to happen."

Anyone lacking in understanding of just what EB meant for its victims, was left in no doubt by the time interviewer Kirsty Wark had concluded the programme. Skilled and devoted as were both Virginia and Dianne Forsyth in dressing their children – both had performed this awesome task many hundreds of times – graphic scenes showing Alex and Adana squealing in agony as bandages and areas of skin were peeled made it impossible not to be affected by their pain ; viewers were left with a sense of relief that it was not their burden to hear the terrible screams on a daily basis.

Virginia and Alex had agreed to take part, believing their contributions would help Robin's fundraising mission. But neither enjoyed publicity and even Robin, the master advocate of publicity, admitted, 'Alex just wants to be normal. She doesn't enjoy having her face in the newspapers.'

Would a cure be discovered? Professor Mclean was in no doubt but maintained the caution of the scientist faced with resolving a problem that had been around for centuries. 'I am absolutely certain there will be a cure one day,' he said. Robin on the other hand honestly believed a solution lay just around the corner. Seen calling on Dianne and her daughter he told them, 'Adana will definitely live into the period when a cure is available without a doubt.' It was a prediction of which in the future he would often remind himself . His championing of EB children earned high praise from Dianne. 'Robin being at the frontline of the fundraising makes you feel like the treatment is going to be close, He's not only fighting for his daughter Alex, he's also fighting for Adana and all the other children. He'd doing this from his heart.'

The airing of the programme had an unexpected and not particularly welcome spin-off. It had mentioned how his single minded determination to raise money had led to the destruction of his marriage to Virginia and how he lived a busy but often solitary life. "By this time I worked between an office we had established for Debra in Hamilton on the outskirts of Glasgow and my home. My telephone numbers for both addresses were well known, especially as I'd used Lochside Cottage as a base in the early years. Shortly after the documentary was screened a woman rang me up and said, 'What the hell are you doing? You didn't tell us that your marriage had broken up.' I don't know who she was but assumed she'd helped support Debra. She certainly sounded angry. But the fact was there were people involved with our cause who felt as if they owned me. This is something fairly common to anyone regularly in the public eye. And because I founded my fundraising on telling Alex's story and how it affected our family, I was always giving out lots of personal information with the result that some people took the view that I shouldn't have kept back any of the details, even about my private life. On the other hand it was very flattering and encouraging to frequently pick up the telephone to be told, 'Robin you're a fantastic guy, you do a wonderful job, please keep it up.'

Periodically he looked forward to visits from Alex and Robin junior. It was for these happy times, the return of Alex to Lochside Cottage, that Virginia had insisted he get to grips with the tricky job of bandaging his daughter. When the television team had followed him to Leamington Spa he had been seen giving Alex a double dose of morphine before doing her dressings. But in his efforts to carry out the task without hurting her, he was slow in comparison to Virginia and when the soothing effects of the morphine began wearing off Virginia had to complete the work. Virginia had changed her daughter's dressings so many times, she was completely familiar with the operation. Even so she took nothing for granted. "I had an entry system to buzz people in because otherwise I would be up and down the stairs while I was trying to do dressings, bath Alex and cook a meal all at the same time. It was very, very intense. While I was bandaging her I'd watch television, but I could never take my eyes off what I was doing." While Virginia had confidence in the ability of her ex husband to change Alex's dressings, she was happier when she knew her son was also on hand, because Robin junior was always willing to help his father.

Robin never ceased to be amazed by the achievements of his daughter. She was an extremely talented artist and considering her frequent absences caused by hospital visits and stays, a gifted pupil, admired by her lecturers. "Even though she used to have her hands in bandages and splints to try to slow the process of the fingers fusing together, she could still, somehow, do up the buttons on her tee shirt. And one time when she was with me at Lochside Cottage, I'd just got her ready for bed with all her bandages done when she said, 'Daddy, pass me my phone, I have to text my mother.' I asked her, 'Alex, you don't expect me to take off all the bandages do you?' and she said, 'Oh no daddy, get a grip' and she pulled the phone over and used the end of her thumb to write the text message. And it wasn't a message strewn with errors. It was articulate, adept and accurate.

"I was always so stressed when I was bandaging Alex. I tried my best but didn't want to hurt her. I found it very, very demanding and you forget to be a dad because you're basically a nurse and that's where I went wrong. It became something I just wanted to do and get out of the way. Sometimes I think I got on Alex's nerves. If she dropped something, she wanted to pick it up for herself but I'd always step forward and do it for her. 'There you go Alex' I'd say and she would tell me, 'I don't need you to do things for me, I can do things on my own'. Or I'd ask, 'Alex are you all right? Alex how do you feel?' and she would say, 'Will you stop asking me how I am, I've got EB. Just get on with being normal'."

"I loved having my children with me at Lochside Cottage, but didn't cherish the good times when we had them. And I was selfish. I had to give Alex all the medicines she took through her gastrostomy and it took time. The procedure was to give her one batch of medicine, give her an hour's break to let it be absorbed by her body and then pop in the next lot. If the second batch was given too soon after the first, she would throw up and be sick and that meant all the skin coming off the back of her throat. So sometimes, even at four in the afternoon, I would be starting to get her ready for bed although her bedtime was usually ten o'clock. The trouble was I just couldn't be bothered to wait, I didn't want to start doing bandages at nine or ten o'clock at night. And so, solely for my sake, I would start early even though the idea of the break was to give Alex more time with me. But I just wanted to get it all done and finished with, get her into bed and out of harm's way.

"I didn't mean that in any nasty way, I only wanted to do my best and if I started late I'd be rushing and almost certainly hurting her more. Because I never skimped on any of the dressings. If Alex wanted an hour's break to give her some relief from pain, or if it took me two hours to bandage an area that was really sensitive, I would do that. I would never short cut on anything for her special needs.

"So when she came to Scotland I looked on it as a good time for her, whereas I should have thought of it as a good time for me too. Because it was. These were special times between us, but I never realised until it was too late just how special. Sometimes when all the bandages were done and she just didn't want to go to bed, then we would sit and watch television, I'd cuddle her gently and she would be mine. I was a very loving, touchy, feely person.

"Once when Alex and Robin were visiting, we were all playing cards. I said, 'Come on Alex, bedtime'. It was late afternoon. She said, 'Dad, it's six o'clock,' but I said, 'I've got to give you this, I've got to give you that, it's going to be two hours to do this, it's going to be nine o'clock and then I've got three hours of bandaging to do.' Poor dad, that was how I felt. I should have told myself, 'Come on, she's your daughter, she's on her holidays, she deserves a good time and she doesn't see you very often'. And now, looking back, I wonder if that's how Alex felt at the time too. Only if she did, she was too nice a person to have said it.

"At that my son said, 'Dad, relax, I'll do the bandages tonight. Let's chill out. Let's play cards. Have a glass of wine.' I never drank when Alex was in the house because if she woke up in the middle of the night with the gastrostomy machine playing up, which it did regularly, I'd be on edge. So I'd leave the door open. She had a baby monitor by the side of the bed so if she wanted me she just had to call, but I was still nervous. Robin said, 'Have a glass of wine, chill out.' Do you know, they spiked my drinks because after two glasses of wine I was drunk. We were playing this card game that I played at school when I was a 12-year-old and I taught the kids how to play it. It was quite a complicated game and they accused me of changing the rules so I'd win. Then when Alex made a particular move I slurred, 'You can't do that, you're a cheat.' They said, 'You just called your daughter a cheat' and I said, 'You're a cheat you little bugger.' I was so drunk I was calling my disabled daughter a bugger and a cheat.

"The next morning I woke up and both of them were laughing about what had happened. Alex told me, 'You went to bed drunk, Robin did the bandages and we stayed up until eleven o'clock.' She had evidently told Robin, 'I love my dad so much, that's one of the few times that I've ever seen him so relaxed and just being who he is.'

"Only twice during her entire life did I hear her complain. Once had been the day we were at the slipway at Lochside Cottage, the other was when she was again in Scotland. She loved being there, sitting in her wheelchair looking out over Loch Ken. There was a buoy where we used to tie the boats up and one day I said to Alex, 'Let's see, I'm going to try and hit the buoy with stones'. We started a game with her urging me on. I was there all day until my arm was in agony. Sometimes we'd go and do that for hours, but on one of those days she turned to me and said, 'Daddy, I hate EB. I'm sick of the pain'.

CHAPTER TWENTY NINE

Cherie Blair had been as good as her word when she promised her backing to Robin. Somehow she found time from a sometimes manic schedule of looking after four children, being the Prime Minister's wife, supporting a host of good causes, working as a brilliant Queen's Counsel, acting as a part-time Recorder and being 3rd Chancellor of Liverpool John Moores University to encourage the work of Debra.

She had twice arranged prestigious Downing Street receptions for the charity and now she made her feelings about EB very public in a candid statement about the condition backing campaigners supporting the charity. In part of that moving testimony Mrs Blair said: 'I readily admit that until I became involved with the charity that helps those suffering from EB, as it is called, I wouldn't have had a clue what it was. But for the children who suffer from EB and half a million people worldwide, it means a life of constant pain, increasing disability and, for many, early death.

'There is no effective treatment or cure but Debra is working hard to put that right. Established in 1978, Debra is the only medical research and patient-support charity in the UK working on behalf of people living with EB. Debra in Scotland was started by a man called Robin Hood. Robin's daughter Alex was born with EB and it is through him that I first became aware of this dreadful condition after he wrote to Tony and me. Any parent would be touched by what he wrote and by Alex's incredible bravery. It is, of course, an enormous privilege to live at No 10, but one of the things I enjoy most about it is the chance it gives to raise the profile of some of our superb charities. So I have been able to invite Alex and Robin here to gain publicity for the condition and to host receptions for the charity. Anyone who meets Alex can't fail to be astonished at how cheerful she is and at the courage and dignity with which she copes with her condition.

'Robin's work has been relentless. Good health is the gift we most want for our children. Robin just wants a day in his daughter's life that is free of pain. And the work of the charity is funding the hope of relief for EB sufferers ever closer. Debra leads the world in identifying and funding specific research projects likely to lead to a cure and successful treatment for EB. The extraordinary advances in genetics hold out real hope for the future. Over the past few years the genes for all main forms of EB have been identified and, in the laboratory, the defects can be corrected at cellular level.

'But Debra does much more than just support and fund research. It campaigns ceaselessly to raise awareness of the issues surrounding EB to the general public, health-care professionals, schools and other interested parties. EB is a terrible condition and everyone who suffers from it needs not just our sympathy but also our help. It would be wonderful if we could find a way of eliminating the pain and suffering that it causes.'

Robin had realised the value of support from public figures. He had won support from Prince Charles, Bill Clinton and the Blairs. Michael Portillo, the well-known former Cabinet Minister had agreed to come on board as Debra's president while golfing television commentator Peter Alliss was a committed backer.

At the Guildhall in London he was asked to make a speech to raise funds for a new mobile home. Debra had bought three of these, one then sited at Blackpool and two others at Weymouth in Dorset. They were specially adapted for the needs of EB victims and their carers and allowed families a holiday with the security of knowing their surroundings had all the necessary facilities. The availability of the caravans had allowed Robin and Virginia to spend a happy and relaxed week at Weymouth when Alex had been much younger. Now one the mobile homes was in need of replacement and that meant somehow finding £50,000.

"At the Guildhall that evening one of my colleagues said to me, 'Right, Robin, your address has got to raise enough for a new mobile home.' How do you make a speech about a mobile home? I just used our story. I told them about Alex, about Virginia, about bandages and dressings and what we were doing to try to end the misery of it all. I said, 'When my daughter was born, we couldn't go on holiday because if we took Alex to a hotel, you didn't know about the facilities, whether they were good enough or clean enough and Alex bleeds a lot during the night so the bed and mattresses would be covered in blood. There would be lots of bandages and the smell from her body might upset the other guests so we just didn't bother.' I told them how everybody needed a break some time but said,

'When you have a child with EB, you can't go anywhere because people stare at your child. You can't even use the bathroom'. I've made better speeches than that but it raised £184,000. Frank Warren, the boxing promoter put his hand up and donated £50,000. Someone else gave the same. And we were able to get a new mobile home."

Guest of honour that night had been Baroness Margaret Thatcher, once termed the 'Iron Lady'. Was the heart of this wonderful lady melted by what she heard? At another later party hosted by author and one-time politician Jeffrey Archer and in aid of Debra, Baroness Thatcher accepted an invitation to be there. Nor would she forget Debra. The event made newspaper headlines when the former Prime Minister took to one side the colourful nightclub owner Peter Stringfellow and ticked him off for not having married his fiancé despite a two-year long engagement. Robin chuckled when he read of the incident. It may have been mere tittle tattle, but the significance of it was that it produced publicity and mentioned Debra in the same breath.

Such incidents, such generosity, such gestures were what kept the wheels of the charity turning. They allowed workers to carry on with their unrelenting battles to relieve suffering. Workers such as a Debra nurse who told a newspaper, 'There is something that shines out from within the children, despite the fact that they may have no fingers and can't do things that other kids can do. It's a job I love; it's good to feel you are making a difference.'

Robin knew he too was making a difference. But the truth was that children were continuing to die and he could sense time was beginning to run out for Alex.

This incredible little girl had matured into a wonderful young woman, her achievements a daily source of admiration for Virginia. "Alex used to go for singing lessons. Although she would sometimes have a bad throat, generally she'd be fine. She used to love to sing and even belonged to a music theatre. That meant her sometimes being on stage. She had a fantastic sense of humour. Some of the roles she played were really humorous and she had such a great turn of phrase that she'd make things sound so funny simply by the way she said them. We used to go to London, to the theatre. We both loved arts and crafts, always had something organised. She was always looking for things about which she could laugh."

Despite his fundraising successes, Robin found it difficult to justify relaxing.

One incident in particular would leave him with especially painful memories that his mind could never erase. Alex had joined him at Lochside Cottage for a birthday celebration and the plan was for a friend to collect her and drive her to Glasgow to link up with Virginia. "I feel really guilty in telling this, but the truth was I was glad when Alex went back to her mother. While she was with me I was very attentive and caring to her, but I just wanted her to go. Isn't that dreadful to say? I just wanted to enjoy the day. Nobody can ever say that I haven't done fantastically for Debra, but I have also got a life and I haven't been put on this planet to fundraise for the whole of my life have I? There were times when I just thought to myself, 'I need some space, I need some time for me'. That's what I was thinking that day and then the moment she's gone, going up the road, waving to me from the car, I was missing her and feeling guilty. I've never talked about this before, probably because I feel so guilty over that day. But once it happened, I just wanted to try even harder to fund a cure. I could miss her then, but I knew I could see her again. I didn't want a day to come when I could no longer see Alex."

He did not want her to join the daily list of children all over the world who were dying from EB. From the outset of his mission to raise funds by heightening the profile of the condition, he had known he was as a man trying to light the moonless sky with a candle. Ignorance of EB was as much his enemy as the condition itself. He was not alone in discovering this sad fact. In England a researcher attempting to compile a register of victims had discovered a woman in her 60s who had been born with the simplex strain. 'You had better talk to my family, there are a dozen of them with this,' she said and was astonished to be told work was actually being done to eradicate the condition. When the same researcher interviewed older victims of simplex most of these assured her 'we're getting better with age.'

One area of research that interested scientists was fibroblasts, parts of cells that contributed towards the production of Collagen VII, the glue-like protein which stuck the layers of skin together. It was the absence of Collagen VII that led to EB. In California, genetically corrected fibroblasts had been injected into the veins of mice with dystrophic EB and within two months normal Collagen appeared at their wounds, seemingly an indication that fibroblasts might help heal these. In Japan researchers were experimenting with genetically corrected bone marrow cells, again with promising results.

Developments were encouraging. Scientists had told Robin they had identified 14 of the genes responsible for EB. But one huge hurdle facing the researchers was that the family of each EB victim appeared to have its own individual version of the condition. What might help one was not guaranteed to solve the problem for another. The best the researchers could do was to find a means of alleviating the condition and then tailor it to individual needs.

Fibroblasts were of especial interest. Tests carried out on Melissa Smith, a dystrophic EB victim in her 20s from the English Midlands had been encouraging. Melissa had bravely suffered 106 injections of fibroblasts into an area of her badly affected back and significantly the wounds had first shrunk in size and then disappeared. They had remained healed for up to a month. This was an incredibly wonderful development for Melissa, meaning the time taken to bandage her ravaged body was reduced from two hours to ten minutes. It was particularly comforting on areas of her body, such as her armpits.

But it was not a cure. However victims had now at least hope of being relieved of some of their pain, a brilliant achievement on the part of the scientists. But they would still live with EB. And in their demands to be healed wounds would still place unbearable strains on the bodies of victims, all too often leading to fatal cancers.

CHAPTER THIRTY

Robin and Alex knew fibroblast injections would never help her. Yet even though the treatment had been developed with the aid of money he had helped raise, his commitment to Debra never slackened. Friends wondered why it was he continued with his work when time was so clearly running out for his daughter. Yet he had worked on through other setbacks, especially the loss of Virginia, had never contemplated ending his fundraising and now his attitude was no different.

"I received a letter from a close friend who asked, 'You gave up everything to raise money absolutely believing you were going to find a cure for Alex. Don't you feel bitter knowing these injections won't be trialled on her? Haven't you thought, "Here I am, all this money I've raised, it's helping to pay for this for others but it will do nothing for my daughter".

"I told him that hadn't affected my thinking. John McGrath and his team had carefully explained how everybody's genes were different and Alex simply didn't fit into the trials because her genetic makeup didn't suit the fibroblast injections. From a very early stage she and I had been aware she was never going to benefit. Other children had hoped to be considered but had to be told they were not suitable. And although they both technically suffered from dystrophic EB, Alex's was much more severe than that of Melissa."

What was hard to take was the fact that the good, the hopeful news about fibroblasts coincided with the worst possible for Alex. Like her parents, she had always known her body was slowly draining of the ability to heal the open wounds caused by skin loss, the peeling off that was a consequence of EB and the removal during grafts.

Not long before her daughter's 17th birthday in February 2006, Virginia's concerns over the deteriorating state of Alex's skin, led to worries cancer was developing. Mother and daughter travelled to Great Ormond Street for tests but after a series of biopsies doctors gave the all-clear. Robin recalls waiting for a telephone call from Virginia to give him the results. "Now I believe I know how someone must have felt sitting in a condemned cell on the morning of their execution waiting for the door to open and the hangman to appear. Time dragged but when the waiting was over being told there was no cancer was the most enormous relief."

It wasn't just her defiance of adversity that amazed Alex's family and friends. At school she forged ahead with studies that would win her a remarkable eleven GCSEs and gain her a scholarship to De Montfort University in Leicester to study Innovation, Design Management and Interior Design. One day a week she had travelled to Stratford-upon-Avon College of Further and Higher Education to study Performing Art and Design. "She was just brilliant, this girl with deformed hands, unbelievable," said Virginia. "Alex had such a wonderful strength of character, and she was great fun.

SMILE DADDY – I'M DYING

But to achieve what she did was exceptional. She was such an inspiration." And all of this while fighting daily excruciating pain and cancer.

But while she worked away at her schoolbooks, her body was failing to achieve the same levels of success. One of her injury sites, on a leg, had been especially horrific and had never closed after developing when she was a toddler. Regular hospital checks now showed the wound had become cancerous, the existence of a tumour in the region of her left thigh and buttock was confirmed and it would need to be removed.

Robin remembers, "The diagnosis was made just before her 18th birthday and Alex said to the surgeons, 'Can I enjoy my birthday? Can you take the tumour off afterwards?' I wondered to myself, 'How can you have a tumour and not want to get rid of it straight away? I'd have wanted the bastard thing off my leg immediately'. But the doctors told Alex, 'Okay, it's not aggressive. Have your birthday then come in and have the operation'."

Alex awoke, high up in her mother's town house, on the morning of her birthday wired up to her gastrostomy machine, her hands in splints and preparing for what she was determined would be a special day. 'Hello Mummy,' she called to Virginia and smiled as she heard the reply, 'Happy Birthday Alex, I'll be in shortly'.

She heard a noise and wondered if one of the slatted screens covering her window outside was loose and blowing against the wall of the building in the morning breeze. 'Kerchunk, kerchunk' seemed to be the sound. 'What's happening, what's wrong,' asked Alex, but received no answer or response. 'Kerchunk, kerchunk' and whatever the source of the noise was, it seemed to be getting close to her window. 'Mummy, what's going on?' called Alex. She was about to get the answer. Outside, her brother was on an extending ladder, gradually easing it higher and higher towards her window, the sound of the extension scraping up and thudding against the wall making a 'kerchunk, kerchunk'. Finally when it reached her window ledge and when he knocked on the window and Alex pulled back the curtains, much to her astonishment and the amazement of passing citizens of Royal Leamington Spa, her soldier-brother turned around on the ladder, dropped his trousers and mooned, giving his sister a birthday treat not just she would never forget.

The removal of the tumour was expected to be a relatively straightforward operation for the team of the experienced surgeons, but in Alex's case it was complicated by the inevitability that her skin was unlikely to heal after the operation. However once the procedure was under way, the surgeons discovered an even more terrible development. A second tumour lay beneath the first and its' removal necessitated leaving, in effect, a hole in her thigh. The medical team, skilled as they were, could not guarantee the cancer had now gone for good. The Hood family could only hope. Cancer had seeped away the life of Jonny Kennedy. It had accounted for so many child victims of EB.

Robin said, "Her body was by this time in a dreadful state. She had no skin on her shoulders, buttocks or legs. The hole where they had been forced to operate was huge, absolutely huge. Imagine a hole being carved out of your thigh. Yet it's amazing how the body recovers. I saw it months later and the flesh had begun to fill back in, the extent of the wound was decreasing, although the skin hadn't healed. But her toes were fused together and so was her right hand. Yet she refused to let any of this get her down or destroy her wonderful sense of humour."

Alex knew she faced a battle to live. But never once did she lose her dignity or throw in the towel. "When she knew about the double tumour Alex told me, 'Dad there's no point in hoping a cure will come soon, I just have to live with knowing that. If I didn't have EB I'd be a totally different person and having it is part of my make-up, it makes me the girl I am. I love what I've made of my life and there are so many things I'd love to be able to do but know I never shall, like swinging on monkey bars in a playground. I'm just going to make the best of what I have'. Sometimes it was very difficult not to cave in under her bravery."

After recovering from the removal of the tumours, Alex continued to be regularly monitored by doctors in London, who feared further tumours. Robin accompanied her on one of these visits and after her check-up went with his daughter on a trip around central London. But he could not resist another opportunity to cash in on her sickness on behalf of Debra. "Because Alex had skin cancer and Debra were funding a research project into this type of cancer, I thought, 'I know what we'll do, we'll go and see Mohammed Al Fayed and see if he'll give us – I don't know how much I was going to ask him for – maybe £300,000'. So I went along to see him with Alex and again he immediately agreed to meet us and once more he was only interested in her. I was talking about this and that and the other but he wasn't really listening to me. He knew about the tumours and probably, like all the Debra staff, suspected it was only a matter of time before the cancer returned. But because I'm an eternal optimist I was thinking, 'I'll work harder, raise more money, we'll get the money for this cancer, we'll get rid of the cancer then we'll get it cured'. That's what I'd told Alex. Mr Al Fayed listened and then pushed an envelope across the table. Later we discovered £1,000 inside. He smiled and said, 'There you are Alex, that's for you and your daddy to spend on the way home'. Alex gave me the money and I said, 'Thank you very much Mr Al Fayed, we are going to put this towards a disabled car'. Alex had been assessed and she could have a disabled car adapted to her needs. He looked at Alex and said, 'Well done, send me the bill. He never asked how much it would cost, simply told us, 'Send me the bill'.

"On the train returning to Leamington Spa, I said, 'Did he really say, send me the bill?' So then Virginia and I made inquiries and found a suitably modified car would cost about £22,000. I rang the office of his Charitable Foundation to tell them about our conversation with Mr Al Fayed and asked, 'How does this work?' They said simply, 'Just tell the garage to send us the bill'. What an incredibly kind man."

In July that year a fully modified, automatic Renault Kangoo, equipped with a hoist for her motorised scooter, remote controlled doors and the main functions operated by an array of buttons was handed over to Alex. For once, it was her speech for which the Media waited. 'The car is amazing. It is going to be so helpful in my everyday life and provide a lot of independence for me. I've had a mobility scooter since I was nine which is great but it means I'm restricted to Leamington Spa. But next September I'm starting at De Montfort University and, with the car, I'll be able to commute. I've just got to get a driving licence now.' "I'll never forget the look of joy on her little face when she took delivery of the car," said Robin. "And her smile was all down to Mr Al Fayed."

Alex began driving lessons, but it was apparent her legs in particular were becoming weaker. "One day I was sitting beside her when she'd been out driving and when we returned home I thought she'd put the handbrake on. But when I went to get out, all of a sudden I realised she hadn't, and the car went straight into the garage door," said Virginia. "That unnerved her because she realised she didn't have enough control with her hands." Alex did not give up hope of sitting and passing her test, she had further lessons, but her confidence was badly shaken and events would conspire to bring her motoring days to an end. She would never pass her driving test.

However not long after taking delivery of the car she had more good news when she was told she had won a holiday to Japan through the wonderful Make-a-Wish Foundation, which makes "magical" wishes comes true for children and young people with life threatening illnesses. Virginia arranged to take a nurse with she and her daughter so that bandaging could be speeded up, giving them more time to travel around Japan. No one begrudged the little blonde-haired girl her happiness. And as Christmas approached doctors at St Thomas' Hospital gave her their own gift with a three-hour operation to separate the fingers of her right hand from her thumb allowing her use of it for the first time in four years. On her left hand the digits were fused up to her knuckles. "Daddy I can unwrap my presents by myself," she told her father. "It's so wonderful."

Virginia was determined Alex would have a truly Happy Christmas, because she had fears that all was not well. Worried by Alex's appearance and by the manner in which she seemed to tire more quickly, she suspected the cancer had returned. She arranged for further tests.

CHAPTER THIRTY ONE

On the morning of February 5, 2008 Robin rang his daughter early. He was attending a conference in Edinburgh and wanted his call to her to be the first of her day and to be the first to wish her 'Happy Birthday'. But he was not her first caller. "Virginia answered the telephone and almost before I could say anything I heard Alex call out in the background, 'Not good news daddy' and Virginia said, 'The cancer is back'. I was stunned. Virginia said, 'We've just had a call from St Thomas' to say the cancer is there again. Speak to your daughter, wish her Happy Birthday'. How do you say, 'Happy Birthday' to your 19-year-old daughter when a couple of minutes earlier she's been told she has cancer? I didn't know what to do. I was all flummoxed but, typical of Alex, she just said, 'Don't talk about it Daddy, just sing Happy Birthday down the phone'. And so, there I was, trying to sing and I lost it a bit, tried to hold on to my self control but struggled. She was such a courageous kid. I was then, and I am now, so proud that she was my daughter."

For Virginia, that moment was one of the saddest of her life. "There were lots of sad times, but she'd had three birthdays that were pretty crap. On her 17th her eyes had been so sore she couldn't open them, that was followed by her being told she had cancer. And now this, although I knew she had cancer and I'd told my mother, in private, 'She's got it back'. But what it was all about was trying to be as happy as possible; it doesn't mean you must feel sad.

"It meant going into hospital again of course and she said she wasn't going in on her 19th birthday. She and her friends had arranged a Teddy Bears Picnic where everybody would bring a teddy bear. Alex had made these disgusting jellies and they all sat around chatting and laughing while Alex and I hid from everybody that she had cancer."

After the Picnic the teenager returned to St Thomas Hospital. "Alex didn't care about herself, she cared about other people," said Robin. "EB was in her face 24/7 and she didn't want to talk about it, she wanted to talk about people's lives."

Alex would spend three months in hospital. "She was in room 26 on the ninth floor of St Thomas' while the doctors tried to remove the tumour from her left leg and buttock. After an operation, Alex rang me. She was very excited and said, 'Daddy, daddy all the cancer's gone, I'm not going to die'. But I knew otherwise, because Virginia had seen some tell-tale spots on Alex's back and told me, 'I think it's gone into her spine'.

The family did their best to cheer one another through the darkness. After weeks in hospital while she recovered from the tumour removal, Alex went into decline and Virginia rang her ex-husband who was fundraising in Scotland. 'You need to get to London as quickly as you can,' she said. 'Alex is in intensive care and it's the end.' Robin raced to Glasgow Airport and was at the intensive care unit of St Thomas' Hospital by mid-afternoon. "Virginia was there when I arrived and I just managed to reach her bedside as Alex was dropping into unconsciousness. I asked, 'Alex, are you all right?' and she simply mumbled. Then she went away from us. That was it, she was gone."

Virginia too was convinced her daughter's long fight against pain was coming to a close. "Before she went into intensive care I was saying to the staff, 'Please don't wake her up, she's obviously exhausted' and I'd go outside the room only to come back to find three or four people had been in to this poor kid who was obviously shattered, because you don't sleep in hospital. It seemed to be just one thing after another, always somebody coming in to do something with her. But in the end, I could see something wasn't right with her and I asked for the doctors to come and look at her. When they did, she was immediately taken to intensive care. And in intensive care she got septicaemia very badly. Her eyes kept closing, she kept dropping off. But the EB nurses were amazing, one in particular, Claire, was with her until five in the morning."

Septicaemia was a consequence of the anaemia caused by the increasing demands of her body for blood to try healing the wounds resulting from skin loss. Despite the regular blood transfusions, her blood quality and count were both poor and worsening.

"Robin junior arrived and the two Robins and I had a meeting with the hospital consultants who said, 'We haven't gone through the paperwork about what to do if she doesn't revive. Do you want us to revive her?' I told them, 'No, I don't' and the two Robins were very good, they went along with me on this even though

I knew they didn't necessarily agree with me. I said, 'Look I just don't want Alex suffering any more'. It seemed to me that if, as was clearly the case, she had just a few more months to live, then there didn't seem to be any point in it. She'd already suffered enough. But maybe, somehow, Alex sensed I wasn't ready for her to die yet'."

Robin could see the dilemma facing his ex-wife. She didn't want to lose her daughter, but at the same time wanted her pain to end. However it looked as though nature itself would resolve the situation. "I gave Virginia some support, cuddling her and spoke to the consultant who told us, 'Sorry Mr Hood, this is the end. All the vital organs are failing. I'm afraid it's only a matter of time'.

The tragedy unfolding around them as their daughter slowly died was not the only concern for Virginia and Robin Hood. Robin junior had sacrificed his father's hopes of his son becoming an Army officer by joining the Royal Marines. A tall, good looking young man he had lost friends as they died beneath the bullets of snipers and roadside bombs planted by unseen enemies in Iraq and had been given a desk job. His prospects of promotion were sound but then he announced he was transferring to the Royal Marines as a Marine Cadet. It meant dropping in rank.

He and his sister had always been close, each proud and protective of the other. Learning Robin's sister was dying, the Marines had been considerate and compassionate, allowing him to spend time with her, and his fellow soldiers rally around to give their support. On one occasion he had taken Alex in her wheelchair to a spot on the banks of the River Thames where they drank champagne, puffed on cigars, although neither was a smoker, and Alex told her brother how she wanted her funeral to be arranged. He wondered if it was time to tell his parents the details. The Royal Marines had made sure Robin, undergoing rigorous training at the Commando training centre at Lympstone in Devon, reached the hospital in time after he was contacted by his mother to be told of Alex's condition.

Dad Robin said, "The three of us were talking about old times, reminiscing, passing time, waiting for the call and around midnight the consultant came to tell us, 'Everything is slowing down, it's not going to be long'. We went into the room in intensive care where Alex lay and two nurses were watching monitors, never taking their eyes from the screens that recorded what was happening with her body, checking her heart, lungs, kidneys, heartbeat, blood pressure and a dozen other things. I was trying to cheer Robin and Virginia. She had said to me earlier in the day that one of the male consultants was very pleasant. I began laughing and joking, aping an upper crust voice, pretending to be the consultant, saying, 'Hello Virginia, can I have your e-mail address?' It was just a form of small talk, trying to drag them out of what must have been the same terrible sadness I felt.

"Suddenly, Alex opened her eyes, made a half gesture with her eyes as if she wanted her head raised in the bed and said to her brother, 'Give me a cuddle me before I die'. It was absolutely remarkable and we couldn't believe it. Robin, who had seen a lot of action in Afghanistan and Iraq and who was no stranger to suffering and death, went across and tenderly cuddled his sister. Then he told her, 'You're not dying yet, get a grip'. And what happened next was amazing. Within minutes the monitors began buzzing back into life and four days later she was back on the ward.

"Because I was still in the TA and Robin was a serving soldier, I'd got free accommodation courtesy of the London Scottish Regiment, close by St Thomas'. A stay in a hotel would have been hugely expensive whereas they allowed me to sleep for free in the Officers' Mess. That morning after Alex had revived and was obviously now not going to die, Robin and I were walking over Westminster Bridge to the Regiment when I told him, 'She should have died. She should have gone tonight because this is just staving off the inevitable'. My son took my arm and told me, 'Dad, what we are going to do now is give her the time of her life'.

"Back on the ward she was in a sorry state, but having resolved to make her remaining time happy, we did our best to keep the promise we'd made to one another. We took her to shows in London including Les Miserables, which was one of her favourites and to see Joseph and the Amazing Technicolour Dreamcoat where at the end of the performance I went backstage and said, 'My daughter is dying, She loves this show' and the wonderful cast came out from their dressing room to spend time with her. It was a kind, spontaneous gesture, one we all appreciated and they had their photographs taken with Alex. But whenever I look at these, the expression on her face seems to be saying, 'I know I'm dying but I want to stay cheerful for you because you are doing all of this for me'."

It was as if Alex had the gift of second sight. The doctors confirmed cancer was indeed at her spine. They carried out a minor procedure to see whether it was possible to carry out more major surgery but the prognosis was as disappointing as it could possibly be. Robin was with Virginia when the news was broken. "The doctors said, 'Alex, the cancer has reached your spine and there's nothing more we can do'. I began to get upset but she put her arm around me and said, 'Daddy, I'm dying, not you. Smile for every day for the rest of your life and don't give up your fundraising work'."

Virginia had talked to the hospital staff about the fact her daughter was aware hope had faded. "We'd discussed how to deal with it when Alex talked of dying," she said. "The doctors and consultants were amazing. Sometimes Alex would be in floods of tears and they would be on their knees at the side of her bed talking to her for hours. I knew she was really upset that there was nothing more anyone could do, but she didn't talk of her distress to me because she didn't want me upset. That was the amazing girl she was."

Alex's thoughts were continually of the feelings of others, conscious of how difficult it must have been for those treating her knowing death had beckoned. Indeed EB victims rarely complain about their own suffering, preferring sympathy to be reserved for those who minister to them. These young people, constantly in pain, unselfishly continually apologise for the distress their condition causes others. Their thoughts are never for themselves but those around them, trying to help. Robin said, "Alex would say to one of the nurses, 'Oh, that's a lovely blouse you have on underneath your tunic. I wish I could have lived longer so I could go to buy a blouse like that'. Sometimes nurses would ask, 'Where does your daughter get this strength from?' And I wondered myself."

Now Alex learned Robin had been told he would be spending a tour of duty with the Royal Marines in Helmand Province, the huge Taliban stronghold in Afghanistan that supplied most of the world's opium and which was being policed by British forces. 'Isn't it stupid,' Alex told a nurse one day. 'My mum and dad having two kids, I'm going to die with EB and my brother is going to get killed in action with the Marines.'

With all hope of recovery gone, Alex left hospital. Because Virginia had been at hospital so much, she needed time to prepare her home for her daughter. A stair lift was one facility that might have proved helpful but an assessment soon showed that in the town house it was not a practical proposition. And so for two weeks Alex became a patient at Warwick Myton Hospice. She faced her forthcoming death as she had faced the agonies that had embraced her entire life, with a refusal to knuckle under. Then the family went off to Weymouth to spend a last holiday in the adapted mobile home operated by Debra. It was fitting that Robin, his former wife and children should at least have shared some pleasure from the homes. Helping find the money to buy and maintain them had cost the adults their marriage and deprived the children of having a father living with them.

"Robin and I were in one caravan, Virginia and Alex in the other. But Alex was in a really sorry state. It was my birthday on June 15 and Alex said, 'Oh Daddy, I'm so sorry, there's nothing we can do' but I told her, 'No, Alex, there is something we can do'. And so we went kite flying. Weymouth has always been a special place to me since my childhood. Robin and I took Alex to a hill at Bowleaze Cove, a spectacular beauty spot overlooking Weymouth Harbour where Alex flew a kite, watching it soar high in the wind as though it had been called by angels. That memory will stay with me forever. I didn't want that day or that time to end. Because I knew when it did, Alex would soon be gone from me for ever."

CHAPTER THIRTY TWO

When the holiday at Weymouth was over, the Hoods took their daughter and sister home to die. In her bedroom Alex, knowing she was dying, spent her time making Christmas gifts for her mother to sell at a craft fayre in Leamington Spa later in the year. She knew she would not be alive by the time the fayre took place. "She wasn't feeling sorry for herself that was never her way. Rather she wanted to help raise money that would maybe mean other children did not have to suffer as she had done and continued to do," said Robin. "That kind of strength is phenomenal, inspirational."

He continued his fundraising work. He knew now nothing could save Alex, but there were children everywhere and others yet unborn who were suffering or would suffer the same agonies of his daughter, of Georgia, Freya, Jonny Kennedy. And he thought of little Adana and his promise to her.

Just over a year earlier, in June 2007, Tony and Cherie Blair had made way at Downing Street for a new Prime Minister, Gordon Brown. Gordon and his wife Sarah had themselves experienced great personal sorrow. In December 2001 Sarah had given birth to their first child, Jennifer Jane but tragically the mite died when only ten days old after suffering a brain haemorrhage. They had two further children, John in October 2003 and in July 2006 another son, James Fraser who was sadly diagnosed with cystic fibrosis. Despite these tragedies Sarah and her husband still made time to help others and she would found the charity Piggy Bank Kids to help disadvantaged children.

Robin had sought the help of the Browns in publicising Debra and they had responded positively with the result that a Downing Street reception for the charity was arranged for July 15. He debated whether to turn up and knew that had he absented himself no one would think badly of him. He wondered what Alex would have said to him and in the end believed she would have wanted him to attend. Two days earlier he had visited her and when friends inquired about her had told them, 'She's poorly, but she's okay. At least she's still with us all'. And so he went to London, chatting to the wife of the Prime Minister and her 120 guests with his mind a whirlwind of fear as to what was happening in Leamington Spa and even managing to make a speech, leaving some guests visibly moved when he told them of Alex and said, 'I might have lost my own, personal battle against the condition, but together we can go on and win the war'. Ben Merrett the chief operating officer of Debra told him, 'Robin I just don't know how you manage to do this'. That evening he rang Virginia's home to be told there was no change in his daughter's condition. The following morning, July 16, he set off for Luton Airport and a flight back to Scotland when his telephone rang. It was his son who had been given emergency leave by the Royal Marines and was heading to join his mother and sister. He told him,

'Dad, it's not looking good for Alex. You need to get there'.

That morning Alex had demanded to be helped from her bed. "She told me, 'I'm a 19-year-old girl, I just can't lie in bed all day', said Virginia. "I'd watched her working away at making things for the Christmas sale she would never see and kept asking myself, 'How does she do this? How brave can she be? Could I do it if I was dying?' Eventually I persuaded her to go back to bed."

She was in bed when her father arrived. "I went straight in to see her. She was absolutely tranquil and still a little coherent, but we knew she wasn't far from death. She had deteriorated so much. We had a little chat and she told me 'I've done some paintings for Debra Daddy, get as much money as you can for them. I don't want other people to have to go through what I have'. She suddenly announced she was getting up. We urged her to stay in bed but she said, 'No, I'm going to sit in my chair one more time'. And she did for 40 minutes."

Her face drawn in pain despite being given morphine but trying to make light of her life draining away, she told him, 'One good thing about dying is I will not have to watch any more Harry Potter films'. "She was trying to lift our spirits, make it easier for us," said Robin. Finally she acceded to the pleadings of her parents and nurses to get back into her bed. "She went to the toilet and it was really difficult because she couldn't walk. We had to put her on a type of commode and she really baulked at anything like that. But we finally managed to get her back into bed," said Virginia. "When she had been in hospital earlier I hadn't been ready for her to die; now I think I was."

In the little bedroom, Alex, her parents and four nurses were joined by Robin junior. The young soldier's parents knew just how much this must be hurting their son. From the very first moment his sister had been brought home after her birth he had wanted to be with her, to be the big brother guarding over her only too often to be pushed aside as his parents and father in particular fretted over her safety. Now Virginia and Robin knew Alex would die content knowing her brother was at her side.

Robin looked at his daughter as the nurses prepared to inject a continuous flow of morphine. He had been warned this might be the last act they could perform for their patient. Once the painkiller was delivered into her body, Alex would drift into unconsciousness but at least her sleep would be free of pain and she would sleep for all time, never to awaken. Despite his own achievements, Robin had always felt humbled by the gentleness and conscientiousness of the nurses who were constantly on hand to care for Alex and give Virginia some respite. Now he saw at close hand why, to most, they were 'Angels', ministering to the dying young woman with patience and total commitment to making her as comfortable in her last hours as they could. Always on hand, but never intruding into the grief of the family as they watched death draw ever nearer, they knew the time was fast approaching when they would have to give the Hoods the news they dreaded.

Finally the nurses told the family, 'Now is the time to say your goodbyes'. "Alex was an absolute horror, a wreck," said Robin. "Her eyes had sunk, she had dehydrated, her skin was wrinkled, she had such a gaunt appearance, a 'Death is looming' look. I knew it wasn't

long. I kissed her and told her, 'Goodbye darling Alex'.
"We began taking it in turn, Robin and me, to sit by her
and keep watch over her. She went through a really frantic
stage, thrashing around in the bed. She was delirious and
unfortunately in the last few hours of her life developed
diarrhoea. That made it really difficult for the nurses.
Because of all the bandages her body was swathed in,
rather than trying to change her we just put a big nappy
underneath her."

Virginia was exhausted. She had cared for Alex for
well over 19 years and in the last few days her house had
been filled with nurses, doctors and friends. "After the
morphine went in, the nurses might have managed to get
a couple of words out of Alex but we could no longer get
through to her. Her eyes just stared. It was really weird.
I just couldn't cope any more and thought, 'I'm not
needed. I'll get out of here'. I don't even remember the
last words I spoke to Alex. A friend arrived and we went
out. Then my son telephoned and said, 'Mum, I think
this is it'. I told him, 'I'll be back in a minute' and I was.
Alex was still alive then."

Alex's father was watching over her when Virginia
arrived. She looked at her daughter and told him, 'This
is it, I'm going to bed. Don't wake me up until the end'.
Robin gave way at his daughter's bedside to his son and
in the early hours of the next morning, July 17, felt
himself being shaken and a familiar voice telling him,
'Dad, I think it's nearly at the end now'.

"By now she had become very, very calm and her
breathing was very, very faint until it ceased altogether.
She looked so peaceful at last, free of any suffering."
Her son woke Virginia from fitful sleep to break the
news telling her, 'I think she's gone'. She looked at Alex

and knew it was all over. Now it was a time for a strong character to take command. "Virginia took everything in her stride," said Robin. "She told us, 'Okay, you both know what you have to do now'. I hadn't a clue what she meant and she could see by the way I looked at her I was confused so Virginia said, 'You have to re-bandage her, we can't let the undertakers do this'. And so after we contacted the undertaker and waited for his arrival we began to put clean dressings on Alex. Fathers and brothers don't expect to have to do things like that. I'm quite an emotional guy and Robin could see I was losing it. He said, 'Dad, there's a first' and I asked, 'What?' He told me, 'Well this is the first time that you've ever bandaged Alex without hurting her.' It wasn't meant to be funny, but it knocked me out of my gloom and doom.

"We bandaged her, sat with her for a while, I cut off a lock of her hair that I wanted to keep, and still have, and then the undertaker arrived and took away Alex."

Trying to sleep, Virginia heard noises of activity as a doctor confirmed death, nurses tidied up their equipment and then an undertaker arrived. She could hear the noise of her daughter being carried away. When she surrendered hopes of sleeping she went into Alex's bedroom and was briefly shocked by movement beneath the sheets. For a flash of time she wondered whether she had simply dreamt her daughter's passing. But then she realised it was her former husband who had gone to sleep in his daughter's bed.

Robin could not allow the news of Alex's passing to go unnoticed. Later that morning he contacted the offices in Carlisle of Border Television who arranged for both himself and his son to be interviewed. "Some people criticised me for going on television so soon after Alex's death,' he admitted. "But it was important for everyone to be aware just what the effects of EB ultimately were."

He and his son set off on the customary round of visiting the family doctor to collect Alex's death certificate, visiting the Registrar to formally give notice of the death and of discussing with the undertaker the arrangements for her funeral. "When we arrived home and went into Alex's room, Virginia had cleared it of everything, even her bandages and I found these in boxes in the garage. I was really upset, indignant even, but Virginia told me, 'Robin, I need to move on' and, looking back, she did the right thing. Nobody could have done more for our daughter and she had the rest of her life to live with the memory of Alex. It had all been such an emotional roller coaster. There were times when I wanted her to die, wanted her to go, wanted her suffering to close out. I kept asking, 'Why Alex? Why us? Why my family?' If she had just died sooner then we could have got on with our lives, with the healing process, but it was as though somewhere, someone was saying, 'Keep going, we're not ready for her yet'. Now I knew they were ready."

That night the Hoods went out for a meal, ordered a bottle of champagne and made a toast to Alex, celebrating that she was finally at a place where there was no pain. During the days that followed came messages of sympathy including condolences from Gordon Brown who wrote, 'Sarah and I are so sorry to hear of Alex's loss. We are thinking of you and your family at this time. Alex was such a courageous and strong person and she bore her condition with great bravery all of her life. You have done so much over the years to raise funds for EB research and you have my deepest admiration for your efforts. You were her greatest champion and I'm sure she was very proud of your great love for her."

Eventually Bill Clinton would learn of the death of the gifted young woman so early in her life. 'I want you to know that I'm keeping you and your family in my thoughts and prayers,' he told Robin, who never doubted the sincerity of the former American leader.

That day by the River Thames Alex had outlined the arrangements for her funeral to her brother. The result was, by funeral standards, fairly bizarre. No one was allowed to wear black. Her father recalls the gathering, before the service at Mid-Warwickshire Crematorium, of her best and closest friends. "It was an odd sensation. Everyone wore colourful outfits and yet you could feel the sorrow draining everybody of energy. I was struggling to uplift everybody, but not doing too well."

The Crematorium was filled to bursting. Many of the mourners had to stand and Robin junior lifted spirits by recounting his 'mooning' act on the morning of his sister's 18th birthday. When her grandfather Dennis Hood had died in 2005, Alex wrote a poem that was read at his funeral. Now it was repeated at her own. 'You are the shooting star that falls, You are the wind through the trees that soars, You are a thousand raindrops that pour, To you compared I feel so small, Because you are a friend of all, You are the sun up so high, You are the earth and you are the sky, You are a million birds that fly'.

Her father, still an officer in the Territorial Army had somehow managed to retain his self control until the moment when the curtains began to close around the coffin. Sixteen years earlier, as he lay close to death following his road accident, Robin had been celebrated by his children singing 'You Are My Sunshine'. Now as those words echoed the enormity of his loss began to penetrate his heart and mind. "I started to lose it and turned to Robin so people wouldn't know I was beginning to cry and see my tears. I suppose I was looking for some TLC and was about to lay my head on his shoulder when he saw what was happening, looked at me in his true Marines style and said, 'Trust the TA to let you down'. It was exactly what I needed to get hold of myself."

And so the butterfly child was finally free to spread her wings without fear of pain. As mourners left the Crematorium they were able to read these words, written by a close friend of the Hood family:

'If velvet was vicious and silk had claws
To rip, rasp and dig then tear at your pores
If the wool on your back was a form of attack
And cotton just stuck to your sores
No chance of this child playing carefree in the sun
Imagine the effort to get simple things done
No rough and tumble with dad on the bed
It's bathing, it's peeling then pricking instead
The life of a butterfly is fragile and short
For butterfly children it's equally fraught
The future uncertain but a goal is in sight
With help from those able we'll fight the good fight.

Robin had one further sad chore to perform. "Four or five days later I went to collect Alex's ashes from the funeral parlour. After picking them up I sat in my car in a car park with the ashes in an urn beside me on the front seat. I hadn't cried the night she died. I hadn't cried in the days that followed. I hadn't cried at her funeral. Now for the first time I let the tears come. I must have sat in the car for an hour and a half crying. Then a parking attendant came up, tapped on the window and said I needed a ticket. I went loopy and got out of the car. 'I've just picked my daughter's ashes up and all you can do is to tell me I need a parking ticket,' I told him. I felt angry, bitter, cheated that somebody like that could interfere after all we'd been through. Suddenly all the sacrifices, all the effort seemed a waste of time. I had promised Alex so many times I'd find her a cure and those promises had helped not just her but me to keep going. Then when I mourned some stranger wanted to give me a parking ticket."

CHAPTER THIRTY THREE

His family and friends worried that the death of Alex might be too much for Robin to handle, that he might even seek to follow her. He admits to being angry and devastated. "When she died I felt deflated, cheated. I kept asking why, when I'd given so much, I hadn't got the tick in the box, why my daughter had been taken'. For the next three months I went around thinking, 'What a waste of time. It's cost me hundreds of thousands of pounds, my business has gone, my wife, my home is mortgaged to the hilt, I've used up all my savings, travelled everywhere, driven hundreds of thousands of miles, burned out cars.' Ten days after her death, I sank to the lowest point of my life. But I kept going, driving around with Alex's ashes in my car and one of the reasons for carrying on was that I don't like giving in after a defeat but, more important was the fact that Alex had asked me to carry on. Was there ever a time when I thought of packing it all in? No, never, not even now when I was on the bottom."

His marriage to Samantha, never a normal husband and wife relationship, much as had been his latter time with Virginia, had ended in acrimony and ultimately they would divorce. As summer began to fade into August

Robin, on leave from the Royal Marines, took him to one side and told him, 'Dad you're coming with me to Greece. You need a holiday'. They decided to fly to the island of Zakynthos, famous as the breeding ground of the endangered Loggerhead Turtle species. Robin did not know Virginia had suggested to her son she was worried about his father. When he told his mother where they were headed she warned him, 'Keep an eye on your father, I don't want him throwing himself off a cliff'.

"I wasn't suicidal, just washed out," said Robin. "I still felt cheated. We got to our hotel about three in the afternoon. Robin went off for a walk and I drank two bottles of vile Greek wine. Then I telephoned a friend in Scotland and told him, 'What a waste of time it has all been'." Next day, August 17, exactly one month since the death of Alex, as he wandered aimlessly around the pool he met stunning Greek teacher Christina Ntagka, working as a volunteer on the island raising money to support the dwindling turtle population.

Christina had been due to leave the island days earlier. Deeply spiritual, she had pleaded with her spiritual guide, 'Send me the man who is right for me'. She felt a sudden need to remain until the 20th and, puzzled by this sensation, delayed returning to the mainland. At that first meeting Robin offered advice on how to fundraise. "I was moping about shell shocked, and told her about Alex. Somehow I wanted Christina to know about my daughter. Christina told me later that she spotted me from the other side of the pool and said, 'I knew it was you, you were for me'. Two days later I knew she was the one and said to her, 'You're going to be the next Mrs Hood'.

"I hadn't gone to Zakynthos with the idea of meeting another woman but felt drawn to her. Telling her about

Alex almost seemed to bring my daughter back to life, as if she was there. Christina had an uncanny understanding of what I was going through. She told me, 'Everything happens for a reason. Your daughter is here with you and she has brought us together'. I'd gone there as a broken man and came back completely revitalised. When the holiday was over and we were back in Britain I called on Virginia who looked at me and said, 'You've met somebody'." From that holiday encounter, Robin and Christina would be inseparable.

He threw himself into his fundraising with a renewed vigour. Before his daughter's death Debra, close to bankruptcy, asked him to become Head of Fundraising and Communications. He discovered that had all their creditors invoiced the charity together, Debra would have gone under. His aggressive attitude might not have pleased everyone, but it was effective. A Mansion House reception, originally budgeted to raise £17,000 brought in £90,000 after his intervention and a speech in which he told guests about Alex.

He regained the sense of humour that had borne him through so many years of sadness. During a function at which he was introduced to the Countess of Wessex, he showed her a photograph of himself with Prince Charles and asked the Royal guest, 'You will recognise one of the men on there because it's me, but do you recognise the other?' The Countess had smiled and inquired about Alex. Later she asked for a further meeting with Robin at which he asked her to become Debra's Patron. Much to the delight of everyone she accepted. In October, three months after the loss of Alex, he was given a Special Achievement Award' at the annual prestigious Bighearted Scotland ceremony.

It was not always smooth going. At a special boxing evening laid on by Frank Warren whose generous charity work all too often went unsung, he was introduced by a fading one-time celebrity comedian who began by insisting upon singing, 'Robin Hood, Robin Hood, riding through the glen', words from the jingle that had accompanied the old television series. The crowd, boisterous and noisy needed to be calmed. Even for a man who had once persuaded Mike Tyson to break a 'No autograph' rule for Alex, it was no easy task but he did so by telling them about his daughter's valiant fight and his own determination to deliver a knockout blow to EB. He received a standing ovation.

CHAPTER THIRTY FOUR

Adana Forsyth often asked her mother, 'Am I going to die?' 'No, honey they are going to get a cure,' Dianne would tell her daughter. Indeed during his own television documentary, Robin had very publicly said a cure would be discovered in time. From time to time journalists would call with news of a development here, progress there, on occasions even tell Dianne, 'There's a cure' and ask for her response. "I would be over the moon, filled with elation when I believed it to be true and then I'd discover it wasn't, but I would never tell Adana that it had been a false hope. The hope of a cure was really what kept her going. I'd insist, 'They are going to find a cure honey, you are going to be fine'.

Like Alex, like all the others, it was the bravery of their children that gave mothers the energy to keep going. Because so often they were left to carry on alone after marriages collapsed. She and Peter had tried to hold their marriage together, but agreed to formally separate when Adana was aged three by which time Dianne had established a routine for caring for her daughter and was content knowing it would not now be disrupted by marital problems. Nevertheless Peter generously supported his family even though he no longer lived with them. Dianne marvelled at the strength and love of Tanis and Cody and tried desperately to avoid their having to take a back seat in the running of the family while she concentrated on Adana. Somehow she managed to spread her time over all her children, never forgetting that had the wheel of misfortune spun differently it could have been one or other of Tanis and Cody or even both who had been afflicted with EB rather than Adana. Among her friends many wondered why Adana and not the others. Neither they nor Dianne would ever discover the answer.

"Because of Adana, the others had to grow up quickly. Tanis was such a good girl. She went off to school when she was four, but she was already grown up by then and, to me, amazing. It was as though she knew even then that helping me was to help her sister. I'd take her off to the school bus with Cody beside me and Adana in her pram. Cody wasn't so happy about leaving me when I needed to place him in a nursery school at the age of two. An older lady came to collect him and he put up a huge fight when she tried to put him in her car. There was nothing naughty about it, he just wanted his mum.

"The children weren't jealous. They were aware of having a sister who had a terrible condition. And they saw the horrors, horrors that thankfully most adults don't have to see. They hurt Adana by accident; sometimes in trying to show their love for her by playing games with her. They did really well with her because they were lively kids and I think the four of us got the balance of everything quite well. They cared for their sister and knew if I was doing Adana's dressings to leave me to get on with it and not be naughty or a nuisance. I talked to them about EB and never hid any of the horrors of it

289

from them. I talked to them a lot because being on my own meant they were my companions, my friends. Tanis took everything in her stride while Cody was a very boisterous boy, but Adana was always really close to her brother."

As Adana grew older, Dianne took her to a local playgroup which organised events in aid of Debra and succeeded in raising lots of money for the charity. There were some, concerned at the pressure on her of raising Tanis and Cody while looking after Adana who urged her to think about having Adana taken into care but it was never an option as far as she was concerned. She realised that the higher the incidence of awareness of EB, the more generous would be the public, (even strangers) when asked for cash support. Dianne continued to keep the Media abreast of her daughter's progress, knowing that each mention in a newspaper, on radio or television brought in further donations. It also helped that the public knew the unique problems that faced EB children and their parents.

Adana's beginning formal schooling in 2002 was by no means straightforward. Her mother needed to shop around for a school uniform with no hard edges such as stiff collars, zips or prominent seams that might chafe against her so delicate skin. She needed a specially tailored classroom chair with sheepskin armrests while a beanbag protected her feet and legs against accidental knocks from her classmates. Because her hands were fused together she was unable to use regulation school exercise books, instead tapping out answers on a board. She carried with her an emergency supply of medication that could be fed into her body through the gastrostomy valve in her stomach. Like other dystrophic EB victims including Alex, she was accompanied to her lessons by a specially trained carer. But each day, while her school friends played and laughed, Adana underwent the never-ending misery of having her dressings changed, frequently resulting in skin being pulled from her body.

There were regular absences while she underwent treatment at Great Ormond Street in particular throat stretching to allow her to swallow. And yet she never complained. On the day she began school Dianne told worried friends, as to how her daughter would handle being in such close proximity to others of her age with the freedom to tumble and fall, 'It breaks my heart to see her watching her friends running and playing outside when she is in so much constant pain. I know she thinks, 'Why me?' but she's been through so much and doesn't bat an eyelid.

Mother and daughter lived in constant hope that scientists in Dundee, just a few miles off, would discover a cure. Robin urged them not to abandon hope, to continue the Media exposure that brought in money, but as time went by Adana became increasingly conscious of her appearance and much as Alex had done, developed a reluctance to see herself in the Media.

"We did lots and lots until she was about five and became more aware of herself and her condition," said Dianne. "There was an enormous amount of publicity when she started school, but then she just wanted to be like the rest of the kids. She didn't want the attention but I'd say, 'Honey we have to do this because this is going to help towards getting a cure' and she and I would talk about what was the right thing to do and how she felt. The hope of a cure was really what kept her going."

Adana was aged eight and by now confined to a wheelchair as a result of deformed feet when, in August 2006, Robin announced that scientists in Dundee had identified the gene types that could cause EB and newspapers carried headlines including words such as 'hope' and 'cure'. And giving hope was important; all too often it was the only strand in the rope by which so many young victims clung to life.

However hope was all there was and Dianne was forced to watch helplessly as her daughter's condition now visibly worsened. Sometimes even nurses who came to their home to help with dressings and bandages fainted at the sight of the jellied mess that was the child's body. "She had really gone into decline once she could no longer move about on her own and had to permanently use her wheelchair,' said Dianne. "That meant her bones no longer stretched and her body slowly became deformed. Up until that point Adana had loved having her friends over to visit her. She had made some really close friends at school but now she seemed to no longer be herself, the happy little girl we knew and loved so much and who had little time for others who felt sorry for themselves. As she got older one of her favourite phrases was, 'Get over it.' She used to use that all the time. If somebody was moaning about something and she overheard you would hear her say, 'Get over it.' It was as if she was saying, 'What have you got to moan about?' And if anyone had a right to say that it was her."

But one day when she had reached the age of ten, Adana told Dianne, 'I'm dying, aren't I mum?' It wasn't a question, simply a statement of fact. Those words remain vivid in Dianne's memory. "I was washing my hands after doing her dressings through in her room, when she said it. I told her, 'No darling, you can't give up hope. There will be a cure.' I knew the truth by then, but I couldn't tell her, 'You're dying.' It was too frightening for a little girl so young when all of her friends were planning how they would spend their own lives.

"She wanted me to take all the mirrors down in our house, because she became quite bloated at the end and didn't like looking at herself. I'd approached Great Ormond Street to get a psychologist involved because emotionally, towards the end, I kept trying to be positive towards her. I think that's why I kind of blocked out that she was going to die myself. You don't say to someone, 'Yeah. You're dying.' She knew from the way she looked and felt and she was telling me I was a liar when I was telling her she'd live. I'd say, 'Adana you've not got to stop, you've not to give up hope,' but then I'd feel so distressed within me that there were times when I'd be dressing and bandaging her and would have to come out of the room and have a cry. You wouldn't let a dog suffer the way she was at the end. It was ridiculous, terrible. She was allergic to morphine and so didn't get proper pain relief. I could see her deteriorating before me every day.

"Along with all her other problems, Adana's body was unable to break down proteins as a result of suffering from a stomach syndrome. So she was taken off all proteins including dairy products which was really difficult because these were her favourites. Because she had hardly any tongue and was unable to chew things properly, her throat suffered from blistering and the stretching was necessary. She was prescribed medicines for the stomach syndrome which caused internal bleeding and then placed on a course of steroids. It turned out to be a stupid thing to do because the steroids caused her bones to be even more brittle and when it was decided to cut down her intake of steroids her skin became really soft and started to shed leaving it a mess and with wounds open to infection. So the steroids would be increased, her skin would shed again leaving more wounds. It took Adana a while to get off steroids and she never really recovered.

"We weren't supposed to give her any milk products at all. But life is too short and if she wanted a milk chocolate button I'd give her one. At first, when the doctors discovered my little secret, they would tick me off. But it only happened very occasionally and frankly I don't believe it would have made much difference in the long run. For her birthday I would make her a tiny plate of macaroni cheese, but with other different types of vegetable milk and vegetable cheese. But Adana didn't like it. Then I tried her with macaroni without cheese sauce.

"So the protein simply went under her skin and as her body deteriorated everything just collapsed and her kidneys started to fail. She had no veins left and then the problems began affecting her brain. I took her to Great Ormond Street for more tests and treatment. Adana loved going to the theatre when we were in London, but this time she was really upset because the doctors wouldn't allow her out. They kept trying to take blood from her. It was really distressing having to watch this. She hated needles and because she no longer had any veins they were getting nowhere while she became more and more uncomfortable. Finally I could stand it no longer and decided I was taking her out of there. When I shouted at a doctor, 'You're not taking any more blood from my daughter', Adana said, 'Yeah, mum, you tell them'.

"We went off shopping and into a DVD store where the guys could see my little girl was desperately ill and wouldn't let us pay for anything. It was as if they too knew she was going to die. When I tried to pay and opened my purse, inside was a beautiful white feather. Where it had come from I don't know, but I looked upon it as a sign that she was going to another place. I told the doctors I wanted Adana to be with us at home because I was going to nurse her until the end."

As her life drew to a close and by now sure she would not live to enjoy Christmas 2008 with her family, Adana was taken to a shopping mall where she was made the special guest of Santa. She sat on Dianne's knee, barely able to communicate as she went on a special sleigh ride. It was the last time the family would enjoy an outing together.

"The day before she died there was a film over her eyes and she wasn't with us. I was with her when she died at home, all of us there. The night we closed the lid on her coffin, I did a tarot card reading. That told me Adana was laughing at some of the things we had placed in the coffin with her and I found that very helpful. When she died, one of the doctors who had dealt with her all her life said 'It was a very right decision, a correct decision and a very brave decision to keep her at home'. That helped too. So many people missed Adana and had been struck by her courage. She was such a brave little girl and when she died it was as though the whole town was in mourning."

The passing of Adana stunned Robin. "It was a total shock. Adana died after Alex and was my next hope, my next driving force. I felt very guilty and didn't go to her funeral as I'd promised Adana's mum 'Don't worry she's young enough to live into a period where a cure will be available'. I'd told them both she wasn't going to die and when it happened I just didn't have the balls to go. Because of that promise I was worried somebody would tell me, 'You're a liar'."

On the day of her funeral he thought about a Bible passage from Saint Luke; 'But Jesus called unto him and said, Suffer little children to come unto me and forbid them not for such is the Kingdom of God'. At that moment he knew where all the EB children were; Georgia, Freya, Johnny Kennedy, Alex and now Adana and he knew they were safe and happy, their pure unblemished skins free of all pain and fault.

Despite her own worries, Dianne felt no bitterness towards Robin. Nor does she today. She prefers to remember the hope and help he gave and his work to try saving Adana. And the good times with her daughter. "The first two years were hell and the last two years were hell but the period in the middle, yes she had pain, yes we had a hectic time, yes we had sadness but there was such a lot of happiness in there too. It was the small, maybe seemingly insignificant things that I'm glad we shared, and that I still appreciate. Like she and me sitting together watching 'Supernanny' on television, seeing her dealing with problem kids. A lot of parents never spend that sort of time with their children, they never experience the closeness of Adana and me.

"My other kids are much more appreciative of what they have, of having their health. They've lost their sister so they know how your life can just be taken away from you. I was crippled initially with her death and they stayed strong for me.

"People always want to know whether Peter and me would have had another baby because we both carried the defective gene. We would, but only if there had been a cure in place, maybe some sort of stem cell treatment that could have been given to Adana. I wouldn't have put another child through what Adana experienced. If tests showed that another baby would be born with EB then, heart-breaking though it would be, I wouldn't have brought another child into the world with that condition. Often the fact is overlooked that it's not only the children who are victims, but their families too. I never had one New Year when I wasn't in the house with Adana because I had dressings to do the next day. And Peter and I never argued until Adana was born.

"Robin may have run away from caring for his daughter, but maybe he and Virginia too would be biting at one another, squabbling over how to best bandage Alex. He was so passionate at what he was doing. It was after seeing him that I decided to go to the newspapers, and I don't regret that because at least it gave me some sort of hope. Eventually all the promises of a cure started to get to me. But then I began to realise there probably wouldn't be a solution to EB in this lifetime although after speaking to some of the researchers I did think they might be able to develop some sort of therapy that could replace the skin.

"I learned a lot from Adana, she made me a stronger person. I was so lucky to know her; to spend time with her was a privilege. I'm a spiritual person and know she watches over me. She's here, just on a different phase in her creation."

Dianne, a highly skilled and sought-after artist, remains on good terms with Peter.

CHAPTER THIRTY FIVE

Ten months after Alex died, Robin scattered her ashes over Loch Ken at the side of the home on Loch Ken she had so loved. It came as little surprise that the ceremony was filmed. An opportunity such as this to gain Media coverage about EB was too good to lose. The delay was caused by frequent cancellations by television stations. And so in a spring drizzle with just a piper, cameraman, photographer and David Leslie as witnesses, Alex came home. Weeks later on the anniversary of her death, Virginia took Robin and Christina to a hill not far from her home where they flew kites in memory of her daughter.

By then Robin was based in Dublin, desperately dragging the Irish Debra back from the slough of near bankruptcy. A 15-minute meeting with representatives of one of the country's most successful businessmen resulted in a £100,000 donation. He told Christina, 'If as a result of talking to someone for a quarter of an hour about Alex and my journey with her, I can get so much money to help cure this condition then I knew she's not really dead.

'But now that Alex has gone on, I think I have got my life back into balance. Initially I felt very cheated and very lost. I wanted to hug my daughter but to think I had never really cuddled her, never picked her up under her arms, been afraid to touch her always consoled though by the certainty that we were going to get a cure. Now that hasn't happened and for a long time I felt very bitter about it, but I've come to terms with it now and moaning and crying about things changes nothing.'

Robin worked for Debra International, the worldwide network of the growing number of national Debras, trying to replicate what he had achieved in the UK but he had little impact.

He returned from Dublin in October 2013 and his paid time with DEBRA had come to an end, and he opted to become Chairman as Roger Wakefield who was Chair had died earlier that year.

This is an unpaid demanding role which Robin did for six months, but it was time-consuming and he needed to earn a living as his 20 years with DEBRA had left him financially worse-off.

In 2013 Robin ran the London Marathon for the third time again with Alex as he has kept a small pot of her ashes which accompanied him on the 26 mile route.

After fourteen months of looking for the right role Robin has decided to go back on the road talking about his work and promoting this book.

I am very proud to have been a big part of DEBRA for so many years.

"This is the most horrific condition known to mankind and I'm really pleased to say that I was part of the fight to put this condition in the history books. Initially, all I wanted was a cure for Alex. But now there is going to be a cure for others and though my daughter was a casualty along the way, nevertheless, it has all been worthwhile. Alex was an inspiration and I am privileged to have not just been her father but to have known her. She achieved so much despite all her disabilities. She made me a nicer person to be with because she was so caring. I miss her cheerful personality and she had wisdom far beyond her years.

"I've lost all my material possessions, even my home is owned by the building society. I've lost Virginia, I've lost Alex but I am very pleased to say I am rebuilding my relationship with my son Robin.

Robin is now happily married to Christina who knows her husband and Virginia still share a remarkable affection. In many ways Virginia is the unsung hero of the story, although it is true to say that all those caring for EB victims are worthy of being described as heroes. Despite the acrimony of their split, Virginia is as proud of Robin's achievements as ever. "He's brilliant for Debra because he's done a wonderful job, a wonderful, wonderful job." She now works for Warwickshire's highly respected and admired Integrated Disability Service supporting families with children with disabilities, doing what she did for so long as a wife and mother.

She misses her daughter. "Alex had a wonderful strength of character and she was great friend. We had a brilliant friendship. Did I become immune to emotion? I don't think you can get immune to it. It's to do with your personality. I just tried putting it to the back of my mind so as not to get upset. But at times I did get upset. In order to deal with situations like that it's no good being in floods of tears, you've got to get on with it. I'm in front of a daughter who has a condition and I might be upset but I just have to get on with what I'm doing and not let her see I'm upset. On occasions I'd ask, 'Why me?' but there was no point in worrying about what you can't have. That is your life and that's what you have to do. There's no choice. When we lost her I wondered, 'Christ what was the point of it all?' But in the end I'd had a loving, talented daughter who never stopped giving back all the love I gave her."

Robin junior, a fine man who is looked on with considerable pride by his parents, politely declined to be interviewed for this story, sending an e-mail to explain why. "This is in no way any reflection on my feelings about my father or the book itself. Alex was a very special young lady, and an exceptional example of most, if not all of the values and standards, that we, as a society, are lacking today. She was an inspiration to all who met her, maybe even many who didn't. She was a loyal friend and most importantly to me, a loving sister who managed to achieve all this whilst being tormented by one of the most horrendous conditions that many could imagine.

"I do have many fond memories of her, as a child and growing into a young woman, memories of a sister, and as a best friend. Alex shared many things about her thoughts and her life with me, mainly because of our relaxed bond, that made talking and confiding easy. However the stories, laughs and life that we shared, are there for me and those closest with me, who I feel worthy of her brilliance, they are there for times when I need them.

"I feel that talking about my father, would only allow a negative response on my part, merely marring the amazing feats that he has achieved thus far. In no way did Alex or I ever blame him for his dedication to succeeding in, or pursuing his goals.

301

"When Alex died the first time in March 2008, before the doctors brought her back to life, I was in emotional turmoil, she was so special, and I was so selfish and upset, I didn't want to lose her, and I was thankful for her revival, and having her to stay with us for longer. As the months passed between March and July, it became more obvious how selfish that we had all been, when her pain and suffering increased to new levels. On that morning of the 17th of July, as Alex passed away we knew she had pain no more.